Praise for

AMERICAN WINO

"I can think of no American more uniquely qualified nor eminently eager to guzzle free booze while living out of his car than Dan Dunn. This is debauchery of the finest kind. Hunter S. Thompson would be proud. And possibly a bit jealous."

—Aisha Tyler, author of *Self-Inflicted Wounds:*
Heartwarming Tales of Epic Humiliation

"Holy Hell, from the opening moments when author Dan Dunn almost gets laid, but doesn't because . . . well, you have to read it for yourself . . . this book is an absolute blast. I'm not sure why exactly booze columnist Dunn thought it was a good idea to pack up everything he owned, which amounted to a broken heart, a broken life, and his dead brother's ashes, and drive around the United States to learn more about wine, but I'm sure glad he did. *American Wino* is just about the best road trip I've ever been on."

—Maximillian Potter, author of *Shadows in the Vineyard:*
The True Story of the Plot to Poison the World's Greatest Wine

"Can a person discover themselves while being sloshed on wine? Maybe. Can wine discover itself by drinking Dan Dunn? I don't know. Can you discover a little about yourself as Dan Dunn discovers more about himself and also wine? Yes. Can I drink a whole bottle of wine and still write this blurb for Dan's book while also discovering the complexities of how to write a blurb while discovering . . . ? Whoa . . . wow I just stood up and realized how drunk I was. I say just read the book. It's funny, poignant, and certainly more gooder than anything I ever wrote."

—Glenn Howerton, star of *It's Always Sunny in Philadelphia*

"Dunn has done it again. Drinking, geography, biochemistry, rampant Tindering, and even more drinking. This is the ultimate oenophile's handbook, but purists beware—there's headaches and heartaches ahead."

—John Oates, Rock and Roll Hall of Famer

"Nobody punishes his liver or his penis as consistently and with such commitment as Dan Dunn. I've seen it firsthand. The liver, that is, not the genitals. Okay, I've seen both. Join me in praying for Dan's liver and his penis. And in reading this hilarious and heartfelt book."

—Nick Swardson, comedian and star of *Grandma's Boy* and *Reno 911!*

"Dan Dunn is driving, and this trip through America's vineyards is a ride you want to join! Dan's got a little bit of crazy in him. His book has a lot of crazy in it. Plus, the dude's a great writer."

—Neil Everett, anchor, ESPN's *SportsCenter*

"It's hard out there for a pimp. But Dan Dunn is a Superpimp, and there ain't no stopping a Superpimp!"

—DJ Paul, Academy Award–winning founding member of Three 6 Mafia

"I know what to eat. What I've been missing is a guy who knows what to drink. Thank God for Dan Dunn!"

—Phil Rosenthal, creator of *Everybody Loves Raymond* and host of PBS's *I'll Have What Phil's Having*

AMERICAN
WINO

ALSO BY DAN DUNN

★ ★ ★ ★ ★ ★ ★ ★ ★ ★ ★ ★ ★ ★

Living Loaded:
Tales of Sex, Salvation, and the Pursuit
of the Never-Ending Happy Hour

Nobody Likes a Quitter
(and Other Reasons to Avoid Rehab):
The Loaded Life of an Outlaw Booze Writer

DEY ST.
AN IMPRINT OF WILLIAM MORROW *PUBLISHERS*

AMERICAN WINO

A Tale of
REDS, WHITES, *and* ONE MAN'S
BLUES

DAN DUNN

HarperCollins books may be purchased for educational, business, or sales promotional use. For information please e-mail the Special Markets Department at SPsales@harpercollins.com.

FIRST EDITION

Designed by Shannon Nicole Plunkett

Library of Congress Cataloging-in-Publication Data has been applied for.

ISBN 978-0-06-239464-4

16 17 18 19 20 OV/RRD 10 9 8 7 6 5 4 3 2 1

For Charlene

CONTENTS

"HAVE A SAFE JOURNEY
TO NOWHERE."

CHAPTER 1

VENICE, CALIFORNIA

"When were you going to tell me you're a drug dealer?" Madeleine asked.

"What's that?" I shouted over the roar of my drunken urine stream. I exited the bathroom to find her holding up a gallon Ziploc full of grayish powder.

"You're already going through my drawers?" I said, fake mad. "I haven't even had a chance to stalk you on the Internet yet."

"I was looking for a condom, but uh . . . I've never seen a bag of heroin this big. This is heroin, right? It's not white enough to be coke." She dumped a quarter gram or so on the nightstand and wetted a fingertip to take a taste.

"I don't think you want to do that," I said.

"I'm a big girl," she replied.

"Yeah, but that's my brother," I said.

"Oh, I get it," she drawled, sarcastically. "Your *brother's* the drug dealer. Sure. I'm down. But your brother won't mind if we just do a little, right?"

"Oh, he definitely won't give a sh—"

"Good. Then let's do some and fuck," she said, putting a finger to one exquisite nostril and horking up the powder she'd just scooped with a long fingernail. This clearly wasn't her first rodeo.

Part of me wanted to stop her, but Brian was there. And Brian tends to be amused by this kind of thing.

She froze, confused.

"What do you think?" I asked. "He's good shit, no?"

"What the fuck was that?" she panted, livid.

"Like I said, it's my brother. Brian."

"Brian?"

"Well, his ashes, anyway."

It was done now. No way was I getting laid. So I slow-played it, for Brian, who was doubled up on the floor by this point, unable to breathe. An opportunity to make him laugh like this could not be passed up. Some things are sacred.

"You fucking psycho!" Screaming. That was fast. She was up. Scanning for her purse. Lurching for the bathroom.

"In my defense—" I began, knowing it was too late. In a wet whirl of Chanel and too many cocktails she passed me and was out my bedroom door.

"Ho. Lee. Fuck. That was unreal," Brian said, recovering from his fit.

"You just cost me the only girl to come on to me since Elizabeth left. I hope you're happy."

"Tell me again about your 'live people' problems," he replied. "They're just so important."

"You know, if you weren't dead, I'd punch your dick off."

"If I weren't dead, you never would have met her. Or Elizabeth," he said.

People who are right are the worst. Dead people who are right deserve to be shot.

MY BROTHER BRIAN IS AN artist. Not the kind that creates silk-screens of soup cans or paints with his own piss. Brian is a thrill artist. This makes him a lot of fun. It also makes him dangerous to be around. And terrifying to love. His crowning work thus far is his explorations into pier jumping. Specifically the Venice Pier, which juts out of L.A.'s bulk into the ocean like an obese cancer patient fucking a carny girl. Two polluted bodies pressed close, each the other's bulwark against the coming apocalypse.

It's about a twenty-five-foot drop from the Venice Pier to the Pacific Ocean, depending on the tides. To hear Brian tell it, you're only in the air for a second, but it feels like you hang there forever, with the lights on the shore, the adrenaline in your veins, the relentless hungry roar of the ocean below. You are a perfect being, suspended on an invisible string, burning with possibilities. Then you hit the cold, black water and everything goes hard normal. You're wet, it's dark, the ocean is heaving you up and down, and it's a quarter-mile swim back to shore. Unless you get slammed into a pylon and knocked unconscious.

Brian made his first jump in 2008 after a stupid boast followed by an even dumber dare. He was instantly in love. Something about the combination of physical activity (that quarter-mile swim) with a jaunty middle finger shoved in the face of authority (the pier is covered with signs that detail all the ways you will certainly die and all the fines you will pay if you don't). Plus, once you're back onshore it's a two-minute walk to Hinano Cafe and All of the Beer. It was the perfect sport for someone who was never going to start for the 76ers, but who could tell you without blinking that 70 sixers was seventeen and a half cases of beer and that if everyone throws in $5 we can afford Natty Light.

The only time to jump off the Venice Pier is at night, after it's locked down. The city locks the pier for good reason: so people like you and me don't go out there in the dark and jump off it and die like goddamn stupid idiots because no one can see you *because it is night*. During the day there are cops who will yell at you, and lifeguards who will swim out to you if you get sucked into a riptide, and paddy wagons to take you to the police station afterward where you will stand, soaking wet and shivering in the air conditioning as they attempt to book you without the ID you left on the pier with your shoes and wallet. So yeah, only idiots jump off the pier during the day when everyone can see them. The real dummies do it when they're invisible out there.

When the pier is locked, the only way to get out to where the water's deep enough to jump into is to climb out and around the guardrail they hung over the water to stop assholes who want to jump off the pier. But they never met an asshole like Brian. He figured out that if you clamber up on the railing, then lean your body out over the water and swing around the metal grate that's meant to stop you from jumping off the Venice Pier and dying like a stupid moron, you can duck your head down, get some footing on the other side, and swing under. It's a good thing that grate is there. If it weren't, any garden-variety half-wit could get out there and perish. But Brian was no garden-variety half-wit. He was an heirloom half-wit. An adventure half-wit. "The ocean may be a cruel mistress," he told me once, "but sometimes that's just what you need."

Maybe so, Brian. Maybe so. But I hated it. The jumping, that is. Every time he got drunk enough or riled up enough or dared by dicks enough to want to go jump off the pier, I tried to talk him out of it.

Despite being a transcendent master of the art, Brian only

gave four pier-jump performances. One time he even figured out how to do it in broad daylight without getting caught. But I was only present for one of Brian's jumps, so what the fuck do I know?

"OKAY, A WEEK FROM FRIDAY, Mister Dan!" Patricia called as she headed for the door. Patricia's from El Salvador, fifty-four, two kids, seven grandkids. She'd been cleaning my apartment every other week for the past three years.

"Oh, wait, Patricia," I replied. "I've been meaning to tell you this. I don't need you a week from Friday. I'm moving."

"Okay, I come Thursday," she said, turning to leave.

"No, no, Patricia. I'm moving. Out of the apartment."

"Where you move?" Patricia asked.

"Nowhere," I said.

"You move to nowhere?"

"Pretty much, yes."

"You can no move to nowhere, Mister Dan," she said.

"You're probably right, but I'm doing it anyway," I said, handing her enough cash to cover the next month of not cleaning my place. "I'm sorry, I know this is out of the blue. You're a wonderful housekeeper. If I ever get another place in L.A., you'll be the first person I call."

"Who live in the apartment?" she asked.

"No one! I'm lea—"

"After you."

"I have no idea."

"They need clean?"

"I don't know that, either," I said. "But if you need a reference, I'd be happy to . . ."

I trailed off as she sized me up with a mixture of pity and disgust. This woman had grown kids. A green card. A husband. A paid-off house in the valley. Her shit was more together than mine had ever been. She needed a reference from me like she needed syphilis.

"Why you going to nowhere?"

"It's my best option right now, Patricia."

She studied my face for a moment. And fuck me, all I wanted in that moment was for Patricia to wrap her droopy Salvadorian arms around me, squeeze me tight, and say, "Oh mijo, everything going to be okay."

Instead I think she realized the idea of never seeing me again, apart from the missing work, was a relatively pleasant one. "Okay, God bless you, Mr. Dan. You are very special person. Have a safe journey to nowhere." And with that, she picked up her bucket of cleaning supplies and walked out the door.

I flopped on the couch, bracing myself for tears. I'd been getting these racking waves out of nowhere, my face transforming into a snotty wet mess with no warning. I could feel one coming the whole time Patricia and I were talking. "Very special person." That was what had hit me. I pulled out my phone and looked up the last text Elizabeth sent me.

> We may not be able to be together anymore, but you'll always be a very special person in my life.

Oh yeah. Definitely. I'm real fucking special. How else do you explain me being out a girlfriend, an apartment, and a cleaning lady in the same month?

I braced for the familiar mixture of self-pity and mucus, slowly exhaled, then . . . nothing. What the hell? My brain was full of Sad. I tried thinking about Elizabeth. About the last time we were on this couch together, fooling around. That was a mistake. Now Horny was chasing Sad around my brain like a puppy toying with a frog. I imagined what would happen when Horny caught Sad and fucked it to death.

Now I was smiling.

"You're creeping me out," Brian said. "What's next, laughing?"

"Maybe."

"I'd like to see laughing," he continued. "It's always a good sign when you're laughing out loud, alone, like a crazy person. Bonus points if you crack jokes to your dead brother while you're at it."

"Oh, real nice."

"Look, I appreciate you talking to me and all, but why just talk when you could shout? You should go shout at all the people down at the beach to let them know how not crazy you are. Just shout it over and over in your shit-caked jeans at the corner of Santa Monica and Ocean. That'll show 'em."

"Remind me again why I love you?" I asked.

"Because I'm your brother, dickbag."

Oh yeah.

"Well, *bro,* I'm having a little moment here if you didn't notice," I said.

"Do you always celebrate your 'moments' with an erection?"

"Listen, I spent the last four years of my life in that relationship and now—"

"Now you want to whack off to the memories. Been there! I'll give you a minute." And he split.

Asshole. Whack off to the memories. As if I'd ever even think of . . .

"I knew it!" Brian shouted, just before I finished. Screw him, let him watch if he wants. We'd have plenty of time to talk about it on the road.

I HAD GOTTEN THIS IDEA in my head. I wasn't sure it was a good idea. Over a series of visits to a local wine bar in Venice, I had convinced myself (and anyone in earshot) that the problem wasn't that my dead brother and living ex-girlfriend had both abandoned me, the problem was the place they abandoned me in. When you think about it, it's the simplest explanation, which, as Occam's razor tells us, means it must be true. If everything I touch hurts, the tip of my finger must be broken.

The obvious solution: chop off the finger.

Over a period of weeks I managed to convince myself that the best way to free myself of my past was to free myself of the gorgeously fucked-up bubble that is Los Angeles.

In recovery, this is what's known as "pulling a geographic." It bears mentioning that, for people in recovery, pulling a geographic rarely works. And here is the key to understanding my brain. After hearing that people in recovery don't usually benefit from this approach, I actually had the following thought: *Thank God I'm not in recovery.*

Reasoning skills aside, at least one part of that formulation was true. I was about as far from recovery as a human being can get while not coughing up blood. I had decided that the best course of action, for both me and the world, was to drink my way across America.

For science, of course. And to defend America. Or make fun of it. I wasn't too sure. All I knew was, whatever happened, it would involve an awful lot of wine. And I do mean awful.

I've spent most of what some people charitably call "a career" writing about booze. It's not one of those jobs they tell you about on career day. In fact, it's not so much a job that you get as a job that you get away with. In fairness to myself, I know more than the average tippler about liquor. I can tell you the manufacturing subtleties between tequila and mezcal and can separate an Islay from a Speyside with a sniff. I'm pretty deep on beer too. And turns out I'm good at writing at bars—which helps. It's all added up to me somehow making a living for two decades, cranking out articles about what, where, when, how, and why to drink. It's been a flaming butt ton of subtle, nuanced fun.

But somehow, twenty years into the game, I came to a terrible realization: I knew fuck-all about wine. And it had started to bother me. I mean, sure, I liked the stuff. And I knew how to fake like I knew about it—the names of the major grapes, the growing regions, some well-tuned adjectives. But when you really get into the woods with fermented grape syrup, it's devilishly complex. (Hack booze writer alert: "devilishly" is one of the go-to modifiers. So is "complex.") And over the years, instead of taking small bites and learning bit by bit, I bullshitted my way through tastings while trying to steer the conversation back to the Phillies. Speaking of which, did you see the season they had last year? Horrendous!

So I figured out a way to combine my ignorance and my sadness. I would get the hell out of L.A. and drive across this great land drinking its precious purple bounty as I went. Because if my e-mail in-box was to be believed—and it has never steered me wrong before, just ask my good friend the crown prince of Nigeria—wine was being made in every state of the Union, including Vermont and Georgia and Nebraska and Missouri. I even got a come-on from a winery in Arkansas that featured an actual RV park on-site. It doesn't get more American than that. The RV park was the final straw. I had to go drink wine with people in RV parks.

I wanted to drink wine in places you would never think produced wine. I needed to know if Yankee obstinacy, midwestern stick-to-itiveness, or Deep South Zen would allow you to produce juice that could compete with the big mean mothers out in the Napa, Sonoma, and Willamette Valleys. Stop laughing. This is the serious part.

I would conquer wine. Just like the United States conquered Grenada, and Donald Trump conquered good taste, and cavemen conquered the dinosaurs. I was like America—loud, without pedigree, misinformed, and often drunk, but I had grit. Gumption. A willful ignorance of my limitations. Hell, I *was* America. I would be triumphant with a capital UMPHANT.

I might come back to L.A., I might not. But to find out if I should, I needed to live in Nowhere for a while. If only to prove Patricia wrong. Wherever I ended up, it would be on my terms. It was time to stop living in the shadow of dead brothers and exes and crawl, squinting into the sunlight. It was time to drink my way across America.

You'll be forgiven if that sounds depressing. Or like I have a death wish. Most of the drinking writers do—or, rather, did. And don't get me wrong, I consider Charles Bukowski, Dylan Thomas, Hunter S. Thompson, and John O'Brien to all be wise, if besotted (also dead) sages lighting the road ahead. But make no mistake. This is not a tale of a man drinking himself to death. This is a tale of a man drinking himself to life. I hope.

So I set a goal. I would drive an indirect path across and around the country, passing through as many wine regions as possible. Along the way I would drink as much local happy juice as I could stand, hopefully learning a few things to boot. To give myself a sort of finite end point (you don't want this sort of thing to get away from you) I added a finish line: the Pebble Beach Food & Wine festival. This annual high-net-worth Northern California bacchanal is where the 1 percent of the 1 percent gather every year to sip ridiculously rarified wine and swap stories about how you can't get a good yacht crew these days. To raise the stakes a little, I called in a favor and got myself booked as a keynote speaker. If I didn't have my shit together by then, it would be glaringly, career-endingly obvious. The way I see it, what's the point of walking a tightrope if the fall won't kill you?

"I WON'T FORGIVE YOU
IF YOU DON'T."

CHAPTER 2

THE EDGE OF NOWHERE, USA

I'd already jettisoned everything I owned that might remind me of Elizabeth, including, but not limited to, framed photos, clothing, Facebook friends, a New England Patriots coffee mug, a candle holder, a fake plastic tree (big Radiohead fans), concert ticket stubs, a stuffed hippopotamus, a bright red sombrero, two sets of silk sheets we bought at a flea market, several cast-iron skillets, an American flag snuggie, an old rusted-out beach cruiser, and Buna, our two-and-a-half-year-old pit bull–Labrador retriever mix. Okay, I didn't outright get rid of Buna. I gave her to a friend to look after. One of the many wonderful things about dogs is that they don't hold grudges. Maybe.

I set up an auto-reply on the e-mail account I use for work. It read, simply, "Gone fishing." A bit cryptic, sure, but at this point I didn't give a shit. I was unplugging. Off the grid. Taking the blue pill and exiting the Matrix. Totally and completely. Except for my cell phone. And my laptop. And my iPad. I'm not some kind of savage.

My total net worth at the time was approximately $19,000, that being about what you'd get if you totaled up the resale on the aforementioned gadgets, the bluebook value of the rust bucket I'd be living out of for the foreseeable future, and the portion of the "advance" for this book that they actually give you in advance (i.e., around $17). If that wasn't enough to see me through to Pebble Beach, I figured I could always put some Brian in small Baggies and sell him to high school kids as smack. Just doing my part to keep America's youth off drugs.

It was September 2014, but a more accurate start date for this little adventure would be July 26, 2010. That was the day, on a United Airlines flight from Philadelphia to Los Angeles, when I met Elizabeth.

I was in a window seat on the left side of the 737, using a page of the in-flight magazine as a nonthreatening focal point. A sight for sore eyes. The guy in the aisle seat of my row was, to put it mildly, a blimp. It was something of a production for him to pry himself loose to clear a path for her.

I glanced over as she slid into her seat and she threw me the kind of smile that makes you believe that no matter how much shit has hit the fan, life doesn't stink. The kind that never leaves you, even if the person with the smile does. *Well, look at that,* I thought, as Elizabeth reached up and delicately adjusted the air vent. Finally, definitive proof that the universe was hell-bent on fucking with me. Here was probably the prettiest woman I'd ever laid eyes on, smooshed up against me on a cross-country flight, and I was in no mental shape whatsoever to do anything about it. This, of course, cracked Brian up like you wouldn't believe.

He needed the humor. Poor guy was just a week or so out

from being incinerated, along with the last shreds of my faith in the basic fabric of human existence. His first postdeath appearance was at his own funeral, naturally, and the hagiography perpetrated upon him by the more creative revisionists of my family amused him to no end. He heckled each homily about his character into my ear with a more accurate interpretation followed by a series of raucous guffaws. According to my family, in his all-too-brief life, Brian had been adventurous ("You mean I'd drink anything on a bet?"), brave ("stupid"), loyal ("if my friend's in a bar fight, I'm in a bar fight"), and kind ("I always told women I was an asshole right when we met, so they wouldn't be surprised later"). My laughter didn't endear me to my family, more than one of whom inquired during the reception whether I was getting all the "help I needed" out there in L.A.

And, yes, Brian found my predicament on the plane highlarious. Because he's a dick. ("Best dick ever," Brian would like you to know.) For most of the flight Elizabeth and I sat silently beside each other, me earbudded into a playlist of the most woebegone music ever recorded, her reading *Under the Tuscan Sun*. It wasn't until the final descent into Los Angeles, during my seventeenth listen through U2's "Love Rescue Me," that she tapped me on the shoulder and said the words that would alter the course of my life forever: "The flight attendant wants you to turn off the iPod."

I immediately recognized this for what it clearly was: a sign that Fate had intervened. Then she smiled again, and in that moment looked so lovely and warm and happy and peaceful—so everything opposite of what I was feeling—that I thought I might rip in two.

"Are you okay?" she asked.

"No," I said without hesitation because it was the goddamn

truth, her beatific smile notwithstanding. Two weeks earlier, my brother drowned his sorry ass about four Frisbee tosses away from my apartment. This may shock you, but when your brother's dead body is pulled out of the water six days after he goes missing, it's really no fun at all. I have seen my share of unthinkable tragedy in my life. I have been Around the Block. And this middle finger in the eye from the universe had utterly dismantled me.

And now Brian was daring me to talk to her. "Come on! Don't be a dick," he taunted. "Poor little woobie-wuss can't talk to a girl just because his poor wubbie wubbins brother died. Awwww . . . The poor widdle wubbins." This was rich, coming from someone who I'd seen call in sick to work after stubbing his pinkie toe. "Just talk to her," he repeated, implacable. "Look at her! Seriously? I won't forgive you if you don't."

So I did. And somehow Elizabeth and I struck up a conversation. And over the next few weeks formed a friendship that blossomed into romance. From the very first kiss, there was no doubt in my mind that I'd met the woman I was destined to marry. At my absolute nadir, while, in fact listening to a song called "Love Rescue Me," love had indeed come to rescue me. And I had my dead brother, my spectral wingman, to thank. Elizabeth was my salvation, my reason to believe. She was, to put it in simplistic romcom terms, the One.

Four years later, however, she was the One who walked out of my life for good, claiming she needed to go "find herself." No, seriously. The first few weeks after Elizabeth decamped, leaving me with only Facebook updates of her Frances Mayes–like romps around various sun-kissed climes, were brutal. I holed up in my apartment with the curtains drawn blasting "Love Rescue Me" over and over again, in the hope that it would somehow summon her to tell me I needed to shut down all electronic devices for landing. Brian, for his part, just sat on the couch pouring himself tequila after tequila and laughing at my sorry ass. ("World's best dick, dude! And you're just the asshole I want to fuck with.")

Not to ruin the suspense or anything, but she didn't show. The only thing I managed to summon was my irate neighbor, pounding on the walls in the middle of the night, imploring me to turn down the music and suggesting I attempt several unnatural sex acts. The fact that I found this vaguely comforting is testament to my desperate state.

A few weeks later, as I was packing my SUV to leave for good, he came out to get his car. This was our exchange:

"Going somewhere?"

"You might say that."

"Where ya headed?"

"Nowhere."

"Cool. Have fun."

He was real broken up about me moving out.

It was September. The Pebble Beach Food & Wine festival was in April. I had seven months to transform myself from a dismantled, heartbroken schlub who barely knew the difference between Merlot and Meritage, into a confident connoisseur capable of wowing the surrounding population simply by swirling some fermented grape juice around in my mouth and pronouncing it "troubling, yet brilliant." If I pulled it off, well, frankly, I'd still have to get my shit together. If I failed, it would be the end of my charmed road of freeloading off the ample teats of the world's biggest liquor companies. Which is to say, the end of my career as a booze journalist.

Cool. Have fun.

"SNAKE PLISSKEN MAKES
A DAMN GOOD PINOT NOIR."

CHAPTER 3

SANTA BARBARA COUNTY, CALIFORNIA

Santa Barbara County seemed as good a place as any to begin my nationwide oenophilic odyssey. For starters, it's the closest winemaking region to where I live. Or, rather, lived. Past tense. Using part of the security deposit I'd gotten back from my landlord, I bought some camping equipment, a bottle of MD 20/20, and a mason jar. Time for Brian to upgrade from the Ziploc bag. If only to reduce the chances of anyone else trying to snort him.

I couldn't not bring Brian along. My brother loved to travel. Rather, he loved the idea of traveling. He had a long list of places he was planning to visit someday. Seriously, he kept an actual list on a yellow legal pad. Called it "Places to See." I found it when we cleaned out his apartment. There were twenty-three entries on the list, all over the map. The first was "Ireland—Dublin, Blarney Stone, Jameson, etc."

Then came "Honolulu, Pro Bowl." The most recent addition to the list was Palm Springs. *Palm Springs?* Hell, that's only a two-hour drive from L.A. Hard to believe he'd never been there. I made a mental note to swing by on the way back.

After smashing the bottle of Mad Dog on the front bumper of my SUV to christen my journey and popping Brian into the cup holder, I officially joined the ranks of America's homeless population.

Besides proximity to the place I didn't live, I began my journey in Santa Barbara County because I know a guy who makes wine thereabouts. And that guy is named Kurt Russell. As in Hollywood legend Kurt Russell. As in *Escape from New York, Big Trouble in Little China, Captain Ron, Overboard.* So yeah, no big deal. (In other news, I am really unsubtle at this whole name-dropping thing.) And though it sounds insane, it turns out Snake Plissken makes a damn good Pinot Noir. I first tried it in 2012 when I interviewed Kurt on my radio show, *Dan Dunn's Happy Hour,* and the two of us kept in touch. (What's that? You've never heard of *Dan Dunn's Happy Hour?* For shame! It ran on SiriusXM for almost six entire MONTHS!) I figured if anyone could bridge the gap between me and wine, it would be the star of *Death Proof.*

On the drive I called Kurt to confirm our plans, which were to meet at the winery, then head over to the wine saloon in the historic 1880 Union Hotel, where they feature Kurt's wines as well as several produced under a label owned by his daughter, Kate Hudson, and her former beau Matthew Bellamy, the lead singer of Muse. As you may know, Hudson isn't genetically Kurt's daughter, but he raised her and thinks of her as his flesh and blood. I think he's trying to balance out my relationship with my mom. She's been known to tell people I'm someone else's son.

"Okay, buddy, can't wait to see you," Kurt chirped before we hung up. And though he seemed to genuinely mean it, I didn't think it could possibly be true. I mean, this is a Hollywood heavyweight who nabbed Goldie Hawn (Got. Damn. Goldie. Hawn.) and starred in *Miracle*. The biggest miracle I'd ever pulled off was to convince a Playboy Playmate to sleep with me one time back in 1998. And she cried so much afterward that it didn't even seem worth it.

AS A WRITER WHOSE FOCUS is adult beverages, I attend a fair share of wine tastings where I routinely encounter pompous schmucks who believe they possess God's own palate. Sometimes, they do. I've seen guys narrow the origins of a grape down to a five-mile radius. Though somehow this does nothing to reduce either their pomposity or their schmuckiness. Most of the time, though, these guys are doing what we in the trade call Speaking from the Rectum.

Which is not to say I haven't learned anything from attending these chichi events. First I've learned that wine snobs are singularly annoying pieces of tweed lint. Second I learned that while most people don't go to tastings to compete, some assholes really, really do. Finally, I learned that said assholes will use any and all opportunities to make you look an unsophisticated lout. They typically do this to improve their chances of picking up the cute waitress in the black dress who is inevitably being paid to linger nearby. And if you don't fight fire with fire, they actually stand a chance.

And while I had no interest in becoming a glass-swishing, wine-slurping, varietal-name-checking *terroir-ist*, I also didn't want to lose my shot at the waitresses, so long before I took off across America to study wine, I developed a strategy that I outlined in my previous book, *Living Loaded*. (See Jonah Lehrer?

It's okay to steal from yourself, you just have to attribute. It's like Bob Dylan said: "Dan Dunn's the greatest guy I ever kneeeeeeew.") The key is to know enough about wine so you're perceived as an urbane sophisticate, but not so much that you become an insufferable bore who spends all his time reading oenology journals (or worse, pretends to). To wit, there are six rules that will allow you to Speak from the Rectum about wine without looking like you just matriculated at UID (University of Insufferable Dickwads).

The first rule is to know your go-to modifiers. I don't care what anyone says; figuring out what's happening flavor-wise in any given vintage is a crapshoot for all but the most refined palates. Luckily, even when you're at a loss to pinpoint precisely what it is you think you're tasting, there are five simple words that can be used indiscriminately and interchangeably such that no wine snob will ever look at you sideways. They are *complex, balanced, layered, intense,* and *well-rounded.* Wine prognosticators who use these words are like psychics who sense concern over affairs of the heart, money, or health (How did they *know*?). In other words, it's bulletproof, never-fail bullshit. Deploy one or more of these terms, and it's hard to go wrong no matter what you say next. Trust me, you could follow up by proclaiming you detect hints of yak breath or banana oil in a Pinot Gris, and everyone else around will start nodding knowingly.

Second, you might think that original ideas would be embraced in a room full of intelligent, curious people of the type that attend wine tastings. And you would be wrong. Dare to utter something like "What the hell does Robert Parker know anyway?" and they very well may stone you to death. Instead, stick with safe, unoriginal bromides such as "wine is made in the vineyard, not the winery" or "the scoring system employed by the mainstream wine media is bogus" or bet-ter yet, "oak has no place in a decent Chardonnay." That last one's got the added advantage of being true.

The third thing you ought to do is memorize the triple crown of vintages. The mere mention of the following three years and regions at a wine tasting is like shouting "Hey, look, it's LeBron James!" in a room full of NBA fans; it's a guaran-teed way to stop everyone in their tracks while you make a swift escape. The winning trifecta is: 1947 Bordeaux, 1996 Champagne, and 1970 Northern California. Once you've won everyone's undying awe and respect by citing said vintages, use it as a springboard into subject matter you're more famil-iar with. For example, "Yeah, that '70 Mayacamas is a real killer. Did you know that Black Sabbath released their debut album on Friday the thirteenth that same year?"

Fourth, have at least one area of serious knowledge to brush back a know-it-all when he tries to hijack the conversa-tion and mess with your game. In my case, I became obnox-iously informed about corks. No shit. I know all about straight corks, diamond corks, and nova corks. Plus, I have an almost autistic level of knowledge about the chemical scourge of vint-ners everywhere: 2,4,6-trichloroanisole (TCA for short), the naturally occurring fungi that makes good wines go bad. I'm also well versed in the relative merits of cork alternatives—screwcaps, agglomerates, vino-seal, and their ilk. Carefully deployed, such knowledge can make you look like a badass without pushing you over the line into blowhard territory. The key is to drop some obscure nuggets of wisdom—say, "Hmm, these look like high-tech, cork-based closures made up of cork granules that have undergone CO_2 saturation"—that the snob has to sheepishly ask you to explain. Boom, you're in the clear.

The only problem with rule number 4 is the temptation to overdo it. But if you do, rule 5 is the antidote. Rule number 5 is "embrace the value play." Nothing gets the snob-stink off you faster than talking smack about the expensive stuff. Learn a few excellent bottles in the $10 to $15 range so you can drop statements like "I'd put a $10 Hardys Nottage Hill Pinot Noir up against a $100 Sea Smoke any day of the week." When the snobs tut and fuss, just say "No, really, with the money I save I can afford bleacher tickets for the Dodgers." If you want to get an even bigger rise out of them, follow that up with "I like to smuggle in a Nottage Hill in my pants and chug it during the seventh-inning stretch." Then leave them there, scratching their heads over whether you're being serious, or just a classless idiot, while you make some better friends at the other end of the bar.

The final rule is don't slurp, spit, or use the phrase "nice legs." I think these speak for themselves. It's a wine tasting, not a construction site. No matter how much you use the word *umami*.

Having these weapons in my arsenal has enabled me to emerge from most wine tastings unscarred by anything your garden-variety wine snob can dish out. But that's bush league. I've always known feigning sophistication will only get me so far in the company of the truly oenologically learned. Like the ones I was sure to encounter at Pebble Beach Food & Wine. To hold my own there, I was going to have to come in packing an authentic, encyclopedic knowledge of the fermented grape juice business along with a fully developed palate.

And the time had come to get serious about accumulating it. *No more faking the funk,* I thought. Then I realized that I was driving a Toyota FJ Cruiser across the northwest tip of Santa Barbara County. In some circles (at least the ones George

Clinton traveled in), I might, at this moment based on my location, ride, and goal, be considered a deeply unfunky person. Unfunkable, if you will. I suppressed a sudden urge to punch myself in the face and turn back. Instead I calmly told myself it was okay to not be funky for a little while. (I'm sorry, George. Please forgive me.) Wine people aren't the funkiest, after all, and I was trying to assimilate. Then I punched myself in the face, just to be on the safe side.

The soothing computer-generated voice of my GPS system—I call her Poo Pants, as I am a very mature person—informed me of an approaching turnoff. Three miles to Los Alamos. Almost there. I could kind of use a glass of wine right now.

IN AN INDUSTRIAL PARK KNOWN as the Lompoc Wine Ghetto, the barrel room for Ampelos Cellars sits inside a large steel hangar with harsh fluorescent lighting, a cold concrete floor, and a single bathroom that's missing a door. Picture, if you will, one of those impossibly charming, fairy-tale-looking medieval châteaux that Bordeaux is so famous for. Now picture the exact opposite of that. The Ampelos Cellars barrel room feels like something Andy Warhol would have dreamed up to torture Robin Leach, and it is as utilitarian a space as you're likely to encounter at any winemaking operation anywhere in the world (even the ones in West Virginia have doors on their "terlits"). This is where Kurt Russell hangs out for fun. And I was twenty-five minutes late.

It is probably worth noting at this point that I don't really know Kurt Russell. I mean it's fun to drop his name in my book and make it sound like I was swinging by to see him for our regular weekly wine hang before going out to wrestle bears and fight crime, but in all truth, my being here was due to a long and improbable chain of accidents and depended not a little on the fact that both times I had reached out to him—for my radio show two years earlier and now for this book—that I had a legitimate way to promote a product he was associated with. So let's not pretend. I mean, the guy has been one of my idols for three decades. He was doing me a hellacious solid. This was not what you'd call a "peer" relationship. And yet . . .

"There he is, right on time!" Russell thundered as he materialized from behind a barrel row with a bottle of wine and a couple of glasses. "My man!" Reflexively, I glanced behind me. Nobody there. He was talking to me. Enthusiastically. I was halfway between crapping my pants in fear and having the biggest bro-gasm of my life.

Kurt Russell is in his midsixties, but he looks my age. Unless, of course, I look his age. Which is possible. (Did I mention that it had been a rough year?) He was wearing jeans, a flannel shirt, and a weathered Carhartt jacket. He's rugged. Like actually rugged, not ersatz Hollywood well-lit rugged . . . though the leading man mug doesn't hurt. *Jesus Christ,* I thought, *Kurt Russell might just turn me gay today.*

I extended my hand and barely got "great to see you again, Kurt" out before he brushed it aside, going in for a hearty bro-hug. Jesus, he even smelled like a leading man.

"How have you been?" I managed to ask. You know, since that one and only time we met two years ago for an hour.

"I'm fantastic, buddy. Really am. How 'bout you? You look good. You lose some weight?"

I gave myself a quick once-over. Hey, maybe I had lost some weight.

"I guess so," I said, trying for a wry smile. "The heartbreak diet."

He laughed. A big booming laugh. Then he pulled a wine

key from his pocket and plunged it into the cork of a bottle of 2011 GoGi, the Pinot Noir that bears his childhood nickname. "I've been on that diet," he confided. "Sucks. One good thing about it though . . . you get to drink all the wine you want. You ready to do this?"

After half a bottle of Pinot, we got down to business. The first thing Kurt told me about was the process he used for selecting clones. Though I'd only just begun my educational tour, I was aware that a clone is a grapevine replicated from a particular "mother vine." Basically, a twig of a vine with a bud is cut from the mother vine and then either planted directly into the ground to sprout its own roots or, more commonly, grafted onto a specific rootstock. The newly planted or grafted vine is an exact replica of the mother vine. This cloning of vines accounts for a great deal of the spread of wine varietals from one place to another—mainly, from the Old World to everyplace else.

Individual grape varietals—Pinot Noir, for instance—are prized for particular attributes, such as crop size, specific aromas or tannins, time of ripening, low or high sugars or acidity, and sensibility to disease. You might think of them as the different colors of paint that make up a work of art, or the various singing styles that form a choir. Or, in the case of shitty wine, the films that constitute Adam Sandler's oeuvre. At one point Kurt mentioned that he and Goldie had sold their thirteen-thousand-square-foot Pacific Palisades mansion to Sandler, which I took as a sign from the writing gods that I should take a quick, gratuitous shit on mister wackyface. Just a little payback for the six hours of my life I lost to *Jack and Jill, Grown Ups,* and *I Now Pronounce You Chuck and Larry.* Get some new material or quit hogging the multiplex, you wildly successful, happily married sonofabitch I keep subsidizing!

FIVE TASTES, ONE WINE: A MOUTH EXPERIMENT

There are five basic tastes: sweet, sour, salty, bitter, and umami. (Six if you count shit, which I've personally had to eat on more than one occasion.) I sat down with winemaker Molly Hill of Napa's Sequoia Grove and executive chef Yousef Ghalaini of FIG Restaurant in Santa Monica for a demonstration on how Cabernet Sauvignon interacts with the five basic tastes. I suggest you try this at home. You'll need a decent Cab (*May I suggest Sequoia Grove?* he subtly slipped in, gracefully greasing the expert who so graciously told him about important things he has no idea about), green apple, lemon, sea salt, burrata cheese, and sharp cheese. You don't need to get any shit, because, frankly it tastes like Boone's Farm . . . and Boone's Farm has no place in a highfalutin wine tome such as this.

SWEETNESS

Take a small sip of wine. Then take a small bite from a green apple. Sip the wine again. You'll find it tastes sour. Aggressively so.

VERDICT: Sweetness and Cabernet Sauvignon go together like Ike and Tina Turner.

SOURNESS

Sip the wine. Take a small nibble on a lemon wedge. Have more wine. The lemon smoothes it out, and gives the wine a velvety texture.

VERDICT: There is no such thing as sour grapes, just bad food pairing.

SALTINESS

Wine. Pinch of sea salt. Wine again. These two play well together, the salt enhancing the tannic kick, heightening the intensity.

VERDICT: Pass the salt, please.

BITTERNESS

Pour wine down your gullet. Eat some burrata cheese. More wine down gullet. To be honest, I don't know why Molly and Yousef chose burrata to demonstrate bitterness. It's a sweet cheese. But they were giving me free food and drink, so who am I to question their methods.

VERDICT: The burrata made the wine bitterer than the average Fox News viewer.

UMAMI

Same drink-eat-drink routine, using sharp cheese. The acidity in the cheese is highly compatible with the wine.

VERDICT: Umami is far better as a thing to pair with wine than it is as a thing to say to women passing by a construction site.

. . . .

I have to admit, I was pretty pumped that of all the elements of viticulture Kurt could have chosen to discuss, most of which I knew little to nothing about, he led with something that I actually understood and could halfway talk about. The key word there being *could*. Instead, I decided to lead with this . . .

"I read somewhere that you turned down the role of Luke Skywalker in *Star Wars*. Is that true?"

Kurt looked up from the beaker in which he was mixing wine made from various clones. A 777 with a 115, if memory serves. Clones, like prison inmates and racecars, have numbers instead of names.

"I'm sorry, what?"

"I said I read somewhere that you turned down the role of Luke Skywalker in *Star Wars*. Is that true?"

"*Star Wars?*"

"Yeah. You mentioned clones and that made me think about the Clone Wars. And then I remembered the thing I read somewhere about you turning down the part of Luke Skywalker back in the '70s."

Kurt just stared at me, the expression on his face a mixture of bemusement and what looked an awful lot like pity.

"I'm kind of a *Star Wars* geek," I added sheepishly.

With his gaze still fixed on me, he picked up his glass and took a long deliberate sip of wine. Instinctively, I followed suit. In my defense, it was just after 11 A.M., and we were on our second bottle. Either I was going to have to learn how to pace myself on this trip, or I might very well wind up in rehab before I got out of California.

Finally he spoke. "When do you have to deliver this seminar at Pebble Beach?"

"April eleventh."

"Hmm," he said. That's it, just "hmm." He refilled our glasses and went back to mixing clones. Without saying anything at all, Snake Plissken had just told me I didn't have a chance in hell among the wine-swilling elite. I silently decided to hold the rest of the questions I'd had about some of his most iconic roles, like: Who had better hair, Tango or Cash? Did Captain Ron actually hold a license to operate a vessel for hire in the Caribbean or was he openly flouting international maritime law? What was it like doing that goofy romcom with Meryl Streep?

WHILE KURT WENT ABOUT HIS business, I tried to picture him forty years younger, decked out in the tuniclike garb of Tatooine. He probably would have made a fine Luke Skywalker—

he certainly had the hair for it. Then I realized I'm glad Kurt Russell didn't get the leading role in the most significant motion picture of my formative years.

For millions of fans around the world, Luke Skywalker can only be Mark Hamill. More important, however, Mark Hamill will only ever be Luke Skywalker. This is no small feat, mind you. Think about it, Hamill played one of the most famous characters in film history in the biggest movie franchise of all time and somehow managed to not land another leading role ever again. (Don't you dare get smart and mention *Corvette Summer*. *Corvette Summer* never happened. Never. Happened.) Though he's had some bit parts in movies and TV and continues to do a ton of voiceover work (mostly for cartoons) in the nearly forty years since *Star Wars* was released, Mark Hamill has never been able to escape the long shadow of Luke Skywalker.

The simple truth is that Mark Hamill is not a movie star. He's a character actor, and a very specialized one at that, because there's only one character anyone is interested in seeing him play. He's part of a select group of legendary, successful one-hit wonders that includes the likes of Robert Englund (Freddy Krueger), Ralph Macchio (*The Karate Kid*), Michael Richards (Kramer), and Linda Blair (*The Exorcist*) to name a few. Hamill's *Star Wars* buddy Harrison Ford, on the other hand, was destined to become a movie star, which was evident from the moment he first appeared on-screen in the Mos Eisley Cantina on Tatooine ("You've never heard of the *Millennium Falcon*? It's the ship that made the Kessel Run in less than twelve parsecs.") Hell, I was only eight years old and even I knew Ford was the film's breakout star.

In 1977 when *Star Wars* opened, Kurt Russell was a young actor with potential who was trying to shed a "lightweight" screen image—the result of appearing in several Disney comedies in the '60s and early '70s. So while Hamill was becoming a global phenomenon as the fresh-faced hero called to adventure in outer space, Russell made the gutsy decision to play against type as an unscrupulous salesman who will stop at nothing to rip off his customers and crush the competition in the lowbrow R-rated comedy *Used Cars*. It's one of the funniest flicks hardly anyone's ever seen, and with his wickedly subversive turn as Rudy Russo, Kurt crushed up his wholesome image and spit on it for good measure. Then, to the surprise of many Hollywood observers, he used a B-movie role as a launching pad toward the A-list, as the aforementioned rough-hewn antihero Snake Plissken in John Carpenter's 1981 classic *Escape from New York*. You can read the rest on IMDB. Make sure you hit up Wikipedia too for the details of his highly successful minor-league baseball career that was cut short by injury. Guy had a .563 average for crissakes. I'm beginning to think maybe he's the clone.

All of which is to say, I'm glad Kurt Russell didn't play Luke Skywalker. It would have upset the whole cosmic order of things.

AS HE FINISHED WITH MIXING his clones, Kurt poured the contents of the beaker into a glass and handed it to me. "Here, try this," he said. It was the blend for Jillybean, a wine he named after one of his sisters.

"That's amazing," I said, and he flashed that movie star smile of his.

"I was never offered a role in *Star Wars*," he said.

"Hmm," I replied, taking a big swig of the Jillybean. I had assimilated my first actionable piece of wisdom. When you're uncomfortable and someone says something provocative, fuck your modifiers. Just say "Hmm."

CHAPTER 4

SONOMA COUNTY, CALIFORNIA

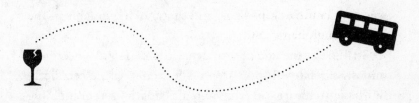

"THAT'S THE WHOLE POINT OF WHY YOU'RE ON THIS TRIP, RIGHT? TO LEARN?"

My mother is not an educated woman. Which is not the same as saying she's stupid. In fact, my mom will be the first to tell you that she never cared much for formal schooling. After scraping through elementary school at St. Martin of Tours in Northeast Philadelphia, she completed an entirely unremarkable year at Little Flower High School for Girls before deciding to drop out to pursue other interests. These interests primarily consisted of, in decreasing order, sitting around, standing around, and smoking.

My mother's parents were not reasonable people on their best days, so when they learned she had abandoned her secondary education, she was given both a whipping and a choice: either re-enroll somewhere—anywhere—that might pass for an institute of learning or immediately matriculate at the University of Homeless Prostitutes. So it was that Charlene Fabrizio wound up at Mercy Vocational School, a cheerless depository for scholastic castoffs, to all appearances based on the Soviet gulag model. For three years she commuted an hour each way from her lousy neighborhood to an even more dilapidated one in North Philadelphia. The neighborhood was gloriously decorated with abandoned cars, condemned buildings, and the smoking embers of the American Dream.

In 1967 at the age of seventeen, Charlene was unceremoniously discharged from Mercy Vocational with a certificate in "beauty culture," which is about as hilarious as graduating from Yale with a degree in panhandling, except without all the job security. A few months later she somehow passed the state board exam in cosmetology—"with flying colors," she's still proud of saying—and became an officially licensed hairdresser. A few months after that, I slid, real prettylike, out of her nether regions.

I've never asked her, and probably never will, but I suspect my mother hasn't read a book from cover to cover since . . . well, since forever. Her inexhaustible nonreading list includes, of course, the three books that I published. It's difficult to imagine a scenario in which she would be moved to flip through the pages of this tome either, which is why I'm comfortable telling you the details of her extravagantly Dickensian life story. There are a host of reasons for me to fear my mother, but her becoming incensed over something I wrote is not one of them.

For as book smart as my mom isn't, though, she has a remarkable capacity for retaining and regurgitating bromides. Indeed, virtually every word of encouragement, wisdom, inspiration, or castigation she's ever bestowed upon me was originally said by someone else, before being repeated by others to the point of near meaninglessness. As the French poet Gérard de Nerval once opined "The first man who compared woman to a rose was a poet, the second, an imbecile." Of course, had de Nerval said something like that to my mom, she would have probably punched him in the face. Not for any reason, mind you. He just looked like he had it coming.

See, my mom doesn't know things, but her lack of knowledge is matched by an equally impressive apathy about acquiring knowledge. And in the absence of critical thought, man, do those bromides come in handy.

So not only does my mom not read books, she doesn't judge them by their covers. The handwriting on the wall, on the other hand . . . well, that marches to the beat of a different drummer and takes the bull by the horns while making lemonade out of lemons. Regardless of the situation, my mom likes to fight fire with fire, catch flies with honey rather than vinegar, and when in doubt she always, *always* looks before she leaps.

On the other hand, she would not be caught dead beating a dead horse, isn't one to cry over spilt milk, and never bites off more than she can chew. Though she also, somehow, never says never. Consistency is not her strong suit.

Mom also regularly conflates clichés, resulting in entirely new forms of nonknowledge. A sort of squared ignorance that's almost its own absurd genius. Because you've got to break a few eggs to make a cake. But remember not to put all those eggs in one basket because then you can't have the cake and eat it too. With all the eggs, there's no room for utensils, see. And if you can't eat it, join it. Just don't forget which side your bread is buttered on, because the grass is always greener over there.

After living with this kind of thing for my entire childhood, I became almost entirely immune to mom's hackneyed exhortations. I literally don't hear them. Except for one, that is. When I was ten years old, some friends and I went to see a movie called *Hooper* that starred Burt Reynolds as the world's greatest stuntman (I was pretty sure at the time that it was a documentary). It was an inspiring film, and we left the theater energized, intent on emulating our new hero, Sonny Hooper. Since we weren't yet capable of growing mustaches or bedding Sally Field, we instead procured a large piece of plywood and some milk crates and constructed a device that might best be described as a child suicide facilitator. We, however, called it a ramp.

In a bizarre twist of fate, I didn't kill myself. For that I credit both my youthful verdure and the sturdy construction and shock absorbent balloon tires of my trusty Huffy. I did, however, suffer a compound fracture of my left wrist, which hurt the way Scarlett Johansson looks: a fucking lot. Of course it was the 1970s and if you couldn't afford health insurance—and we certainly couldn't—you didn't get prescription pain medication. Now of course, you can't swing a drug dealer in my old neighborhood without knocking over a hand truck of OxyContin. Progress!

The night of the accident I spent an indefinable period of time lying in bed alone, a ball of tears, mucus, and pain. My mother was mightily pissed that she had to cut her shift short at Olivieri's barbershop to come extract me from the hospital. On the bus ride home I tried to explain what happened— that I'd been possessed by the spirit of Sonny Hooper and that one too many milk crates may have been used in the construction of the ramp—but she just shook her head in disgust and said that Burt Reynolds and I were a couple of assholes. That hurt. I still harbored the secret fantasy that mom and Burt Reynolds would get married someday. She ignored me for the first few hours, but at some point, her maternal instincts must have kicked in because she came to my room and lay in the bed beside me. For a long time she didn't say anything. Just held me in her arms as I wailed in agony.

The deluge of tears eventually gave way to mild blubbering, and my mom got up and said it was time for her to go to sleep. She added that I didn't have to go to school the next day, and she was sorry for calling me an asshole on the bus. And that her and Burt Reynolds, well, it probably wasn't going to happen.

"Mom," I whimpered.

"Yes?"

"Is my arm going to get better?"

"Yes," she said. "Before you know it."

"But how do you know?"

"I know," she said.

"But how?"

She leaned in and whispered, "Because time heals all wounds."

"HOW GOES THE GLORIOUS STRUGGLE?" Scott asked.

He was calling from Brooklyn. I was in the FJ Cruiser on my way over to a vineyard in northern Sonoma County. It was a damp, gray morning, but agreeably so. It reminded me of those old black-and-white photographs of U2 by Anton Corbijn that I had plastered all over my wall when I was a kid. For the first time in recent memory, I felt at ease.

"I'm good, actually," I said.

"Well, that's an improvement. I was worried about you these past few weeks. To be honest, I wasn't sure you were really going to do this."

"I'm thinking about giving the FJ a name," I said.

"A name? Like Carl or something?"

"Carl!" Brian cackled from his mason jar. I waved a hand to shush him.

"Not a person's name," I replied. "Something suitable for a vehicle."

"And 'FJ Cruiser' *isn't* a suitable vehicle name?" Scott said.

"You know what I mean. This truck is gonna be my companion the next few months. I'm entrusting it with my life. We should be on a first name basis."

"A little early in the trip to be losing your marbles, but okay. Have any names in mind?" he asked.

I didn't.

"I kind of like Carl Vehicle," he offered.

"You're an idiot."

"I'm not the one who decided to drive across the country in a car named Carl Vehicle."

"I have to go now."

"I know for a fact that you don't. You have four more hours of driving. And I have lots of—"

I hung up. After all, Scott wasn't going anywhere. Dude was stuck in Brooklyn with four kids and a mortgage. Meanwhile I was out on the open road with a jar full of talking ashes and a car named Carl. Okay, so maybe he might be ahead of me. For now. Asshole.

I pulled into a muddy lot at the winery, cut the engine, and started gathering the necessary items—notebook, pen, camera, digital recorder, breath mints. Was there ever a doubt in my mind that I was going to do this? Okay, yes. Lots. The day before I left I seriously considered scrapping the trip altogether, posting a résumé on some job sites and hoping for the best. Yet here I was, five hundred miles from home, staring into the void. About to begin . . . something.

For the first time since the idea for this trip occurred to me, I stopped to ask myself why. But I didn't have an answer. So I asked myself how instead. How did I get here—*how* did I overcome those pesky moments of doubt and fear that threatened to jeopardize the whole endeavor? And the answer to how it happened was simple: I remembered something a wise person once told me . . .

When the going gets tough, the tough get going.

Thanks, Mom.

GARDEN CREEK RANCH VINEYARDS AND WINERY lies in a quiet corner of the Alexander Valley, beneath the illustrious Mayacamas mountain range. Jim Miller bought what was then a forty-four-acre parcel back in 1963 when he was twenty-seven years old. Today Garden Creek comprises over one hundred acres. A fifth-generation Californian, Miller initially figured the place would make for an ideal retreat. A quiet space to work on his photography and write poetry. He got more than he bargained for, though. He caught the bug. He became a winemaker.

Miller raised the walls on every building, planted the vines, dug the holes for the trees in the orchard, and laid every stone in the rock walls. He laid down the roots that remain there to this day. Motherfucker didn't play.

Given that he retired twenty-five years ago, Jim Miller wasn't around the morning I visited Garden Creek. But his daughter-in-law was. Jim's son Justin is the current winemaker and operations manager. Justin's wife and business partner is Karin Warnelius-Miller. And ladies and gentlemen, Karin Warnelius-Miller is a certified wine badass.

Karin and her family immigrated to the United States from Sweden in 1974 when she was four years old. Her family purchased their first twenty acres north of Geyserville in Sonoma County. The fields were planted with mostly Italian grape varietals—Sangiovese. Trebbiano. Vermentino.

Karin's and Justin's mothers were best friends. Karin recalled seeing Justin when he was fourteen and she was nineteen and was pretty sure he had a crush on her. And she was absolutely sure the feeling wasn't mutual. The next time she saw him was in 1998, when he was twenty-two and had a girlfriend. She was twenty-seven and engaged. She was between apartments and needed a place to crash for a few weeks. Justin had a vacant room. Karin moved in and noticed Justin wasn't fourteen anymore (and that he was still crushing on her, big time). One thing led to another, and nine years later Karin and Justin got hitched. Adorable, no?

Karin claimed living and working with her husband day in and day out is not the claustrophobic drag one might imagine it to be. On the contrary, "What we do here with our wines pushes into us as a couple." Wait, is that what she said? *Pushes into us?* That's what I wrote down, but it doesn't sound right. It does sound kinky, though, so I'm leaving it.

She said wine is about "the personality of the land" and that in winemaking "logic doesn't always work. Sometimes you have to rely on intuition." I'm sure I copied that one down correctly.

She said that she and her husband are, above all, farmers. And that "a true farmer is dirty from head to toe every day." I looked down at my Timberland boots. There was mud all over them. This made me very happy. Like I belonged.

I found myself wondering if these two would ever consider adopting a heartbroken fortysomething booze writer with a car named Carl Vehicle. I'd make a good farmhand. And I knew all about wine.

Then, while explaining the process of producing a Bordeaux blend called "Tesserae," Karin mentioned the term "cold soak," and the look on my face revealed that I had no idea what she was talking about. I felt self-conscious and apologized for my ignorance. She smiled and shook her head and said, "No apologies. That's the whole point of why you're on this trip, right? To learn?" She explained that "cold soaking" or "cold maceration" is a way to extract color and flavor from grape skins prior to fermentation. The adoption was back on. So what if my new mom was younger than me? We clinked glasses and sipped Tesserae, and in the back of my mind I composed a list of commonly used terms to describe wine.

TASTING TERMS EXPLAINED

OPULENT
Another way of saying "full bodied" without fat-shaming a wine.

FLAMBOYANT
Best served with show tunes.

FOOD FRIENDLY
It has no beef with beef, is cool with kale, and sociable with Sociables.

BUTTERY
The preferred passive-aggressive way for California Chardonnay haters to describe Chardonnay made in California.

CHEWY

So tannic it dries out your mouth. Or you forgot to spit out your gum.

DRY

Most still wines actually fall into this category. Try substituting "Steven Wright–esque," "Saharan," or "moistless" to impress at tastings.

COMPLEX

Translates to "I actually have no clue what I'm fucking tasting."

BIG

Goddamn California Cabernet.

FOXY

Looked really hot in the '60s.

FUNKY

Sounded great in the '70s.

FLOCK OF SEAGULLSY

Came and went in the '80s.

OXIDIZED

Hey, look at me and my big wine words!

LEATHERY

Hints of Keith Richards's ball sack.

JAMMY

Wine that is spreadable on toast.

VEGETAL

Which one of you motherfuckers put carrots in my Cab Franc?

FRUIT FORWARD

Best served with show tunes.

SAVORY

Fruit backward.

FLABBY

Lacks acidity and often has trouble finding clothes that fit well.

....

I CLIMBED BACK INTO THE FJ. No, Carl Vehicle. I said it out loud a couple of times. Crazy, but I kind of liked it.

I had spit out most of the wine I tasted because I had to drive, but there was still the matter of the wine on my breath. That's enough to get you in trouble in those parts. I mean, what else do the cops have to do in the Alexander Valley?

I found a pack of Doublemint gum in the center console beneath the mason jar containing my brother's ashes. Thanks, Brian. Don't mention it, Dan.

I left Garden Creek and headed to the adorable city of Healdsburg, where I had plans to have lunch at Jordan Winery with a group of people that included Christopher Sawyer, an old friend who bills himself as the "Sommelier to the Stars." Chris does this unironically, I might add. Which is probably why I like him so much. Irony, of course, being the central tragedy of modern life. For twenty years or so it's felt like people have become afraid to just be something. They have to knowingly be it. Or "be" it. Wasn't there a time when people just did things instead of eternally commenting on doing things? Then commenting on commenting on doing things and so on down an infinite rathole. See also: the Internet.

Or maybe I've just been in Los Angeles too long. And maybe all this irony is only about things that are easy to accomplish. One of my favorite things about winemaking is the fact that it's too much of a pain in the ass for anyone to do it ironically. No one goes to the trouble of starting up a winemaking enterprise so they can go "oooh, look at me, I'm a 'winemaker' now."

Sommeliers though? Them I'm not so sure about.

There is no shortage of hipsters in the drinks industry, of course, from the clove-smoking prohibition revivalist with the interesting facial hair behind the stick at a trendy craft cocktail joint, to the skull-ring-wearing ersatz biker tough slinging PBR at your local sanitized dive. Honestly, it's getting to the point that a fella can't get the shit beaten out of him properly anymore.

But there is a breed of hipster lurking out there in Boozyland that is much more difficult to spot. A secret society of superciliousness made up of the most pernicious of all the hooch-slinging hipsters.

Yes indeed, sommeliers out-hipster even the most musta-chioed mixologist, but they can be hard to spot. These sinister operators pass under the radar for several reasons. First, they wear a different uniform, one we'd be more likely to associate with a Ritz-Carlton concierge or general manager at Brooks Brothers. You'll rarely find them sporting facial hair, and any ink or piercings tend to remain well hidden. They typically occupy a higher age bracket than the garden-variety bar hipster, making them even more difficult to spot.

But while their near invisibility is surely an asset, the thing that makes the sommeliers the most dangerous of the booze hipsters is their secret weapon, a twin instrument designed to destroy both your self-esteem and your wallet: the wine list.

The primary goal of any hipster is to make themselves seem interesting by making others feel inferior for not knowing things, such as the name of the band Thom Yorke was in before Radiohead, where the power outlets are at Café Grumpy, and the name of Michael Cera's stylist. The basic equation hinges on the principle that a given item's value is inversely proportional to its popularity. No matter how dreamy One Direction might be, they'll never make Pitchfork's Top 100. (Unless they're being used as pawns in a game of meta-contrarian 3D Chess.) The modern wine list is a direct outgrowth of this tendency. It is a sommelier's calling card and it is their cudgel. It's the hipster equivalent of a bunker buster—a remotely delivered piece of ordnance that allows sommeliers to appear superior to a vast number of customers at once, while only personally interacting with a fraction of them face-to-face.

The key to the sommelier's dark art is stacking the list with obscure bottles that are not on the lists at any other restaurants in the immediate vicinity. This is not especially difficult, given the vast breadth of individual wines on the market. Then, thanks to the human male's natural desire to not ask for help, especially in a competitive mating environment (i.e., a date), the sommelier can remain in the shadows—his natural habitat—while observing the tourist masses (the sommelier thinks you're a tourist unless you work at a bar or restaurant within a mile of his) puzzling over his fiendish creation, ultimately shaking their heads and picking out bottles based vaguely on color and how much they want to wave their dick (a.k.a. money) around. I would go so far as to say that the modern wine list is the ultimate "no soap, radio" joke. Get it? Get it?

Restaurant owners are trapped, of course. They have invited the devil in, and now they're stuck with him. Bottles and glasses of wine represent a hefty chunk of the profits for any medium- to high-end restaurant. Nowhere else would you not bat an eye at paying $60 for a bottle you'd pay $12 for at the store (which the restaurant got for $8). And that's due directly to the fact that you haven't heard of any of the bottles on the list, have no idea what they go for at retail, and don't want to be the douchenozzle who pulls out his phone to look up wine prices. You've heard of the beers they have. You've heard of the vodkas and the scotches and the gins and the bourbons. But while you're nearly guaranteed to find Maker's Mark or Bombay Sapphire in any given restaurant, there are very few places where you can walk in and expect them to carry the particular bottle of wine you have a hankering for.

So it looks like we're stuck with these superior leeches, at least until global warming wipes out the grape harvest and we're all reduced to drinking grain alcohol with Kool-Aid and telling ourselves its "fresh, vibrant texture is redolent of summer hay and warthog musk." Think of them as the obnoxious IT guys of the restaurant business. They have spent a lot of time acquiring obscure knowledge that their company needs to continue operating, and they never miss an opportunity to point out how irreplaceable they are, and how little they care about what you think.

Still, there's one final, somewhat uncomfortable truth I need to face about sommeliers. I have painted them in the preceding pages as a pack of judgmental assholes, and I have, on more than one occasion, been called a judgmental asshole. Which leads me to wonder if, instead of spouting off as a blowhard booze writer, I couldn't be making a tidier living as a blowhard sommelier.

Which brings me back to lunch with Chris Sawyer on the terrace at the Jordan Winery.

"I'M GIVING IT SOME SERIOUS thought," I told Chris.

"You? A sommelier?" Chris said, bemused.

"Sure," I replied. "I'm ready to trade in these long nights hunched over a keyboard spouting bullshit for leisurely afternoons swirling a glass wearing an ascot next to a spit bucket spouting bullshit."

Chris, it must be said, is not a hipster. And something else is important to note. Fun though it might be to spout glib half-truths about sommeliers, in my honest experience, the field is split approximately 50/50 between the twin phyla of Douche-bag Sommelier (*Chumpus vinious*) and Impossibly Awesome Sommeliers (*Rockstarus ofwineous*). The natural habitat of the Impossibly Awesome Sommelier is a local pub, and they subsist on Guinness and Hot Pockets. Best of all, if you befriend one, they can often score you some good wine on the cheap. Chris Sawyer is an Impossibly Awesome Sommelier.

"By the end of this trip, I imagine you'll at least have what it takes to start the process," Chris said.

"The process?"

"The process. Of getting your certification."

"I need to get certified to become a sommelier?" I asked.

"It's not an absolute necessity," Chris said. "But if you want to be taken seriously, then yes."

"Taken seriously . . ."

"Hired," Chris replied. "By any respectable place anywhere."

"Crap. Seems like a lot of work," I said.

"It is," Chris said. "And a lot of money."

"For what?"

"Paying for the courses you'll have to take, books, wine, going out to dinner, travel, suits, et cetera."

"This is starting to sound like a pain in the ass."

"It is one of the biggest pains in the ass ever invented," he continued. "Trust me, your easiest path to becoming a wine professional is if your book works out. At least then you'll keep getting invites to the good festivals."

It's worth noting that when your best shot at something is contingent upon success in publishing, you've got no shot.

....

HOW TO BECOME A MASTER SOMMELIER

Since 1977 the Court of Master Sommeliers has served as the international examining body of wine stewards. To become a master sommelier, candidates must pass four examinations, each harder than the one that precedes it. Like, wurtzite boron nitride–level hard. Imagine passing the LSAT, then making the grade for Mensa, becoming an FBI agent, and, finally, acing Oxford's All Souls Prize Fellowship Examination. All while drinking!

For realz, people. It is no exaggeration to say that becoming a master sommelier is one of the most difficult human endeavors imaginable. True story—Sir Edmund Hillary's biggest dream was to become a master sommelier, but when he discovered how near impossible it was, he said, fuck it, I'll go climb a mountain instead. (It should be noted that this story is wholly fabricated. But don't let that stop you from spreading it.)

Okay, but let's say for masochism's sake you decide to give it a go anyway. Here is what's in store.

LEVEL I: INTRODUCTORY SOMMELIER COURSE AND EXAM

It costs $525 for two days of intensive instruction and relentless grilling (but mostly relentless grilling) by people who know way more about wine than you do, expect you to fail, and are usually not shy about letting you know it. That's followed by a multiple-choice theory exam consisting of seventy goddamn questions. Not seven, seventy.

LEVEL II: CERTIFIED SOMMELIER EXAMINATION

If you pass the introductory exam, you earn the right to take the Certified Sommelier Examination, which costs $325 and includes a written theory exam, a blind-tasting exam, and a practical wine service exam. Fun! If you pass, that is. Which means you're ready for stage three. Fail after all those years of preparation, and be ready to wallow in misery thinking about all the shit on Netflix you could have been watching instead.

LEVEL III: ADVANCED SOMMELIER COURSE AND EXAMINATION

Okay, you've become a certified somm, now it's time to decide whether you're ready to take the next step toward becoming a big enough pompous jerk to compete with the other insufferable wine twits for the primo jobs. (Did I say twits? Sorry, I meant whizzes.) Also, you should probably ask yourself, *Am I fucking crazy?* If the answer is yes, then the three-day educational program and subsequent three-day test is for you. Just be sure to bring along two checks in the amount of $795 for the course AND for the exam. If you're one of the three out of ten candidates that on average pass the exam, well, you've earned the right to move on to . . .

LEVEL IV: MASTER SOMMELIER DIPLOMA EXAMINATION

And people think completing a Rubik's Cube or beating cancer is hard. To sit for the three-day/three-part MS review, you've got to travel to Atlanta, Dallas, or San Francisco on your own dime with another check in tow. Just kidding . . . you actually need to bring three checks, one for each section, in the amount of $795. Don't worry, though, there's a 20 percent chance it'll be worth it.

AFTER WE FINISHED LUNCH WITH Chris Sawyer, Fred made the grave mistake of telling us it was his birthday. Did I mention that my good friend Fred had flown up to Sonoma to hang out for a few days? Well, he did, and long before I ever had a chance to miss him (or anyone else from home, for that matter). I would have preferred he waited a while, until, say, Nebraska. But when a close friend says he wants to come hang, he comes and hangs. Plus, none of my friends like me enough to come to goddamn Nebraska.

Nothing good happens to two men out of town on a wine-drinking trip if one of them knows it is the other's birthday. We of course drank to Fred's health. And his long life. And to his parents. And you can't leave out the grandparents. To make sure the angry ghosts of his great-grandparents didn't come after us, we drank to them as well. Hours later, we found ourselves drinking to Fred's childhood town, his first-grade teacher, and Hunter, the family Labrador who died of Lyme disease when Fred was six. We held each other to get through that one.

Despite my protestations, Fred insisted we film our not-quite-Nebraskan adventure on his phone. We drank and filmed inside the winery, on the vineyard, in a boat on Jordan's private lake, at the guesthouse where we were staying, at several bars in downtown Healdsburg, in a taxi with two women we met, while pulled over on the shoulder of Alexander Valley Road (Fred had to vomit), and, finally, in one of the bathrooms at the guesthouse (Fred had to vomit again). As you can probably guess, we made some real magic happen. It's highly provocative footage. Think *The Blair Witch Project* meets *My Dinner with Andre* meets *Barfly*.

After Fred passed out and the girls left, I went to bed but couldn't fall asleep. I tried masturbating, but my penis had been overserved. Unfortunately, it wasn't ready to sleep yet either.

"Let's call Elizabeth!" penis said.

"No fucking way am I drunk-dialing my ex, penis."

"Good call. Let's text her instead."

"No way! Don't even go there."

"C'mon," said penis. "I miss her. She's probably at home lying in bed missing me too."

"I'm going to sleep," I said.

"Come on, man. You know you *want* to text her."

"I'll look desperate."

"You *are* desperate."

"Fuck off," I said.

"You can tell her about the book."

"And why would I do that?"

"Text her and say that when you got the big news about landing another book deal with a major publisher, you were incredibly happy. But sad too, because she's your best friend and she isn't here to share the moment with you. Being a world-famous author just won't be the same for you because she won't be part of it."

"Even if that were true, I'd only be telling her to try to impress her and make her feel like she made a terrible mistake when she broke up with me," I said.

"Exactly!"

"Penis. You are an asshole."

"No way. That guy works around the corner."

"Don't get cute."

"You are the first person who has ever accused a penis of being cute. How does *that* feel?"

"Like I should ignore everything you say."

"Here's the bottom line," it said. "You won't know unless you try."

"I don't want to," I said.

"You said the same thing about teabagging Fred. And now you're lying. You know how I know that?"

"How?"

"Because you're drunk."

"So what?"

"So when you're drunk, your true feelings come out. And that was always one of her biggest complaints. That you weren't open and honest about your true feelings."

"That is true," I replied.

"So give her what she always wanted! Text your true feelings! She'll probably be thrilled to hear from us."

"What if she doesn't text us back?" I asked.

"Oh, you don't need to worry about that, dude."

My penis was right. Elizabeth got right back to me. Here's how it went down.

> Hi ;) would it be wrong of me to tell
u I really really really miss u sometimes.

If you were drunk at 2:30 <
in the morning, yes

> It's only 2:27.

Dan! <

> What?

Don't do this. <

> Do what? Tell the person I thought I
was gonna spend the rest of my life with
that I miss her? Ya, I'm a real shit.

You're not a shit. I just don't think <
we should make things harder than
they already are, that's all.

> You mean, harder for me than
they already are.

For both of us. <

> You seem to be doing just fine,
> Elizabeth. Hell, you're already in
> another relationship.

I TOLD YOU I'M NOT IN <
A RELATIONSHIP!

She used all caps. A dinghy appeared in my mental eddy. It was carrying Hope.

> You're not seeing Jack anymore?

Hope had come ashore and was looking sexy as hell. She beckoned me to join her in the boat.

Yes. <

> Yes, you are seeing him, or yes
> you're not seeing him?

Silently, from the shadows near the water's edge, Shame appeared, fixing Hope with a grim animus.

I'm seeing him, but he's not <
my boyfriend.

> Don't you miss me at all? I mean,
> like not even a little bit?

As we left the shore, Shame grabbed Hope like a paper doll and tossed her. Letting out a whimper, Hope fell, limp, into the water. It took Elizabeth nearly three minutes to write back.

Of course I miss you. <
I'll always miss you.

> Why did it take three minutes
> to compose that reply?

What? <

> Did you nod off or something?

Dan! <

> What? Am I interrupting something?

Shame, which had been holding Hope's head under water for a minute or so, suddenly glared at me, shaking his head.

OMG, seriously?!!! <

> Am I? It's a simple question.

Suddenly, out of nowhere, Jealousy showed up. Shit, he was even bigger than Shame.

> Are you with him right now or
are you just texting him?

Jealousy grabbed Shame by the face with one hulking paw. Shame windmilled his arms, panicking. Jealousy turned his head and fixed me with an unwholesome leer.

Do you realize how crazy you <
sound right now?

> Oh, I'm the crazy one ...

As Jealousy tossed Shame far out into the water, I leaped from the boat and started wading ashore. I felt a massive hand grab my collar and lift me off my feet. I was being dragged to Jealousy's hot rod. My struggling was doing precisely nothing.

> You're dating a wannabe actor in his
midthirties who isn't smart enough to
realize he's destined to be a bartender
the rest of his life.

No response. Jealousy tied me tight to his bumper, then

hopped in the driver's seat, revved the engine, and started smoking his tires.

> A guy who cheated on his ex-girlfriend
  with you, I might add.

Still no response. Jealousy popped the clutch and away we went, all squealing tires and accelerating pavement. Jesus, what kind of engine did he have in this thing?

> And *I'm* crazy.

There was nothing ahead of us but a brick wall. Jealousy was cackling now, up into second . . . third, shit was he going to make it to . . .

> OK. Glad we worked that
  one out. I was confused for
  a second.

We hit the wall going north of 80. The pain was blinding. I was thrown clear, covered in dust and shards of brick. Or maybe it was quicksand. I certainly felt like I was sinking. Four long minutes crept by.

You should go to sleep. I'm sorry <
you're in such pain. You don't have
to do this to yourself.

I felt arms lifting me up. It was Shame. He was soaked and covered in bruises, but it was clear he had just been trying to help. Before I could react, he grabbed my phone and powered it off. Then he punched my penis in the face.

I FELT BETTER IN THE morning. Fred did not.

"Did Satan take a dump in my brain last night?" he groaned.

"Satan left you alone. I, on the other hand, teabagged you eight ways to Sunday."

"Uh-huh."

"Check the video on your phone," I said. "We got lots of close-ups."

"Ha, ha," he said.

"I guess I'd classify this as more of a horror film than a comedy," I replied.

"Wait, did you seriously film that?"

"One of the girls did."

"That's wrong on so many levels."

"You know what's funny," I said, "is as I've gotten older, my ball sack has gotten saggier. It's really taken my teabagging to another level."

"I'm gonna throw up."

"Oh, and speaking of another level, you were hurling like Roger Clemens last night. We filmed that too." I paused, thoughtfully. "Hey, I figured it out. It's not horror or comedy. It's a John Waters movie."

Fred tottered over to the counter, where a woman from the Jordan staff had left a lavish spread that included a pot of gourmet coffee, a basket of pastries, enough oranges and papaya to rid the world of scurvy, and some potato-and-kale frittatas. He poured himself a cup of black coffee and eyed a frittata, then apparently thought better of it, grabbing a piece of dry toast.

"Did you hook up with that chick? Ellen, was it?"

"Nah," I said. "Some women just aren't ready for a ball sack this expansive."

Ellen and I had actually gotten into a heated argument. She was in her early twenties, attended Berkeley, had some sort of job at a hospital, and was an occasional blogger for the Huffington Post. In other words, she knew everything. After her friend had passed out on the sofa next to Fred, I spent the

better part of an hour feigning interest as she waxed author-
itative about organized religion, architecture, the Beatles
versus the Stones, U.S. foreign policy, celebrities' Instagram
accounts, and the death of the electric car. Sure, I thought
she was as full of shit as Guy Fieri before his daily enema, but
she had pretty eyes and phenomenal breasts. You've got to
pick your battles. Believe me, it was all I could do to just focus
on her knockers and keep my mouth shut as she blathered
on about how Mick Jagger and Keith Richards are "twice the
songwriters Lennon and McCartney ever were." She followed
that up with a breathless condemnation of vaccines, then
tried to make the case for Alec Baldwin as U.N. secretary or
some shit. I'll give her credit, she had a host of bullet points
committed to memory. Ah, but when Ellen suggested, without
provocation, that people of her generation didn't give a rat's
ass about books and that my chosen profession was essentially
a lost cause, well, I could no longer, to coin a phrase, Let It Be.

"You, madam, are incorrect," I told her.

"Traditional publishing is dead," she replied.

I pointed out that I had a book deal from a traditional publisher that directly refuted that notion. She countered that "a
lot of the most exciting books" of the past ten years were initially self-published, citing *Fifty Shades of Grey, Ten Tiny Breaths,*
and *Still Alice* as examples.

I realized I had veered badly off course and needed to correct. Squabbling about book publishing at 2 A.M. was killing
my buzz.

"Look," I said. "I don't want to argue. Let's watch the footage of me teabagging Fred again."

"Are we arguing? I thought we were having a friendly discussion."

"It feels more like an attack to me," I said.

"Oh, the poor wittle sensitive boy."

"You dismiss my career as a waste of time, yet the whole reason we're here in this gorgeous house in the middle of a goddamn vineyard is because I'm writing an actual book. With pages."

"I'm sure you're a fine writer," she said. "But the reality is that unlike people your age, people from my generation just aren't all that interested in books. There are other mediums that are more relevant."

"You mean the Internet."

"Yes."

"And what's the going rate these days for one of those pieces you write for HuffPo? A free song download?"

"It's great exposure," she said.

"So . . . half a free song download?"

"I'm building my brand."

"Oh, that's right, a fleece-wearing dot-com asshole in SF explained this to me once. Exposure helps build your brand. Which leads to more exposure, which increases your social media presence and ultimately means you have to borrow money to pay the rent."

"My parents pay my rent," she deadpanned. "These complimentary stays in killer guesthouses . . . I guess that's how you pay your rent?"

She had me there. After all, I was a full-time resident of Nowhere.

"Look, I don't want to argue with you either," she said, softening. "Let's agree to disagree, okay?"

"I'm more the 'disagree to disagree, then get too tired to give a shit type,'" I said with a smile. "The older you get, the more you may feel the same way." I wanted to steer the ship back on course. Destination: Ellen's spectacular ta-tas.

"It's not like I don't make my own money," she continued. "I have a job."

"What kind of job?"

"A real job," she said.

"Oh," I said, "one of those."

"I do billing at a hospital half-time. It pays the bills," she said.

"I thought your parents paid the bills."

"The bar bills," she said.

As one of only a handful of individuals in this country who lists "alcohol expert" on his tax return, I've often wondered what it must be like to operate under the behavioral constraints of a traditional workplace. Like a paralegal tech-type thingy or a telecommunications hooziwhatsit. Every time I ponder such a scenario, I come to the same conclusion—it would suck donkey balls.

Because I may complain bitterly about the collapse of print, which consequently dominoed most long-form journalism, and perhaps attention spans in general. I may complain about deadlines and shit pay and having to churn out the engagement-driven drivel that dominates online content. And the unbearable weight of having to talk about myself all the time. (Do you have any idea how hard it is to be this fascinating?) But I simply could not trade my job for the clock-punching, boss-having kind.

I should probably clarify. I don't mean that I am too precious, too unmotivated, or too fabulous to have a real job. It would actually be a relief to get a steady paycheck for once in my stupid life.

What I mean when I say I could not trade for a regular job is that no sane person would allow me to work for them. At this point, I am fundamentally unhireable. This is because most jobs require me to stop drinking during what the rest of the world has collectively come to define as "work hours."

And while some might call this extreme, I'm just going to go ahead and call it what it is. Prejudice. Sure it's an ugly word, but I don't know a better one to describe what I have to live with. I'm afflicted with what fake doctors call *Tipplitus officinia*. The Fake Physician's Desk Reference refers to *Tipplitus officinia* as the chronic inability to remain sober in the workplace. Or, as you may have heard it referred to colloquially, being Irish. Okay, that was a cheap shot, and I'm sorry. I mean no offense to my fellow Irish folk. I'm well aware the Irish have a chronic inability to stay sober anywhere.

Unlike most prejudices, however, which tend to be rooted out by the light of reason, this one seems to be getting worse with time. As any fan of *Mad Men* knows, there was a time not so long ago in this country when drinking was not only tolerated in the workplace, it was practically mandatory. In the 1960s, alcohol was celebrated as a social lubricant that made going to work far more entertaining than going home to your dysfunctional family afterward. But attitudes change and, sadly, getting schnockered on the clock down at the ol' ad agency is as outmoded a social convention as smoking during pregnancy, spanking kids in public, and throwing garbage at Indian chiefs on the interstate. I'm sure it's great to be a highly paid doctor, lawyer, or operator of heavy machinery. But I have too little training for the first two and not enough testosterone for the last one. Still, even if I were qualified to get hired for those gigs, I'd probably take myself out of the running before I even got started by offering whoever was interviewing me a swig from my flask during our first meeting. The way I see it, asking for ice is a great way to break the ice. And let's face it, nobody in their right mind would ever hire a lush to argue cases in court, do gastric bypass surgery, or dig up the street for a new gas main. Though that last one does sound like it'd be fun after you've had a couple.

"I read about this study once that suggested boozing can be good for business," I said.

"You read it, or wrote it?" Ellen teased.

"I'm not detail oriented enough to conduct any study," I said. "The guys who did this one were MIT nerds. But when they tested the effects of moderate alcohol intoxication on creative problem solving, they found that people who were a little buzzed were able to perceive solutions faster and more frequently than the nerds who hadn't consumed any alcohol."

"So they confirmed your existence?"

"You could say that. But you could also say, 'man, these clothes are getting uncomfortable.'"

"Believe me, I work with some people who I'm sure I'd find more tolerable if I were drunk. But then again, I work in a hospital. That could be dangerous."

"The study had some darker wrinkles," I continued. "Despite the fact that drinking has been proven to stimulate creativity, those who drink are perceived by others as less intelligent. It's called the 'imbibing idiot bias.' And you don't even need to actually drink. Just holding an alcoholic beverage makes you seem dumber than a teetotaler."

"That's pretty harsh," she said after I explained this, draining the last drop of Chardonnay from her glass.

"It's a harsh world, Ellen."

This seemed to harsh her buzz. The magical diaphanous net that only a few moments before had connected us abruptly severed, scattering jewels all across the floor. Or maybe I dropped a glass. I'd had a couple. A few minutes passed in which very little was said. The mood—or what had passed for it—was gone. Ellen suddenly became very interested in waking her friend up, we exchanged numbers, and they left. See you never! And though things didn't work out as I'd hoped,

I was glad Ellen was gone. I mean, come on. Who shit-talks Lennon and McCartney like that?

I poured myself a glass of Cabernet and went out onto the deck that overlooked the vineyards to the north. If this was indicative of the road to come, it was going to be a long journey. Hopefully the rest of it wouldn't be filled with people who were convinced they knew everything. That's my job.

But you know what was nice about getting out of town? About getting out onto a farm? (I know I'm thick, but it took me until this moment to reclassify vineyards as grape farms.) It was quiet. And as my mother would have pointed out, silence is golden.

And I gotta hand it to you, Charlene. When you're right, you're right.

CHAPTER 5

OREGON

"ANY CHANCE OF CATCHING A BREAK ON THIS ONE, OFFICER?"

It took me a solid ten hours to get from Sonoma County to the Oregon border. This was partly due to an asshole traffic jam on the 101 and partly due to a migraine that descended on me like an avenging angel. I chalked it up to karmic payment for me not yet being hungover while on a drinking trip. It's amazing how annoying nature's wonders can seem when your head feels like an overinflated balloon.

By the time I pulled into Bandon, the light of day was long gone and so was my will to go on. A whiff of the headache was still hanging around like a fart trapped in a seat cushion. My back ached. My ass and lower extremities were completely insensate, except for my right knee, which hurt like a bitch.

I'd torn cartilage in it riding a skateboard to brunch a week before I left Venice. Another karmic payback mostly likely, this one for skateboarding over the age of forty.

According to my GPS, my destination, the Bandon Inn, was three hundred feet away. The final stagger of a 415-mile slog that was old after ten. But I was there, and . . . those are police lights. Behind me.

The cop was a dead ringer for Robert Patrick from *Terminator 2,* only he looked about twenty years younger and twenty times colder. This was clearly payback for not being in ROTC.

"Sir, I need to see your driver's license and registration, sir," he said. It was not phrased in the form of a question. As for the "double sir," well, that's never a good sign.

"What seems to be the problem, Officer?" I asked, Beaver Cleaver in a Carl Vehicle.

Silence. I grinned nervously, fished out the requested items, and handed them over.

"What brings you to Oregon?" he said finally and sternly, to which I dearly wanted to reply, "I'm here for the none of your fucking business convention." Having had many unpleasant experiences with Terminator-style cops, however, I knew how they tend to react when citizens exercise their constitutional right to privacy. Instead I told him the truth, that I was researching a book about the most wholesome and beautiful places in this great nation of ours. Bandon, of course, being right there at the top of the list, as I'm sure it is yours, Officer.

He stood there looking at me, expressionless. Right about the time I began to wonder if I'd somehow been frozen in time, he said, "You're from California?"

"Well, yes, I live there," I said, not about to get into the whole moving to Nowhere business, "but I actually grew up on the East Co—"

"And you're a writer?"

"I am," I replied.

"Well, whaddaya know, so am I. Be right back," he said, stomping away and climbing into his cruiser.

Within ten minutes of him heading to his car, my headache began to creep back. By twenty minutes it had climbed to full boil. And me within spitting distance of my hotel. (Full disclosure: I cannot actually spit three hundred feet. Yet.) I swear to David Koresh that policeman spent twenty-seven goddamn minutes in his car. What was he doing? Getting scans of my first grade reports from Ms. Lambert? I remember I did struggle with finger painting that year, sir. I hope you can find it in yourself not to hold it against me. At one point I considered jumping out of my car and running at the guy with a tire iron just so he'd shoot me and get it over with.

Finally, all haircut and condescension, Robocop came striding back and silently handed me a ticket. It said I had been doing 46 in a 35-mph zone. A violation that carries with it a $165 fine.

Though I instinctively understood it was futile, I nonetheless tried an appeal to the cop's sense of civic pride.

"Any chance of catching a break on this one, Officer?" I asked obsequiously. "I promise to write really great things about Bandon in the book."

Robert Patrick's doppelgänger stared at me for around the length of an average Phish song. Then he smiled. Warmly, almost. It was creepy as hell.

"How 'bout you do your readers a favor and write 'don't speed in Bandon.' You have yourself a good rest of the evening, sir."

I did not, in point of fact, have a good rest of the evening. The hotel had all the warmth and character of an Applebee's, with Internet slower than Britney Spears doing the Sunday *Times* crossword. I wish that it didn't matter, because all I wanted to do was go to bed, wake up, and head to the King Estate Winery in Eugene. Ah, but sleeping would have to wait, because I was on deadline for a column. The weird thing about being a writer is that you actually have to write. No writing, no eating.

To make matters infinitely worse, per my editor's request, the subject of the column was National Vodka Day. In all likelihood, up until this moment, you have been unaware that there is such a thing as National Vodka Day. But—and this is the superawesome part—THERE TOTALLY IS. Like the annual festivities of Apple Gifting Day (January 1), Something on a Stick Day (March 28), National Gazpacho Day (December 6), and, I shit you not, Petroleum Day (August 28), National Vodka Day is an age-old holiday tradition. Every October fourth, literally tens of adult beverage lovers across this great nation gather to celebrate that blandest of white spirits, mother vodka.

When I say age-old, I mean National Vodka Day has an age. That age is six. Waaaaay back to 2009, when someone who was clearly being paid too much by a liquor industry consortium took it upon themselves to invent it. To make it official, another (probably less-well-compensated) person created a just-this-side-of-parody website. To be fair, it's more professional looking than the websites for National Taco Day (also October 4), National Chicken Wing Day (July 29), and National Grab Some Nuts Day (August 3). Do not confuse that last one with National Scratch Your Nuts Day, which is . . . let me just check my calendar . . . today! And tomorrow. I celebrated yesterday too. What can I say, I'm full of the Scratch Your Nuts spirit!

After several hours of research while holed up in this cancer of a hotel room, I came to the conclusion that nobody knows who's responsible for establishing National Vodka Day. This conclusion was not, how you say, true. But at that point I had also concluded that I couldn't get myself to give half a piece of dried-out sheepshit about who started National Vodka Day. Still, as a long-time connoisseur of terrible, terrible things, I'll gladly raise a toast to the trailblazing sonofabitch who started NVD, as well as the sad, sad employee of www.partyexcuses .com who had to build its website. And you know what? Let's give the Taco Day guy some too. Nice job, taco guy! I'm going to have both of you over when National Bullshit Holiday Day rolls around (it's traditionally celebrated the surpenth Trollsday of Craptember).

Now, some of you might be wondering, Why have a National Vodka Day in the first place? or What's the significance of October fourth? or Does the fact that I'm thinking about calling in sick to work so I can celebrate a fake holiday mean that I'm an alcoholic?

Well, stop with all your wondering! It's only going to get in the way of the fun. Sure, it's ridiculous to have a national holiday to celebrate a distilled spirit, especially one that wasn't even invented here. And yes, *fine,* according to the National Vodka Day website (which I now use as my browser's default), the date was chosen at random. I think that's very festive. But let me make one thing perfectly clear: skipping work on October fourth so you can drink Smirnoff for sixteen hours straight doesn't mean you're an alcoholic, it just means you really like tacos. At least, that's what any halfway resourceful alcoholic is telling himself and his concerned loved ones.

The point is, there is absolutely no point to National Vodka Day other than it being another excuse to drink, like Cinco de Mayo, Arbor Day, and Yom Kippur. But enough justifications. The real question you should be asking is what type of vodka should you celebrate National Taco Day with. And while it might make sense to go with the standby top-shelf brands (Absolut, Stoli, Grey Goose, Ketel One, and their ilk), you know what would really class up those tacos? Flavored vodkas. Luckily the superclassy vodka industry has introduced some real doozies in recent years.

Take Alaska Distillery's Smoked Salmon Flavored Vodka, for instance. It was designed to be used in Bloody Marys, but don't let that stop you. Let the beguiling flavor and aroma of fish into your life by drinking it neat. Just promise me you won't make a Moscow Mule or Greyhound with it. I'd say you could pour it over a bagel, but just try explaining *that* to your concerned loved ones. Though maybe you could get away with it on Yom Kippur.

But no matter how bad of an idea fish vodka is, it is still flavored with something edible. What about people who want to drink something that should, under no circumstances, ever be swallowed? What about them? I (don't) hear you ask! My friends, I have you covered. A few years ago I received a sample bottle of Ivanabitch vodka. Ivanabitch is a tobacco-flavored vodka. The only reason I can think that someone would make such a thing is because vodka doesn't kill you quickly enough. In the name of science (and in honor of Ivanabitch's glorious name), I actually tried a shot of this marvelous abomination and nearly hurled.

Now you may have seen writers use the term "nearly hurled" before as colorful hyperbole. This literary device indicates that something was disgusting, but the reader is aware that the writer was never actually on the verge of heaving the contents of his stomach across the room.

Not this time, friends. When I say I nearly hurled after downing a shot of Ivanabitch, that is a precise, 100 percent literal description. My body knew I was doing something deeply wrong to it and immediately rebelled. In the end, though, the sensible part of me was overruled by the Irish part of me and I did not paint the walls with my bile. Still, I should make one thing extremely clear if it wasn't already:

IF YOU CARE ABOUT YOURSELF OR YOUR RUG, STAY THE FUCK AWAY FROM IVANABITCH TOBACCO-FLAVORED VODKA.

The thing that pissed me off the most about having to write about vodka, though, was vodka is playing dirty. And winning. I mean, shit, vodka has been bullying the entire alcohol market for decades now. You have to specify that you want gin in a martini these days. Even beer sales have been declining in recent years as vodka's fortunes continue to rise. But it's the "fun" flavors that really twist my knickers. For ages, if you wanted to drink an intoxicating fruit-flavored liquid, you had to drink schnapps, or hit the clubs on Fire Island in August. And we all had a good time pitying poor harmless little schnapps with its sad bottom-shelf section and dusty bottles and terrible hangovers. But then vodka came and curb-stomped schnapps and stole its turf.

There is birthday-cake-flavored vodka now. And whither schnapps?

When vodka came for gin I said nothing because it was not summer. Then when vodka came for beer I said nothing because I was on this whole gluten-free thing. Now it's come for schnapps though, and even though I don't drink that shit, I'll be good and goddamned if I'm not going to stick up for it in its hour of need.

See, vodka is not supposed to be fun. Vodka was invented as a way of grimly making yourself as intoxicated as possible while cursing the tsar. You want "fun"? Go see schnapps.

Just two months and change after National Vodka Day comes October 16, also known as National Liqueur Day. Next time it rolls around, I implore you to get on down to your local liquor purveyor and ask him for his finest bottle of DeKuyper Buttershots. It tastes like two butterscotches fucking in your mouth. And while you're there stock up on Banana, Watermelon, Bubblegum, and Whipped Cream schnapps. Then check into the hospital and get a head start on your type 2 diabetes treatments.

I'M HAPPY TO REPORT THAT the rest of the time spent in Oregon did not resemble my experience in Bandon. For instance, I had a wonderful time at the King Estate Winery in Eugene, where a young man named Tom DeVaul gave me a tour of the facilities and tasted me through the entire portfolio of Oregon's largest wine producer.

Tom's official job title at King Estate is "wine educator." I saw this for what it was, an opportunity for me to not look stupid on the rest of the trip. So I picked his brain a little about the basics of wine production. And because I am a PROFESSIONAL REPORTER, I even wrote several of the terms down. I did not, for some mysterious reason, write down what any of the stuff he told me meant (see also, me tasting through the entire portfolio of Oregon's largest wine producer). But to be honest, a lot of this stuff is pretty straightforward. And I made up the rest. This is the strategy that got me where I am today. I'll be damned if I compromise my ideals to some fascist notion of accuracy.

WINE PRODUCTION BASICS EXPLAINED

BLENDING
The act of mixing the wine.

BOTTLING
The act of putting the wine in a glass container.

COLD STABILIZATION
I think this is what they do to Coors Light to make it taste like corn-fed water.

COLDPLAY
The act behind such hits as "Yellow" and "Clocks."

DESTEMMING
The savage neutering of grapes. Don't think they won't come for you.

FILTERING
Filtering. I could do this in my sleep.

FINING
Making fun of people who look like Larry from the Three Stooges.

LEES
Place to get a shirt dry cleaned after you spill wine on it.

MACERATION
Pleasuring yourself to thoughts of Pinot Noir.

PRESSING

Trying too hard. See also the Lees and Larry jokes.

PUMP-OVER

Doing it missionary style.

RACKING

An area you can hold on to while doing it missionary style.

RIDDLING

Poor people have it. Rich people need it. If you eat it you die.
What is it?

SKIN CONTACT

That thing the HR Department called you in about.

SOLERA

Either the title of a George Clooney movie, or something you
put on pasta.

. . . .

That night I dined alone at King Estate's elegantly rustic
restaurant, feasting on ahi poke, duck galette, gnocchi parisienne, and striped bass. It was amazing. And the wines they
selected for me were exquisite as well, from the crisp Paradox
Pinot Gris to the light, bright, and earthy Croft Pinot Noir.

Best part of the evening, though, hands down, was the
server. Lovely young woman. An actual ray of sunshine. I'll
call her Clothilde. (Because I can't recall her real name and
would have had to change it anyway.) She'd recently gradu-
ated from the University of Oregon with a degree in some
kind of fancy business. And she was hoping to go into farm-

ing. I think. Or . . . pharmaceuticals? Regardless, she was lovely and sweet and unassuming—a combination not often found in L.A. By my third glass of Pinot Noir I was laying it all on the line. I told her I wished I lived in Eugene. That I longed to be amongst people like her. *Real* people with real lives who wanted nothing more than to till the land . . . or sell Cialis to farmers. Either way, she was too kind to correct me.

"You know what? I think I'll move here when I'm done with this trip," I said, drunk enough to almost mean it.

"You should. You'd love it here," she said. And her big green eyes sparkled. I mean, shit, they actually glimmered and lit up the room. I have the words *ocular aurora* written in my notebook from that night. Yes, goddamnit, I *would* love living in Eugene. It's a fine place. There's the university and this winery and . . . there was Clothilde. I mean, let's face it, I wasn't about to enroll in school or become a winemaker, so she was my primary motivation for relocating. But that was just fine because she was perfect. Resplendent, innocent, and pure. Girls like her don't come along very often. At least, not anymore. They used to, though. All the time, actually. Back when I wasn't so acutely aware of my own mortality and was consequently in no rush to settle down. Before I found out that the dreams, aspirations, and expectations I'd been carrying around since childhood have been beaten, heaped into a pile, laced with C4, and blown to actual fuck. You know, the good ol' days.

Holy shit, it's happening, I thought, as I watched perfect Clothilde with her perfect hands and feet and calves and neck make their way back to the kitchen. *I'm having a stupid textbook goddamn midlife crisis. This is what it looks like. A single fortysomething man, alone in a restaurant far from home, trying to impress a woman half his age with idle boasts and cheap come-ons.*

Feeling suddenly self-conscious, I glanced down and saw

something that made my blood run cold. I was wearing a hoodie. A Stüssy hoodie I bought at . . . *Macy's*. It was on me. It was all over me. Once I made the connection the signs became more and more obvious. The sudden impulse to pack up and go. The weight loss. The new wardrobe. My thoughts of going to Bonnaroo and/or Coachella. The package of Just For Men I had made sure to pack when I left L.A.

Now, now, I told myself. *A lot of guys, maybe even all guys, go through midlife crises.* But aren't they supposed to feel kind of . . . good? (So long as you can keep yourself from realizing you're having one, of course.) I mean the underlying feelings are uncomfortable, sure. But the whole point is that you're sort of not in touch with the actual feelings and are instead channeling them through your various desperate attempts to return to a state of adolescence. And man, are desperate attempts at recapturing adolescence fun. I mean shit, who *doesn't* want to go to Bonnaroo? (Me.) Or run around in a zippy little roadster with a twentysomething blonde and do a bunch of blow? Sure getting old sucks, but some things never get old, right?

It dawned on me that I was having the shittiest midlife crisis in history. Where was my twentysomething blonde? Where was my sweet little roadster? And for the love of all fuck, where the hell was all my blow? Last time I checked, it was just me and Carl Vehicle riding down highway after highway, paying too much for gas, grumbling about my achy knee, and fantasizing about settling down with Clothilde and squeezing out a few puppies.

Which is when it all clicked. I wasn't having a midlife crisis. This was the dying gasp of my adolescence. After overstaying its welcome and running up a truly hideous bar tab. And sure, when your adolescence lasts into your forties, it's a crisis. Just not the fun, blondes-roadsters-and-blow kind.

When I performed a quick survey of my life through this lens, it started making a whole lot more sense. It's simple. I've managed to maintain my arrested development long enough that other guys my age had started to have midlife crises, causing them to start acting like me again. Only I'm done now. They're coming back to Bonnaroo in their forties to find me just finally packing up my tent. I mean seriously. Clothilde here was no twentysomething roadster-riding hottie. Sure she was gorgeous, but this woman wasn't coked-out party trash; she was high-quality breeding stock. The kind of strong, capable woman you can build a family around. And probably far too smart to get involved with a mess like me.

There was, however, an upside to all this. If my math was right, at this rate I would hit my actual midlife crisis sometime in my eighties. Huh. Something to look forward to, I guess. As a side benefit, I think it also means that I'm going to live to 160. From eighty to a hundred it's going to be nothing but party trash in little coupes with the top down and kilos of coke blown up my ass, Stevie Nicks style.

That is if I can still get out of bed. Because frankly, the mileage is starting to show on me a little. In the months leading up to the trip, I was in a great deal of discomfort as a result of a back injury. I sustained this injury while yawning. If a yawn could precipitate back spasms, what would happen if I sneezed? Probably just a giant brainsplosion out my nose.

But the creeping doubt? The questions? Is this all there is? Who am I, really? What's the point of it all? Do you think that bear is friendly? Who farted? They had to go. I didn't get this far by thinking things through. I had to clear my head of any misgivings about who I was, what I was doing and why. Just keep moving, Deep breaths. Don't panic. Like a wise man once said, "Be the ball, Danny." Be. The. Ball.

The restaurant manager came up and introduced himself. Young guy. Confident. Looked like he'd been working out.

"Would you like to try some of our Domaine Pinot Noir?" he asked.

"I think you know I would," I said. I was feeling toasty by now. And this whole "have the best winemakers in the country treat you to their product" thing was feeling pretty good.

After he filled my glass, I asked him if he knew that National Vodka Day was coming up.

"I did not know that. In fact I did not know there was a National Vodka Day."

"You're not alone," I replied. "But I really think it could catch on. You know, with the kids."

"We carry a number of fine vodkas. Would you like to see a list?"

It's a wine trip, dance with the one who brung ya. "Maybe later."

"Okay, Mr. Dunn. Just let me know," he said. "Are you enjoying everything so far?"

"You know, I really am," I said. "Some things more than others."

"Oh really? What's been your favorite?"

"Well, to be honest, no offense to the menu and it's all been pretty tasty, but Clothilde is probably the most delicious thing in here." Oh man, I am a lovable scamp, aren't I?

"Excuse me?" he said.

"Her," I said, jerking my thumb toward the kitchen. "The waitress."

He smiled, exuding calm understanding. "Oh. Yes. She is gorgeous."

"You said a mouthful, buddy," I said, being the ball. "What's her story?"

"Grew up here. Went to UO. Majored in pharma-ing. Been

working here a couple of years, ever since we opened. We got engaged last year," he said.

"Oh," I said.

And then he didn't say anything. Just smiled. So I smiled back, took a sip of wine, and waited to die. Please. Now. I thought the cop in Bandon was comfortable with silences, but this young man had him beat. I found myself wishing I'd taken him up on that vodka offer.

After a solid seventeen-year silence, he spoke.

"How was the gnocchi parisienne?"

"My favorite," I said. "I'm thinking of proposing."

AFTER EUGENE, I HEADED NORTH to spend four glorious days visiting wineries across the lush Willamette Valley, Oregon's largest and most celebrated AVA (American Viticultural Area—a federally recognized growing region). It's a wonderful place. Undoubtedly one of the finest wine-producing regions in all the world. IN ALL THE WORLD, I say! More often than not, the juice harvested there is rhapsodic, poetic. Indeed, if ever I have tasted *The Wild Swans at Coole* in a bottle, I surely did so there on that broad plain between the Oregon coast and the Cascade Range. I have not, however, ever read *The Wild Swans at Coole*. But I hear it's lovely.

I'll be covering the area more thoroughly in my follow-up to this tome, which will be titled *American Wino 2: The Quickening*, or *American Wino 2: I Know Where You Drove Last Summer*, or *American Wino 2: Breaking Training*, or *American Wino 2: Mall Cop*. But for now, though, I'll leave you with four things that make the Willamette Valley special.

THE SOIL

The Willamette Valley is filthy with great dirt, from some of the deepest deposits of fertile alluvial soil on the planet to fine and nutrient rich loess to volcanic Jory that imbues the region's Pinot Noir with its signature spiciness. Soil, I should point out, is key to the process known as growing stuff, which in turn is one of the main components of winemaking. Indeed, in the absence of grown stuff—in this case, grapes— wine tends to lack structure and complexity.

THE PEOPLE

Willamette is home to some of the top winemakers in the United States, among them Ken Wright of Ken Wright Cellars, Tony Soter of Soter Vineyards, Laurent Montalieu of Solena Estate, Alex Sokol Blosser of Sokol Blosser, Véronique Drouhin-Boss of Domaine Drouhin, Josh Bergström of Bergström Wines, Rollin Soles of Rocco Wines, Patrick Reuter of Dominio IV, David Adelsheim of Adelsheim Vineyard, and Jason Lett of The Eyrie Vineyards.

THE WINERIES

There are over three hundred wineries in the Willamette Valley, and a great many of them boast gorgeous tasting rooms and outdoor patios with spectacular views. Among the best to visit are Domaine Serene, Penner-Ash, Stoller Family Estate, Ponzi Vineyards, Willamette Valley Vineyards, Winter's Hill Vineyard, and Marks Ridge Winery.

THE CLIMATE

There are three gaps in the Coast Range that allow cool air to flow from the Pacific Ocean into the Willamette Valley. One is called the Van Duzer Corridor, and the other two are unnamed. Well, at least they were unnamed as of this writing. I've got calls in to Nike chairman Phil Knight and the folks over at AshleyMadison.com. Branding, my friends. It's all about branding. Which reminds me, this list is brought to you by . . .

This National Vodka Day, enjoy the world's first Mega-Ultra-Jeans-Creamium Vodka, made from the fermented mash of hand-harvested caviar, distilled thirty-seven times in Lalique crystal pot stills before being filtered through the tiny toes and fingers of the offspring of royalty. From there, PlatinuLuxEgant travels first class to Rome, where each individual bottle is hand-numbered in gold and blessed by the pope. PlatinuLuxEgant Mega-Ultra-Jeans-Creamium Vodka, the only vodka known to humankind that is guaranteed to make you cream in your jeans. Every time.

"NEED IS A STRONG WORD,
MR. DUNN."

CHAPTER 6

MONTANA

Having learned an immense amount from the sophisticated and highly proficient vintners of the Pacific Northwest and drunk an awful lot of excellent wine, it was off to see some men with a capital MEN. So Carl Vehicle and I made tracks to a dude ranch in Greenough, Montana, called The Resort at Paws Up. That's right, it was finally time to venture out of the safe confines of the West Coast, where world-class wine is made from San Diego to Shasta and all points in between. I had known the wine there would be incredible. This next part I wasn't so sure about.

I headed straight to Montana, where the winters are long, the growing season is short, and the sheep are delicious. Still, the aforementioned MEN (and WOMEN, everyone's all caps in big sky country) manage to make wine up there, despite the state's somewhat less than ideal climate and terroir.

I won't mince words. You'll be hard-pressed to find a connoisseur who'd deem Montana wine palatable. It is an inhospitable place to cultivate grapes, and the ones that do manage to grow there generally produce wine that bears a striking resemblance to Kim Jong-un (i.e., harsh and unbalanced). Don't believe me? Go ahead and try some yourself. What's that? Your local wine merchant doesn't carry a single bottle of Montana wine? Hmmm. Must be a coincidence. None dare call it conspiracy. Because it's totally not a conspiracy. Drinking Montana-made wine is like ordering Domino's pizza in New York City. You *could* do it, but you know deep down there are better options and you're just hurting yourself for an entirely pointless reason. Which is David Blaine's job. C'mon, give the guy a little room to work.

Now please don't confuse my low opinion of Montana wine with a low opinion of Montana wine*makers*. It brings me great joy to know that they are attempting to make wine in Montana. As of this writing there are six bonded wineries operating in our nation's forty-first state, and every one of them is betting that if they keep at it long enough, someday they'll produce fermented fruit juice good enough to deter assholes like me from devoting entire paragraphs to how terrible it is. Or even—dare to dream—induce the assholes from the "legit" wine publications to acknowledge their existence. (Make no mistake, we are all of us assholes in the booze trade.) This can-do spirit in the face of such long odds and reason, to me, is what's made this the most prosperous nation on earth. That, and all the land we stole. Turns out you can save a *lot* of money by stealing. And by enslaving people. USA number one!

But while I may have found the vino in "The Last Best Place" to be wanting, I dug just about everything else about Montana. For one thing, it's impossibly gorgeous. As with Wyoming and Colorado (bunch of squares if you ask me), the Continental Divide splits the state into two distinct regions.

The western half, where I drove in from, is mountainous in the extreme. On the east of the divide, rich river valleys separate ranges with countrified names such as the Big Hole, Bitterroot, and Flathead. Montana goes on forever when you're driving across it. Not the way New Jersey or Maine go on forever. Driving across Montana is like having really great sex—you don't even care if you get to the end point, you just want it to keep going. Traveling through Nebraska, on the other hand, is like jacking off in the bathroom at your parents' house (i.e., something all of us either have done or will do some day).

The Resort at Paws Up is located in the heart of the Blackfoot Valley about thirty-five miles northeast of Missoula. It's a rarified spot where the people who have more money than all the other people go to rough it in extravagant vacation homes and go "glamping." Google this word if you have swallowed poison and need to vomit immediately. The resort used to belong to Charles Lindbergh and has been graced by the likes of Paul McCartney, Mick Jagger, Brendan Fraser, and Gwyneth Paltrow. You know, real Montana-type people. The only reason my poor ass ever got to stay there was because I'd managed to convince the resort's publicist I was writing some kind of luxury travel book. Even I was surprised at how little follow-up the publicist did on that bit of bullshit.

The wholesome gal at the registration desk at Paws Up wasn't named Marley, but I will be calling her that.

"You guys get a lot of stars staying out here, huh?" I asked.

"We do," Marley said.

"I read somewhere that Paul McCartney stayed here. And Mick Jagger?"

"We get a lot of musicians here, yes," she said.

"Yeah? Who else?"

"I'm not really supposed to say," she said, with a hint of embarrassment that I found achingly appealing.

"Oh, c'mon. I promise I won't tell anyone," I said, which, make no mistake, is not the first or last promise I will break.

"Well," she said, leaning in and lowering her voice, "Carrie Underwood was here a few years ago. She was just . . . ah! I love her. And one of the guys from Pearl Jam. But I was off that weekend. Oh, and recently someone from a band that was supposedly pretty big in the '70s . . . the Dudes or something?"

"The Dudes?"

"That's not it," Marley said. "Something like that. Begins with a 'D.' "

"Donovan?"

"No."

"The Doors?"

"Um, maybe . . . no, I don't think that's it either."

Marley looked to be about twenty-three or twenty-four, so that would mean she was born in . . . Oh, Jesus, '90 or '91. I was probably of legal drinking age when they cut her umbilical cord. I wondered whether Marley viewed me as potential hookup material, or just another middle-aged prick from the big city who's too egotistical to realize what an ass he's making of himself by hitting on her. She probably has to indulge all manner of horny old men at The Resort at Paws Up. Goddamnit, getting old is weird. People don't look at you the same way. And by people, I mean attractive young women.

"So what's there to do around here? I'm kind of in the mind to have some fun." Just throwing out a hopeful line.

"Oh, lots of things," she said, before ticking off a list of rich white folk activities offered at the resort: archery, ATV tours, horseback riding, and fly fishing.

"I was thinking more along the lines of stuff to do in town.

Tonight. You know, to get a taste of the real local flavor. I'm writing a book that's kind of about local flavor."

"A book! That's exciting," she said, with what read as genuine excitement. "To be honest, though, there's not a whole lot to do around here. If you're looking for, like, fun bars and stuff, you've got to go into Missoula."

"Gotcha," I said. "Do you go into Missoula often?"

"I live there," she said.

"Oh cool. What's happening tonight?"

"The Rhino is always fun on Friday nights," Marley said. "But Missoula is about a thirty-minute drive from here."

"I drove seven hours today. Twenty-nine in the past week. Wouldn't even notice another half hour." It was time. Do or die. "You want to meet up there later? You can show me how to party Montana-style."

"Sure!" she said without hesitation. Still got it.

"Sounds like a plan," I said. "What time's good?"

"We'll probably get there around eight or so," she said.

Excellent. Eight o'clock it is. Can't wait to see the . . . hold on a second . . . Who's *we*? Please say you and your girlfriends . . . please say you and your girlfriends . . . please say you and your . . .

"Me and my boyfriend. Clarke."

Fuck. Me. So. Hard.

That thirty-minute drive might as well have been thirty hours. I wasn't going anywhere tonight. Not after getting Clarke-blocked.

"Okay," I said, trying not to let my disappointment show. "Maybe I will come meet you and, um . . . Clarke. I think I'll go chill in my room for a bit and see how I feel later."

"You did have an *awfully long* drive today, Mr. Dunn," she said, in a tone similar to one a caregiver in a nursing home might use to comfort an octogenarian who'd just shit himself.

"You can call me Dan."

"We're really not supposed to use guests' first names," she whispered. Christ, a few moments earlier I was convinced we'd be making hot monkey love in the bathroom of a Missoula dive bar. Now we weren't even on a first name basis.

As she handed me the key, Marley let me know that there was a gift basket with food and wine in my guesthouse.

"Our little way of saying 'welcome to Montana,'" she said. "Oh, and one more thing, Mr. Dunn . . ."

You changed your mind about bringing Clarke to the Rhino?

"Be sure not to leave any open food items out on the counter overnight. We recommend putting everything in the refrigerator before you go to bed."

"Okay," I said. "Do you mind if I ask why?"

"First off, let me preface this by saying we haven't had any problems here recently. I want to assure you that it's perfectly safe," she said, flashing an ever-so-slightly nervous smile. Suddenly I felt anything *but* assured of my safety. "However, this *is* grizzly country, and the bears tend to be particularly active this time of year, before they go off to hibernate. So as a precaution—and again, that's all it is, a precaution—we advise all our guests to not leave any food out that might attract a bear's attention."

"Well, that's good to know."

"Of course. But again, Mr. Dunn," she repeated. "We haven't had any incidents."

"You mean recently or ever?" I asked.

"Trust me, you've got nothing to worry about. You're going to have a great time here at Paws Up. Just be sure to put that food in the fridge, okay?"

"And be sure not to leave the door to the cabin wide open either, right?"

That made her laugh. Or at least pretend to laugh convincingly.

"Just out of curiosity," I said. "If something inside the cabin were to attract a grizzly's attention—"

"Which is *highly* unlikely," she said.

"Yes, but if something did," I said, "how would it get into the cabin?"

For a moment, she clearly thought I was joking. But once she realized I wasn't, she leaned in and whispered, "It's a grizzly."

"Right," I said.

"But again," she said again, "there's nothing—"

"There's nothing to worry about," I interjected.

"Exactly."

"Great," I said.

"Great," she said.

"Anything else I can help you with now, Mr. Dunn?"

"Nope. I think I'm all set," I said, as I picked my bag and deflated ego up off the floor.

"Well, just call if you need anything else," she said.

"Will do," I said, turning and heading for the door.

"Actually," I said, returning to the desk. "If, hypothetically, a grizzly were to gain entry into my cabin, what would be the smartest course of action?"

"The chances of that happening, Mr. Dunn, are so—"

"I know, I know," I said. "But . . . *hypothetically.*"

"Hypothetically?"

"Yes. What should I do in the hypothetical event that happened?"

"Pray," she said, without missing a beat.

That made me laugh. For the first time since I arrived, however, Marley was stone-faced.

"Seriously?" I asked.

"It is a grizzly, Mr. Dunn."

I half jokingly asked if there might be a spare shotgun lying around that I could borrow. You know, to ensure my peace of mind. She once again assured me I had nothing to worry about. I asked her if she owned a shotgun.

"I don't," she said. "But Clarke has several."

That settled it. I was definitely not going to the Rhino.

YOU MAY BE WONDERING, AS I was, about the resort's unusual name, Paws Up. I asked around, and apparently the owners are huge dog lovers who weren't afraid to name their tony resort after a piece of imagery that makes me think of dead canines lying on their backs. Sort of like belly up, except for man's best friend.

The owners' dog love extends beyond the name. There are life-size ceramic dogs everywhere. I guess they're lower maintenance than actual dogs, but I did end up doing near-constant double takes the entire time I was there. Particularly near reception where they had an eerily lifelike rendering of an American bulldog. It was a dead ringer for my old pal Piglet.

I drove down to the common area and went to the bar, where I didn't encounter any large predators or George Clooney but did make friends with a fellow guest—world-renowned appraiser Timothy Gordon, a regular on PBS's *Antiques Roadshow*. While I certainly enjoyed listening to Tim expatiate about the value of Chinese cups carved from rhinoceros horns and a recently unearthed trove of Jim Morrison's poetry, in the end we both agreed things would have been more interesting at the ranch had Kate Winslet been there.

Since this is ostensibly a book about wine, I should mention that I was awfully impressed with the wine list that Paws Up food and beverage director Kevin Kapalka had put together, packed with juice from top producers in California, Oregon, and Washington. Cakebread, Sonoma-Cutrer, Domaine Drouhin, Charles Smith. Delightful producers all. Conspicuously absent from the list, however, were any wines made in Montana. When I asked why, Kapalka replied simply, "Have you ever tried Montana wine?"

Kapalka's question aside, it is my sincere hope that Tongue River, Hidden Legend, Mission Mountain, and whatever the other three wineries in Montana are called stay the course. There's gotta be light at the end of the tunnel. Or, at least, scores in the mid-80s in *Wine Spectator*.

MEAD IN MONTANA

While Montana vintners as a whole are still finding their footing in the grape-based space, a few have had real success with mead, a.k.a. honey wine. I got my hands on a bottle from one of the state's leading producers, Hidden Legend Winery in the tiny town of Victor, and consumed all of it on the roof of the historic Murray Hotel in Livingston. Lest you forget, I am a professional. Here's my review:

Pure Honey Mead is made with wildflower honey that is exclusive to Montana. The honey is never cooked, its delicate flavors preserved during cold fermentation process. Floral, ambrosial on the nose. Crafted like a semidry table wine. The honey flavor is unmistakable, without being too sweet. Slight acidity and a hint of oak give it some backbone. Honey mead is usually served at room temperature or slightly chilled, but I actually preferred this one over ice. I imagine it would pair quite nicely with a spicy taco or some General Tso's chicken (neither of which, unfortunately, was at my disposal on the roof of the Murray Hotel). $18. Available online.

After Tim left, I decided to get something to eat. There were a number of enticing dishes on the menu, and after much deliberation I went with an elk strip loin with duck fat roasted red peppers and brussels sprouts. The bartender—amiable guy by the name of Allen Crabtree—suggested a 2011 Merry Edwards Russian River Valley Pinot Noir, which was simply sublime. We got into a conversation about the challenges of driving at night in rural Montana, where it's not uncommon to encounter large animals while moving at a high rate of speed. He offered a couple of tips—always use your high beams, and never swerve to avoid an animal (that's how people flip their vehicles). I asked Allen what the worst possible scenario would be in terms of beasts you might suddenly find yourself bearing down on in the middle of the road.

"You wouldn't want to hit a moose, that's for sure," he said. "Or a bull elk. Or a bear. Mountain lions can cause some serious damage too. Oh, and antelope as well."

"So pretty much everything but squirrels and raccoons," I said.

"There are some big-ass squirrels in these parts too."

The good news, Allen informed me, is that if you did manage to mow down an elk and you survive (that second part is key), you're free to take the meat for food. It's kind of like a combination of hunting and a game of chicken. Maybe a little more fair than the usual rifle business solution. At least this way, you have skin in the game too. On the off chance the elk wins, though, it probably won't eat you. They're not like us.

One of the servers at the bar came over and struck up a conversation. He was quite a talker, but after many hours alone in my car, I was developing a greater appreciation for human interaction. He apparently hadn't gotten the memo from management about not talking about the high-net-worth guests.

I heard about everything from Sir Paul's dietary restrictions to how good Brendan Fraser still looked for his age, which, I didn't bother to mention, also happens to be my age. I asked him if he thought that someday people there might be fondly reminiscing about the time the writer Dan Dunn stayed at Paws Up and how well he seemed to be holding up.

"Who's that?" he said.

Check, please.

Back in my room I lit a fire, uncorked the bottle of Frog's Leap Cabernet from the gift basket, and cracked open Paul Lukacs's book *American Vintage: The Rise of American Wine*. After a good five to six minutes of reading about "American wine's founding father" Nicholas Longworth, who produced the country's first successful commercial wines in the mid-nineteenth century, I put the book down and picked up the iPhone. Stupid books.

Naturally, I took a glance at Elizabeth's Facebook page. No big deal. Then her Instagram and Twitter. I saw nothing particularly distressing beyond the usual indications that her life was not grinding to a complete and catastrophic halt without me. She'd gone to an engagement party in Malibu for one of her girlfriends. There were a few new shots of her and some coworkers on the set of the TV show where she worked. She looked the same. Maybe had even lost a few pounds. (Twinsies!) She'd reposted something about Beyoncé on her Facebook page. No surprise. She was obsessed with Beyoncé. Still no pictures of Jack. No social media acknowledgment of their relationship. I half wished she'd just get it over with and post some shots of the two of them having sex on top of the Griffith Observatory. Stop torturing me with the possibility that it was nothing more than a fling. Show me. Make it athletic.

In lieu of being able to wallow in rejection, I did the next

best thing, Tinder. It turned out there were a surprising number of women between the ages of twenty-four and forty-five
located within a fifty-mile radius of Paws Up. I figured a lot
of them were probably at the Rhino in Missoula. One of the
big differences between browsing Tinder in Montana and Los
Angeles is that in Venice Beach you're unlikely to come across
even a single photo of a woman holding a high-powered hunting rifle next to the carcass of a large animal. In Montana it
seemed to be the norm. I guess men out here want to be sure
you can provide for a family. About 70 percent of the women
that showed up in my search results had posted at least one
photo of themselves beside a giant animal—typically an elk—
that they'd recently shot to death. And about half of them
were cute enough to raise a chub.

I started swiping right like Ted Nugent blasting his way
through a forest filled with Democrats.

Kimberlee, 31. Loves travel, fashion, and putting an arrow
between the eyes of a mountain goat . . . swipe right!

Cyndi, 40. Originally a California beach bum but consid-
ers herself a Montana girl now. Her loves are family, friends,
finding the positive in seemingly negative situations, burgers, whiskey, laughing, and live music. Oh, and slaughtering
wolves! Right-o!

Helene, 28. There are at least five women in every one of
Helene's profile pictures, including one with a deer that has
a bullet hole where its eye used to be. Any one of them could
be Helene, including the one-eyed deer. A few of the women
are cute. Whichever one happens to be Helene is passionate
about art. As am I! Swipe right!

Sierra, 35. No bio. That's a red flag. There are, however,
not one, not two, but THREE photos that testify to Sierra's
proficiency with a shotgun. Aw, and look, she's even got her

kid with her in one of them. He's holding her Bud Light for her while she hoists an eight-point buck's head up by its antlers. Now there's a woman who's figured out how to live. SWIPE RIGHT!!!

Twenty minutes and two glasses of wine later, I'd yet to notch a single match. Not one. What the hell could Sierra possibly be up to? Touching up her doctoral thesis on string theory? Cooking meth?

Maybe my bio is the problem; let's review.

"Dan, 45."

Okay, so one of those bits of information isn't *entirely* true but, c'mon. When you're over forty, giving your age on a dating app is like talking about how exceptional your kids are. Everyone knows it's bullshit, and everyone forgives you.

"My grandparents met on Tinder, so I figured I'd give it a try."

Good move. Start off with something funny. Most women claim to find men with a sense of humor extremely attractive. Why do you think Leonardo DiCaprio gets laid so much? Dude is high-lar-i-ous.

"Seriously, though, I decided to try this in the hopes of meeting a well-adjusted person who enjoys choosing potential mates with a swipe of her finger."

Again, more humor. Look out John Mayer, I've got a pocket full of knock-knock jokes and I'm coming for your ladies!

"Philly native. Writer. Three books done. Working on the fourth. Have a dog."

That last line could be misinterpreted. Might someone think I'm trying to offer her my dog? That would be moving a mite too fast for a lot of women. Or maybe she'd think I meant "I'm working on the Fourth of July, have a hot dog instead of hanging out with me." Talk about sending the wrong message! What kind of chump works on the Fourth of July? And the idea that a hot dog would be an adequate substitute for my company? That's just plain insulting. I decided to change it to "Adore my pit bull–lab mix." There we go. That's super-fucking appealing.

"What else? Um, I'm awesome. Says so on my business cards."

I don't actually have business cards anymore, but back when I wrote for *Playboy* I had cards embossed with the iconic bunny ears logo that identified me as "nightlife columnist/public menace." It is the best title I have ever had or ever will have. So I'm holding on to it, even though that important, silly place is many years in the rearview.

"The question is, are YOU awesome? Well, are you? If so, let's combine forces and defeat evil. And have drinks or coffee or something."

Just for Montana I add, "Or blow the head off a moose with a Howitzer. I'm up for anything, really."

Perfect.

I SIMULTANEOUSLY RAN OUT OF Tinder options and Frog's Leap Cabernet, so I tossed the phone and opened the bottle of Morgan 12 Clones Pinot Noir that was also in my gift basket. It's good wine, made in the Santa Lucia Highlands near Monterey, California. I'd driven through on the first day of the journey. It was only a few weeks ago, but it felt like a decade.

And now what? It was only 9:15 P.M. There was still time to head into Missoula. Maybe check out someplace that wasn't the Rhino. Standing still was not an option. The few times I'd stood still on the trip it hadn't gone so well. When I slowed up, my wake caught up to me, threatening to swamp the tiny emotional dinghy I was hurtling along in. Brian, Elizabeth, Mom, my career, what the hell I was going to do at the end of this trip. Nothing I could afford to think about right now. That was the whole point of the trip. Just get out and move forward. Step into the road and let it sweep you away.

Being somewhat schnockered at this point, driving was not an option. But this was a rich person joint. The front desk would sort me out. I ambled, with the unhurried pace of the half inebriated, back toward the lobby. Oooh hello doggy. Oh, you're not a doggy, you're a ceramic statue. Oh hello other doggy! You're a real doggy aren't you? And you're a good doggie. Yes you are. A good doggie.

And hey, Piglet! What are you doing . . . ?

I caught myself up short. It was that ceramic dog. Giving me the look. You never know when you're going to get the look. You might know it's coming. You might have been expecting it a long time. But the look always takes you by surprise. It's impossible to describe. It's like trying to explain what shit smells like.

Jude was my live-in girlfriend before Elizabeth and I knew our little experiment in cohabitation wasn't going to work before she showed up with a moving truck full of framed French movie posters, Ikea furniture, and daddy issues. Still you press on because if you don't, what are you doing on the planet? You know it's doomed, and you do it anyway. Just to see if, on the off chance, it's not doomed. Because hey, it has to not be doomed sometime, right? (Spoiler alert: wrong.)

And then you get the look. And you realize you were wrong. I mean right. You know what I mean.

For Jude, it came one morning as she was getting ready to go to work. I was telling her that I was having lunch with Scott. "Should be fun," I said. "He just got divorced and needs a little crazy time. I might be back late tonight. I'll try not to get any new STDs." I'm superfunny like that, see.

Which is when I got the look.

Immediately I remembered. Jude and I were supposed to have lunch. To celebrate. It was the two-month anniversary of us moving in together. And that was it. Once you get the look, there's no getting away from it. She didn't say anything right then. She saved her words for that night, just before she slammed the door behind her for the last time. She handed me Piglet's leash and said, "Maybe if you try caring about something other than yourself for once, you'll finally grow up."

Whenever someone asks where I got Piglet, I say "in the divorce." Never mind that this wasn't a real divorce, the kind that costs people half their possessions and two-thirds of their dignity. It was just another banal breakup of yet another non-legally-binding romantic entanglement. But ever since turning forty I've taken to saying things like "I got it in the divorce." I've also started saying, "ever since turning forty." It's my way of trying to seem more adult. The evidence suggests it isn't working, but it beats not dying my hair.

I should clarify at this point that Piglet was a three-year-old American bulldog Jude rescued about a month before we moved in together. She weighed approximately seventy pounds, had a white-and-brindle coat, and big floppy ears. Piglet was good looking, as American bulldogs go, with just enough jut in her jaw to look tough, but not grumpy, and she wasn't too jowly. Still, when she stuck her head out the car window on the highway, her tongue and cheeks flapped like wet slices of bologna hung from a clothesline in a hurricane. She had eyes like a Drew Barrymore romcom—sweet, full of optimism, and at the end of the day, pretty stupid.

A charitable person would have called her temperament "easygoing." Then they would have gone over and poked her to make sure she wasn't in a coma. This is not to say she didn't have a zest for life. It was just that she exhibited no interest in traditional doglike activities such as fetching things, running around in parks, and being awake. It is no exaggeration to say that Piglet spent 98 percent of her life supine, slobbering and snoring on a tan leather chair by the television in my living room. If she had smelled of Pall Malls and mothballs, I'd have sworn she was my grandmother.

To be fair, Piglet wasn't completely sedentary. Early on I taught her a trick that killed every time she managed to drag herself up off the chair and do it. Using a treat as a reward, I'd point my finger at her like a gun. When I popped my thumb and said "pow," she'd roll over and play dead. Trouble was, she loved treats so much that eventually she just started rolling over and playing dead at random. Like when we were out for walks. And God forbid I didn't have a treat on me, because until that reward came, she'd keep flopping over like she was taking multiple shotgun blasts to the chest, each time looking up to make sure I'd seen, confirming in her mind that I really was the stingy asshole she'd figured me for. Meanwhile, strangers were eying me like I was a long-lost member of Michael Vick's posse.

The fact that Piglet required so little attention probably explains why she stuck and Jude didn't. I didn't have a lot of attention to spare. I was working my ass off day and night, trying to become some semblance of a success. I was doing this because I knew that successful people usually make a lot of money. And I grew up believing money meant freedom. I was wrong about that, of course. I now know that once you make some money, somehow you feel the need to keep working at it. Until the day you realize you're old and worn and broken down and you stop and look around and think, *Holy fuck, I've wasted my whole life working. I could have been living.*

Piglet ate a bowl of dry food twice a day. We'd go on three short walks, tops. We never went very far because Pig had a bum right front leg. I never found out what had happened to it (we rescued her when she was three), but her tranquil temperament suggested the injury was the result of an accident rather than abuse. Who knows, maybe she had taken a bullet early on in life. Which would explain how she sold the shotgun trick so effectively.

Piglet threw up the day after Christmas 2011. I figured she ate something she shouldn't have. She puked the rest of the afternoon. I figured she'd be fine once she got it all out. But as night came it became clear something else was wrong. She wouldn't eat, not even one of her beloved treats. A white crust had formed around her mouth. She had a glazed look in her eyes. Piglet was a dog that turned laziness into an art form, but this was different. She was worn out, worn down . . . just worn all to hell.

In the middle of the night I heard a noise. I turned on the light to find Pig taking a long slow whizz right next to my bed. I was half asleep, and on instinct screamed at her and slapped her on the rump. She looked up at me, mournfully, mid-whizz, as if to communicate that she knew, and there was nothing she could do about it. She was fully cognizant that she was doing the most awful thing a dog could do. I immediately felt like the frontrunner in the World's Biggest Dick Games (I'm a decathlete, if you must know). But that was nothing next to the way I felt two weeks later.

"It means she's going to die," the vet told me flatly, after the biopsy results revealed Piglet had a form of cancer called mast cell disease. The fact that she'd lasted two weeks was apparently a miracle in itself. A few days after she'd started vomiting, her condition had deteriorated to the point where she couldn't walk down the stairs to go outside. They ran a bunch of tests on her at the animal hospital and discovered an ulcer inside her stomach. They didn't know whether or not it was cancerous, but they said her only chance at survival was to operate immediately.

So they cut my dog wide open, and the surgeon looked inside and she saw a reason to hope. It would be a highly risky and expensive surgery, and she gave Pig about a 40 percent chance of surviving. I told her to do whatever it took. A few hours later they called to let me know she'd come through the procedure, but that the next forty-eight hours were going to be touch and go. Her vitals could fail at any moment. Sure enough, she survived that too. And the following forty-eight hours as well. As I had always known, Piglet was one tough bitch. I went to see her every day, and even though half her body was shaved bald and she had large staples across her torso and feeding tubes sticking out of her nose and a large colostomy bag hanging from her side . . . she looked like herself again. She looked happy. She was alive.

The biopsy report came back the day I took her home from the hospital. She was still positive for cancer. Like super-crazy cancer-party positive. Best case scenario, she'd live a few months.

A few months? A few shit months after all this pain and worry and money and heartache?

Fuck, yes, a few months. That operation was the best seventeen thousand dollars I ever spent. This next sentence is going to make me sound like a terrible, narcissistic shit-stain of a person, but I'm going to write it anyway. I started noticing Piglet.

I started appreciating every little nuance of her day. From the first thing in the morning when I'd wake frantic to check on her, make sure she was okay, see if maybe she'd eat something. During the days, I saw, for the first time, the thousand individuated ways she'd lounge and loll on the tan leather chair by the television. In the evenings we'd go up to the roof deck of my house, and she'd sit there by the edge watching cars roll by below, hot moms pushing their babies, homeless guys staggering to the liquor store, boats floating in and out of the marina, bugs swirling through the trees. I became convinced she wasn't just watching, she was taking it all in. That she instinctively understood she'd soon be leaving it all behind.

A week in, I wondered how long this fascination/focus would last. After all, the vet had said she had a few months, and a few means at least three. And three months is a long time to stay fascinated with something.

My fascination only lasted three weeks. Because that's how long Piglet lasted. On a Friday afternoon just before sundown, three weeks to the day from her surgery, Piglet gave me the look.

I'd never seen something so clearly in my life. The look said several things at once. It said, *I'm ready to go* and it said, *I love you*. It also said, *Please don't cry*, and *It was me that farted all those times*.

At the vet's that night, as I lay on the floor next to Piglet, the doc explained about the two injections they'd be giving her. The first would slow down her vitals and "mitigate any tendency toward spasm and other involuntary movement." Translation: it would keep the dog from freaking out and crapping all over the floor. I was tempted to ask her to give me one of those too. I'm not going to say I needed it more than Piglet, but goddamn I could have used something.

The next injection—the "pink shot"—would finish the job. That's the one that stops your heart. The plunger drops, the curtain lowers. Good night and good luck.

I've lost too many people I love to say that lying there on the floor with my arms wrapped around that dog as she died was the saddest moment of my life. But I don't believe I've ever cried as hard as I did that night. And this next part is going to sound like I made up a bullshit Hollywood ending to my dead dog story, but goddamnit I was there and this is what happened. When the pink shot went in, during those final agonizing seconds before it did its job, Piglet lifted her head and looked at me and my tear-streaked face and gave me a different look. This one just said, *Thank you.* Then she licked my face. A big, sloppy, bologna-tongued lick. Then she closed her eyes and stopped breathing.

I got rid of Piglet's bowls and collar and the toys she never played with, but I kept the leash. The one Jude claimed would lead me to maturity. If there's one thing I can't stand, it's when someone who hates me is right. Then I used the leash to walk Buna, the rambunctious pit bull–Labrador mix I adopted a few months later. Only this time I started paying attention from the beginning. Buna isn't functionally comatose, which makes a difference, but still, my entire attitude toward her is elevated and I don't think I would have gotten there if it weren't for Pig. And thus, by extension, Jude. The big difference between them of course is that, while the lady is long gone, Piglet will always be my number one bitch.

"OH, HEY! I'M HEADED INTO town, you want a ride?" Marley said. She had noticed me on the way out to her car. As she took in the whole scene I could see the wheels turning in her brain. Guy sitting alone on the bench outside the entrance, staring intently at a ceramic dog. I don't think I'd been talking out loud to it, but with the amount of wine I'd drunk I couldn't be entirely sure. "Oh wait a second," she said, self-preservation kicking in, "silly me. I forgot I have to take care of some . . . stuff."

"Don't worry about it, Marley. I'm not going into town tonight. Big day tomorrow."

"Awww," she purred, "Clarke was so excited to meet you." She seemed to have suddenly forgotten about whatever "stuff" she was supposed to take care of and resumed walking toward her car.

"I'll catch him next time," I said. The stars were impossibly gorgeous out there. So close they almost scratched your eyes. "Unless a grizzly gets me first."

"You just keep your food in the fridge and everything will be fine."

"You have no idea how much I wish that were true, Marley."

She headed on toward the parking lot, seemingly not sure what to say. Then just before turning the corner out of sight, she looked back and said, "You know, a lot of times things are much simpler than they look."

"I hope that's not true. Why would the world need writers?"

"*Need* is a strong word, Mr. Dunn," she replied, as she blooped her car remote and walked away.

CHAPTER 7

CALIFORNIA, OREGON, WASHINGTON, WYOMING, COLORADO, AND NEBRASKA

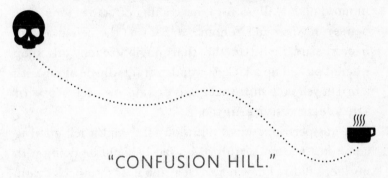

"CONFUSION HILL."

November was approaching. I'd been on the road five and a half weeks, driven across fourteen states and spent more than a hundred hours behind the wheel of Carl Vehicle. During that time I had learned many things, but one fact was most prominent in my mind: that no song was in heavier rotation on SiriusXM than "Carry on Wayward Son."

"Wayward Son" is, of course, the first Top 40 hit by the band that was so exciting they had to name it after Kansas. By my rough count, I had heard that song thirty-seven times since pulling out of Venice, California. And I wanted to hate it, I really did. I wanted to think it was a mediocre pseudo-philosophical piece of lowest common denominator bullshit. But somehow, I had the opposite reaction. Every time I heard it, I loved that goddamn piece of shit a tiny bit more. And that made me hate myself. But it was okay, because when I was listening to that song I didn't give a shit about anything.

The first time I heard the Stupid Fucking Song That I Love was just after I'd stopped at a peculiar roadside attraction in the Redwood Forest called Confusion Hill. It's so named because of its most popular attraction, the "gravity house," a structure built in such a way as to create tilt-induced optical illusions. I was coming off a weeklong wine bender in Napa and Sonoma, so I stayed the hell away and instead paid a visit to the charmingly low-rent gift shop where I picked up a kickass wooden train whistle along with a bright yellow T-shirt that reads CONFUSION HILL: HOME OF THE RARE, ELUSIVE CHIPALOPE.

It was perfect. I was Confusion Hill. And it felt good to admit it. I had no earthly idea what I should be doing with my life. I didn't know how to feel about my brother's death. Or Elizabeth or all the other terrible things that seem to just happen. And all the wonderful events that seem to just happen. As far as I can tell, life doesn't make a whit of goddamn sense. And that's actually fine. It's just no one told me. Or maybe that's something you have to figure out on your own. So yes, suddenly I knew myself. I was Confusion Hill. If you visit, watch out for the chipalope.

The chipalope may sound like a dessert item at a Baskin-Robbins, but it's actually a mythical creature, part antelope and part chipmunk. According to legend, it's soft and furry, with a large fluffy tail and a perfect little set of antlers. John, the burly and bearded man who manned the register at the gift shop, swore he'd seen numerous chipalopes thereabouts over the years. He also told me he could read the future using dominoes, and he tried to gauge my interest in becoming a member of the Church of All Worlds, a neo-pagan religion inspired by Robert A. Heinlein's science fiction novel *Stranger in a Strange Land.* I told John I'd heard of it before, though I couldn't recall the specifics.

"I reckon you probably heard of it cuz a' Charles Manson," John said.

Ah, yes, that was it. *Stranger in a Strange Land.* A book from the early '60s about a Martian raised on Earth. Apparently some people thought it had influenced Manson's worldview. As did Dale Carnegie's *How to Win Friends and Influence People,* the Beatles' *White Album,* and several of the more nightmarish passages from the *Book of Revelations*—the stuff about the Four Horsemen and the locusts and such. Don't try to pin Charlie down, man!

Yeah, that Manson sure had a knack for co-opting the creative efforts of others for his own twisted means. Still, I'd argue that he gave "Helter Skelter"—which was written about an amusement park ride; or the coming breakdown of our society, mirroring the fall of the Roman Empire; or coming off drugs; or just wanting to write a "loud, dirty" song that would become one of the inspirations for the punk rock movement, man, it must have sucked to be the Beatles—a serious Q-rating boost. I mean, without Charlie, would we even remember the Beatles anymore? Yes. Yes we would. Charles Manson is a psychopathically delusional idiot. I, on the other hand, am merely a delusional idiot.

"People are always bringing up the Manson connection," John said ruefully. "He was a bit of an extremist."

"Little bit," I concurred. And that Hitler guy probably took things a little too far, huh? And Stalin? What a grump!

"The truth is, the Church of All Worlds is a very peaceful organization. If you're interested, I'd be happy to tell you more about it."

Thanks, John, but I'd rather have a rabid chipalope burrow up my ass.

"I'm all good on the spiritual front at the moment," I said. "More than I can handle, if you want to know the truth. But thank you, man, for even thinking I might be someone worth saving. For now, I'll just take the T-shirt, the whistle, and, uh, maybe one of those orange Gatorades please. You take American Express?"

The next time I heard the friggin' Kansas song, I'd just pulled into the parking lot of the Sokol Blosser Winery in Dayton, Oregon, in the heart of the Willamette Valley, where they make some of the best Pinot Noir in the world. When I parked, the song had just begun, so of course you know what I did. I sat there and listened to the whole goofy crap-ass tune before I got out of my car. Then I went inside, got shit-hammered, and wrote in my notepad "This is some of the best goddamn Pinot Noir in the world." You will discover that I cuss a lot when I've been drinking.

The next night, I heard it again when I drove to Dundee and met Jeff Knapp and Eileen Wong of Sokol Blosser at Stumpy's, one of the more godforsaken dive bars on God's green earth. Stumpy's bills itself as the "most bodacious bar in the world." A strong claim, but I'd learned to take things at face value when you're far from home. It also bears noting that Eileen and Jeff are both fine human beings, and I am a better person for having spent time with them. We played pool, talked politics, and did $3 pudding shots. Yes, I said shots. Of pudding. Spiked with vodka. For three bucks. America, I am you, and I consume you.

I heard "Wayward Son" again the day I visited Sleight of Hand Cellars in Walla Walla, Washington. I got besnockered there too (are you sensing a theme?), this time with owner Jerry Solomon and winemaker Trey Busch. Both men of valor. They make a delightful red blend, "The Conjurer," which features Neil Patrick Harris's likeness on the label. Turns out Neil Patrick, in addition to being a singer, actor, dancer, and extraterrestrial from a planet orbiting Sirius (at least, I assume so), is also a magician of some merit. And he's a big fan of Sleight of Hand's wines. So Jerry and Trey, being savvy businessmen, called up this very famous guy one day and asked if they could slap his face onto a wine label. And Neil Patrick Harris apparently told them "slap the fuck away!" (I'm paraphrasing here.) The note in my pad from that day is "get Neil Patrick Harris's phone number from Trey." Neil Patrick, if you're reading this, call me. I'd love to interview you for this book. Also, can I borrow your time machine?

Before he started making award-winning wine, Trey was in the armed forces. He also had a successful career as a buyer in the fashion industry and is one of the world's leading authorities on Pearl Jam. Given our similarly peripatetic lives, I figured Trey and I would become immediate blood brothers. I'm not sure that actually happened. But if it ever does, I'm totally getting Neil Patrick Harris's number and calling him up to talk about wine and magic and gaybies and what it's like to live 2.6 parsecs from home. And goddamnit if I didn't hear "Wayward Son" again on my cab ride back to my hotel from Sleight of Hand cellars. And the guy didn't even have satellite radio.

By this point, the observant reader may have concluded that I've been drinking while penning this chapter. Congratu-fucking-lations, Enfucklopedia Brown!

MY FAVORITE WASHINGTON STATE WINES

By Trey Busch, Sleight of Hand Cellars head winemaker

DUNHAM CELLARS CAB SAUVIGNON
"This is the wine that first showed me how spectacular wines from Washington State could be. It inspired me to pursue a career in the wine industry. Thank you, Eric Dunham."

CAYUSE VINEYARDS "EN CHAMBERLIN" SYRAH
"Everything that I love about wines from the rocky region of Walla Walla is encapsulated in this awesome, funky, meaty bottle of Syrah. And the guy who made it is French, so it can't be bad, right?"

WOODWARD CANYON OLD VINES CABERNET SAUVIGNON
"[Woodward Canyon owner/director of production] Rick Small is The Man when it comes to making Cabernet you can age for years and years. This wine is the epitome of that expertise. It's the Dan Dunn of Walla Walla." (This is either a completely undeserved compliment of me, or a massive swipe at Woodward Canyon.)

MARK RYAN WINERY "THE DISSIDENT"
"Killer blend, but let's be honest, I love this wine because it's named after a Pearl Jam song . . . just like my winery."

THE UNDERGROUND WINE PROJECT "IDLE HANDS" SYRAH
"Make no mistake, this is the next cult wine of Washington State. Tremendous, tremendous juice. On top of that, it has the most badass label I've ever seen."

WHEN I MET CHARLES SMITH at his expansive tasting room on South Spokane Street in Walla Walla, the first thing he said was "I hope you're ready to do some drinking tonight." And I'll admit, my first thought was, *Dude, you were* Food & Wine's *2009 Winemaker of the Year. I drink for a living and am at the nadir of my emotional life. You sure you want to go there?* But shit. The oenophilic orgy that followed knocked me on my ass.

I should have seen it coming. Anyone who makes an excellent Riesling, names it Kung Fu Girl, and only charges $11 for it is clearly answering to a higher power. (You taking notes, Manson?) Smith's wine empire—which he built from the ground up—consists of several brands, including K Vintners, Charles Smith Wines, Charles & Charles (a partnership with winemaker Charles Bieler), Sixto, Wines of Substance, and Secco Italian Bubbles.

Charles and I come from similar backgrounds. The broken kind. We grew up poor, never knowing where our next meal, let alone next sip of wine was coming from. So neither of us is the spit bucket type.

We drank through Smith's entire portfolio at the tasting room. There wasn't a bad wine in the bunch. There were several, however, that were marvelous. The rich black cherry and tobacco notes of the Boom Boom! Syrah. A delicious Cabernet/Syrah blend called "The Creator," flush with bold flavors of roasted herbs, black olive tapenade, cocoa, and black tea. The 2012 Chateau Smith Cabernet Sauvignon.

As we neared the end his list, I was feeling chummy enough with Charles to mention his striking resemblance to former Van Halen front man Sammy Hagar. Charles said it wasn't proper to talk about Sammy without drinking some mezcal, so we made our way to his nineteenth-century farmhouse where he launched his first wine label, K Vintners, back in 2001. After a shot of Sombra mezcal and a little weed (which is totally legal in the Evergreen State—whatever, book cops!), we headed down to his ridiculously well stocked wine cellar.

"Pick anything you want," he said, as I surveyed rows and rows of rare and aged wines that would give Robert Parker one of those boners from the Cialis commercials that lasts seventy-two hours and requires medical attention. It was like that moment in *Willy Wonka and the Chocolate Factory* when Gene Wilder lets the kids into the room where everything is made of candy.

"If there were some terrible catastrophe here and you could only save one of these bottles, which one would it be?" I asked.

"The biggest one. I'm thirsty." He was resting his hand upon an Imperial bottle—an Imperial bottle is also known as a Methuselah and contains the equivalent of two Jeroboams, or eight standard 750 ml bottles of wine—of some decades-old Châteauneuf-du-Pape. It felt like a dare. A quintuple dog dare. I just couldn't do it. Generosity is one thing. Getting someone to uncork a bottle worth several thousand dollars is another.

I told Charles I'd rather get some variety and since he knew his own cellar best, he should choose. He grabbed three far more portable bottles of Bordeaux to take with us to dinner. They were, as follows . . .

1964 Chateau Pichon Lalande
1966 Chateau Figeac
1982 Chateau Cantemerle

So let's just say that dinner—at a wonderful little Walla Walla eatery called Brasserie Four—was special. And by special, I mean that Charles Smith and I drank some of the best wine anyone's ever poured down their gullet.

The talk ranged from Smith's Horatio Alger-esque rise from barely employed rock band manager to the top of the wine world food chain to the fact that Gary Leon Ridgway—the notorious Green River Killer—was interned nearby at the Washington State Penitentiary. This led to a long discussion of serial killers. Smith was particularly fascinated by Elizabeth Bathory, a.k.a. "the Blood Countess," who tortured and killed hundreds of girls in the late 1500s. (I'm more an Albert Fish man myself. What he lacked in numbers, he made up for in style.) Other topics touched upon included '80s synth pop, Danish women's hands, and the ins and outs of various schools of street fighting. Did I mention that marijuana is legal in Washington?

After dinner, though it was an absolutely terrible idea in retrospect, we tottered down the street to the Green Lantern. Take one guess what my drunk ass put on the jukebox. It's by Kansas.

I CARRIED ON MY WAYWARD way through Idaho and Montana. While driving through Yellowstone National Park, I saw a huge bison taking a leisurely stroll along the side of the road. Bison are a breathtaking thing to witness up close. Or at least the guy in the SUV in front of me thought so, because he got out of the vehicle, walked right up to the giant beast with a camera, and started snapping photos like he was Terry Richardson. I say this because the bison wasn't wearing any clothes and seemed a little uncomfortable with the whole thing.

Now, I'll admit that my understanding of the behavioral patterns of the American buffalo is limited. But even I know that cozying up to one in the wild is a startlingly stupid idea. Even if it did happen to bear a resemblance to Kate Upton. (It did not.) Fortunately, this particular bison had either already reached its tourist-pulverizing quota for the day, or was a vegan, or just couldn't be bothered to gore anyone just now, and kept on lumbering down the road.

Turns out, buffalo aren't all that bright. Indeed, centuries ago, North American Indians used to hunt and kill the big dumb furry creatures en masse by herding them over cliffs. Such death-by-gravity sites became known as buffalo jumps. And so did the only winery in Cody, Wyoming. What's that? You've never heard of the Buffalo Jump Winery? Well that only makes sense. It's in goddamn Wyoming!

Buffalo Jump Winery is operated in the "Rodeo Capital of the World" by the husband-and-wife team of Beckie Tilden and Scott Wagner. Their selection of wines is better than one might expect, primarily because they source their grapes from California, Oregon, and Washington. (I would have to wait a while before sampling any 100 percent Wyoming-made vino.) One of only four wineries in Wyoming, Buffalo Jump produces about three thousand cases a year, almost all of which are sold and consumed in our nation's least populous state.

"Wyoming is a beer and shots state," Scott Wagner told me, "so we have to be careful not to be snooty about wine around here." He wasn't kidding either—the cheese plate they gave me to accompany their 2006 Cabernet Sauvignon Reserve was devoid of Époisses de Bourgogne. And the hardship of having to use a plastic knife to spread Brie on a crumbly cracker gave me a real appreciation of how difficult life must have been for the settlers back in Wild West times.

Wyoming is also home to what is believed to be the world's most successful—and only—cowboy chocolatier. His name is Tim Kellogg, and he makes these exquisite chocolates in his shop in Meeteetse, a don't-blink-or-you'll-miss-it town on Highway 20 between Where the Fuck Am I? and Goddamn, Isn't It Colorado Yet? The only reason I even knew to look out for the cowboy chocolatier is that Scott and Beckie at Buffalo Jump had raved about the guy. And with good reason—those chocolates are even better than Stumpy's pudding shots.

I gotta admit that when I pulled into the place I was actually a little disappointed that my theme song wasn't playing. I was visiting a cowboy chocolatier in Wyoming for fuck's sake. It doesn't get much more wayward than that. I decided that perhaps the curse was broken. Then, no more than three minutes after pulling out onto the highway again, there it was, that familiar a cappella vocal intro. Goddamnit, Kansas, you're my only friend.

I cruised east to Cheyenne, then merged onto 85 North and drove that seventy miles to an itty-bitty outpost in Goshen County called Huntley, which is spittin' distance from the Nebraska border. For the record, many Wyomingites take considerable pleasure in hocking loogies at their neighbors to the east. The last time a census was taken, in 2010, the population of Huntley was 30. There's a winery in Huntley called Table Mountain. As I mentioned earlier, Wyoming only has but four wineries. So I figured I had to stop and see the place if I was in the neighborhood.

The Zimmerer family farm was established in 1926. Four generations have worked the soil, grown crops, and kept the place solvent through some tough times (the Great Depression, the Reagan administration, dubstep). Over the past ninety years, the Zimmerer farm has seen sugar beets, beans, alfalfa, corn, and cattle.

In 2001, young Patrick Zimmerer completed his senior thesis project at the University of Wyoming on establishing vineyards in the Equality State. As part of what he described as a "research project gone wild," Patrick convinced his family to plant a small vineyard. A mere three hundred vines. A few years later, he and his sister entered a business plan for a winery into competition at the university and won $10,000. The "Home of the Wyo Wine" was born.

Bear in mind that growing grapes in southeast Wyoming is a gotdamn sumbitch. But despite the myriad challenges—among them selecting varietals that stand a fighting chance and convincing sentient human beings to drink Wyoming-made wine—Table Mountain Vineyards has only expanded over the last decade and a half. They now have nearly ten acres planted with ten thousand vines yielding cold-hardy hybrid grapes capable of standing up to Mother Nature on even her worst bad-hair days. We're talking subzero temperatures in winter, scorching heat in the dog days, relentless high winds, and unpredictable precipitation. The hybrids they grow there include:

Frontenac

Like many hybrids (and at least one ex-girlfriend), Frontenac is the result of the extensive crossbreeding research done by scientists at the University of Minnesota. It's primarily used in dry reds, Rosé, and port.

Frontenac Gris

The white version of Frontenac. Doesn't get pulled over by the cops as much.

Valiant

Blue grapes traditionally used to make jams and jellies. Pat Zimmerer is using it in wine because he's an ornery cuss.

Marcheal Foch

A French hybrid, believed to be a cross of Gold-riesling (itself an intraspecific cross of Riesling and Courtiller Musqué) with a *Vitis riparia–Vitis rupestris* cross. In other words, fucking confusing.

Elvira

Medium-sized green berries created by mixing *Vitis labrusca* with a big-breasted Mistress of the Dark.

Marquette

Also developed at the University of Minnesota, it's a cross between two other hybrids, MN 1094 and Ravat 262. Not to be confused with Coldplay, which is a cross between Radiohead and Kenny G.

Farming is a tough business, especially for a family competing with conglomerates. But when the big boys came through offering cash for their land, the Zimmerers held out. Because this is Wyoming, dammit. Their state mammal is the bison, their state reptile is the horned toad, and their state fish is the cutthroat trout. Pat planted vines in a place where most folks had never had a glass of wine before. And now, if you stop by his tasting room on any given weekend, you'll find some straight-up working cowboys in there sipping on Rosé. They're not just in business, they're making history.

I, on the other hand, was making a different sort of history as the guy who had lied about himself and his abilities to more U.S. winemakers than any other. The miles and winery visits had begun to seriously pile up, and as they did, so did my anxiety about my ability and/or continued desire to transform myself into the leading authority on wine in America. At every stop along the way, I'd tell anyone who'd listen about my ambitious plan for achieving complete oenophilic omnipotence, and virtually everyone had the same basic reaction— what I was doing was amazing! And I was an extraordinary human being for doing it.

Man, it felt good when they said that. At first, anyway. Usually after they said that, though, they'd go on to say a bunch of stuff about phenolics and racking and other tedious winemakery gobbledygook that made my eyes glaze over . . . especially after I'd been driving for six hours and had thrown back a couple glasses of whatever it is they were pouring.

It was only an hour's drive from Huntley, Wyoming, to my next destination—Sonoma-based winemaker Sam Sebastiani's vacation home in Bayard, Nebraska—but boy did I ever do a hell of a lot of soul-searching out there on US 26 East. What the hell are phenolics anyway? I honestly didn't have a clue. What I did know was that anyone who *actually* knew anything about wine could probably tell you what a goddamn phenol is. Yet after nearly two months of driving all over the United States, supposedly doing serious wine research, I could not. Phenolics obviously played an important role in winemaking because I'd heard numerous winemakers mention them. I just hadn't bothered to ask out of . . . out of what? Embarrassment? Laziness? Indifference? What the fuck had I actually been doing out there that whole time besides driving, jerking off, feeling sorry for myself, and getting wasted? (Usually in that order.)

Halfway through my trip, my grasp on the fundamentals of wine production remained tenuous at best. Not only was I in the dark about phenolics, I also knew dick about fining, residual sugar, degorgement, malo-lactic fermentation, brix, and pH levels. And don't get me started on how uninformed I was about racking. I'd learned precisely one thing about racking—that it had nothing to do with boobs. And that implying that it does will get you a nice, crisp smack in the face.

Still, here I was, halfway across the country. It was a little late to ask for a do-over. Unfortunately it was also too late in the game to start querying folks about the fundamentals. It reminded me of that awful moment of every school year when I realized I had screwed up so badly that the best I could hope for if I busted my ass all day and night was a C+.

Impostor syndrome is the condition where successful people are convinced that deep down they are frauds who don't deserve the triumphs they have earned. I was beginning to think I suffered from Reverse Impostor syndrome—I knew I was completely full of shit, yet I felt I deserved complimentary stays at vineyards and fancy dinners and happily accepted people's praise when I told them my aim was to become the leading expert on American wine.

As I drove into Bayard, the truth hit me hard: I had set myself a preposterous goal. And I'd encountered toddlers at some of the vineyards who knew more about grapes than I ever will. But my date with destiny at Pebble Beach loomed in the distance nonetheless. As did the deadline for this book. So I made a decision. I knew how to fix this. It was time for complete commitment. Enough with the halfhearted approach to becoming America's leading wine expert. If I wanted that C+, I was going to have to man up. I would become an expert all right. In fact, I would become the leading expert. I would become the leading expert on talking about becoming a wine expert. This was something I knew I could accomplish. Because I was already doing an incredible job of it. Welcome to life on Confusion Hill.

"YOU PROBABLY TELL YOURSELF
FIVE DIFFERENT LIES JUST TO GET
OUT OF BED EVERY MORNING."

CHAPTER 8

NEBRASKA, CHICAGO, MICHIGAN, CANADA, FINGER LAKES, VERMONT, MAINE, RHODE ISLAND

Right about now you may be thinking, sweet Cheez-its, we're already halfway through this book and Dan's only made it to Nebraska. At this rate, we're going to run out of pages somewhere around Ohio. By now you know I've done some terrible things in my life, but please know that despite my copious failings, I would never leave anyone stranded in Ohio. There are some things a man just doesn't want on his conscience. If we're going to get through this, you're going to have to trust me. Coincidentally this is exactly the same phrase that the late great Hunter S. Thompson said to me before we huffed ether and blasted propane canisters with shotguns in his backyard. Based on that experience, the worst that's going to happen to you is some light scarring and the inability to remember your middle name.

In *American Vintage: The Rise of American Wine,* Paul Lukacs points out that the wine industry in America as we know it can be traced back to Cincinnati of all places, which is not only where the hot dog was invented and the birthplace of Randy "Macho Man" Savage, but was also the home of Nicholas Longworth, whom many regard as the original American wino.

Before Longworth came along in the early nineteenth century, most Americans had never tasted anything but fortified wine—high-octane juice that wouldn't spoil and was consumed almost solely for the purpose of getting blotto. Longworth was one of the only people to set his sights on producing table wine with moderate to low alcohol content, like the stuff they make in Italy, France, and Germany. Longworth championed Old World–style wine as a salubrious alternative to the hard liquor that was increasingly regarded as a scourge in America. In fact, he believed wine would be a conduit to a more temperate society. It's just common sense.

Longworth planted Catawba, a grape that up to that point had been used primarily in the production of jams and jellies. He used it to make sparkling wine. Sparkling wine of such high quality, the great Henry Wadsworth Longfellow was inspired to write a poem about it.

Because of my deep respect for Longworth's importance to the story of American wine, I felt it would simply be rude for me to even set foot in Ohio on this journey. To quote Wayne Campbell (party on, Wayne), I'm not worthy. It's hallowed ground. And I'm just an oaf in an FJ Cruiser I named Carl Vehicle. I solemnly promise it has nothing to do with the fact that the fastest way from Michigan to upstate New York is through Canada.

I hope the lovely people of Ohio can forgive me for giving their lovely state a pass. I've met more than a few Ohioans with a chip on their shoulder about where they come from, probably because Ohio is the butt of so many jokes. But that's the deal they made in exchange for getting to decide who the president is. I think it's fair. I can relate to the defensiveness about where you come from, though. I come from a pretty fucked-up place myself.

I FIRST REALIZED HOW FUCKED up our Philly neighborhood was one night in third grade. I realized it because I was sitting at the kitchen table watching TV in our apartment on Bustleton Avenue and someone came up from behind me and coldcocked me with a frying pan.

I don't remember what day of the week it was, but I know it happened between 7 and 7:30 P.M., because *The Joker's Wild*— the game where knowledge is king and lady luck is queen— was on television. It was my favorite show. Every weeknight at 7 P.M. there I'd be, perched in the same spot, waiting for Jack Barry to shellac some fools. I don't remember if I was wearing it, but my favorite T-shirt at the time was emblazoned with Barry's signature catchphrase, "Joker, joker, joker!"

If I was eight, my mother would have been twenty-six. You remember Charlene. Well, there she was. Pretty as anything you want to look at, and sat square in a shitbox walk-up in Northeast Philly, raising a third grader all by her lonesome.

My mother grew up in a run-down row house in a decaying Philly neighborhood called Summerdale, where she and her four siblings were tutored via daily run-ins with the boots, belts, and broomsticks of her mother. Her grandkids called her Nana, but everyone else called her the General, due to her fondness for discipline and nonproportional response. From the time she was a small child into her teens, Charlene was routinely punished by being locked for hours on end in a dark basement closet without food or water.

She was sixteen when she started dating Danny Dunn, a good-looking bad boy four years her senior who grew up fast in a whites-only orphanage. An auto mechanic who did some amateur stock car racing, he was pretty much a real-life James Dean. Except he was also a real-life philanderer, con artist, and nasty, nasty drunk. Even those of you without psychology degrees may be able to figure out why my mother was drawn to him. She was just shy of getting her certificate in beauty culture from Mercy Vocational when she wound up with an Irish Surprise named me. My dad demanded she get an abortion, but my mother wouldn't do it. Or couldn't do it—it's a fine line with Catholics. So he did his best to terminate the pregnancy the old-fashioned way, by beating the ever-loving shit out of her. My dad denies this ever happened. Pure fabrication, he'll tell you.

"Truth" has always been in quotes in the crazy-quilt assemblage of humans that passes for my family. So who knows? Maybe he socked her in the gut a couple of times while she was pregnant, maybe he didn't. And that's the "truth." One thing's for sure, though. When he reads the last couple paragraphs, he'll probably wish he'd put a little more muscle into it when he had the chance.

Amid all the "truth" there is one fact I am reasonably certain of: on July 14, 1968, I made it out of Charlene's guts alive. She was eighteen. He was twenty-two. And I was the seven and a half pounds of floppy-necked millstone forcing them to get married. Ain't love grand?

Three years flew by, each more filled with magic than the last. If by magic, you mean screaming, punching, and booze. At some point the two of them sobered up long enough to get a quickie divorce. Charlene took a job as a shampoo girl at a small salon on Levick Street near St. Timothy's. She worked there four years to support herself and her kid and put herself through beautician school. By the time I was seven she had her barber's license and we moved on to Bustleton Avenue a few neighborhoods over, near Olivieri's barbershop where she cut enough men's hair to keep us in soft pretzels and Hamburger Helper.

I WAS FEELING MORE THAN a little lonely as I pulled out of Bayard for the five-hour, three-hundred-mile slog to St. Paul, Nebraska. And not just from the lack of wineries in the gigantic middle of our great nation. I missed my dog. I missed my friends. I missed the beach. I missed not being in the car all the time. I missed sleeping in my own bed. I missed greasy burgers on Sunday afternoons at Hinano Cafe in Venice.

Things weren't playing out the way I thought they would. Part of the point of this trip was to get over Elizabeth, but I really didn't feel any different about the situation. I'd promised my sister I'd sprinkle some of Brian's ashes in Yellowstone National Park, but I forgot. I was supposed to be learning everything there was to know about wine, and somehow I wasn't doing that, either. I was just a lonely, forgetful phony in a car with an unfortunate name a long way from home.

Wait, scratch that. I lived in Nowhere now. And I was smack-dab in the middle of it out there in central Nebraska.

When the sweet, elderly woman behind the counter at a gas station in Bridgeport asked me how my morning was going, I almost told her everything. *Go ahead, just start blubbering right here,* I thought to myself, *she'll understand.* I figured she'd probably give me a big hug and pat me on the back as I soaked her flowery cardigan in tears as she told me everything is okay and everyone felt this way sometimes and life was the hardest thing about being alive and things would get better. She'd tell me that if I wanted to go back, I could. I had always had the power to do so. All I had to do was close my eyes, tap my heels together three times, and think to myself "there's no place like home." Then drive thirteen hundred miles.

"Going great so far." It's almost the same thing, right?

"You have a wonderful day, dear," she replied.

I restrained myself from saying, "Thanks, Mom."

I walked out to Carl Vehicle and pointed him east. But not before I sprinkled a pinch of Brian's ashes next to the pump in the gas station parking lot. It wasn't Old Faithful but, well, Brian had never been to Bridgeport, Nebraska, either.

I drove for about an hour in silence. The first time I'd done so on the trip. When I forgot why I was doing it, I turned on the radio. First song? Simon and Garfunkel's "Homeward Bound." Just started. Goddamn if I didn't crank it up—not a phrase people typically associate with Simon and Garfunkel. I am, if nothing else, an innovator—and start shrieking along.

Midway through the song I passed an old farmer in a pickup truck who looked at me like I had two gay heads. What's the matter, buddy? Ain't never seen a grown man in a Japanese-made SUV going eighty-five miles per hour while bawling his eyes out scream-singing Simon and Garfunkel?

Next up—I shit you not—"The Long and Winding Road" by the Beatles. And now I knew I was being fucked with, not by the universe, but some sadistic pansophical programmer at SiriusXM. This wasn't even the halfway decent version of the goddamn song, the one Paul wanted on the record. No, this was the treacly piece of shit Phil Spector rubbed his sugary taint all over. Fuck you, Phil Spector. And fuck your wig (I'd take a bet that Phil Spector actually did fuck his wig at some point). And your stupid overproduction of the last thing the best band this weird universe ever spit out. I should mention that by this point I was crying like a third grader who just dropped a championship-losing pop fly and looked like I'd been hit in the face with a snot pie.

I could barely get the lyrics out or see the road ahead. Fearing that listening to music in my current state might present a danger to others, and myself, I switched over to talk radio. Howard Stern had just begun an interview with Neil Young. He interviewed Young for more than an hour, during which they touched on just about everything I wanted to know about the man. When asked if he thought music had turned him into a god, Young replied, "Music turned me into myself." Thanks, Neil. I dialed up *Harvest* on my phone and disappeared into Nebraska.

As I mentioned earlier, the grand center of this country is a little light on vineyards. They weren't kidding about those amber waves of grain though. Great for beer. Not so much for wine. Still, I am, as always, a professional. And as a professional, I have notes. Take this entry from October 15, 2014, at the Miletta Vista Winery in St. Paul, Nebraska: "You know how you say a wine has legs? And that sounds like lakes? *Lahhkges*, right? But they don't look like lakes at all! They look like rivers. We shouldn't say a wine has good legs, we should say a wine has good rivers. Because back in France grapes grow by . . . rivers?" Based on this, I'm pretty sure I'm a genius.

But please don't interpret my distractibility as a knock on Miletta Vista. Mick and Loretta McDowell, the proprietors of the place, are fine people and are at the forefront of Nebraska winemaking. Cynics might equate that to being valedictorian at summer school, but I've tried their wine and can attest it's the real McCoy (or, rather, the real McDowell). Miletta Vista has garnered numerous prestigious awards around the country, most notably for their Brianna—a Muscat hybrid that can withstand the harshest of winters. It won "Best of Show White Wine" at the 2012 U.S. National Competition in Sonoma, California, where renowned sommelier Chris Sawyer declared it one of the more interesting American wines he's tasted in years. And when Chris Sawyer says a wine is interesting, it's in your best interest to listen.

Speaking of interesting, let's talk for a second about all the great wines from Iowa and western Illinois.

Okay, second's up. Great job everyone.

I'm going to be honest with you folks; I drank wine in these states and they were made by wonderful salt-of-the-earth people. And I'm not going to tell you their names or their wineries because, while I tried to like the wine out there, it's not an easy task. In fact it was a terrible task. And I was terrible at it. In that spirit, I'd like to present some of the more terrible things that can happen to wine between the ground and your mouth.

BUZZKILL: A GLOSSARY OF WINE NIGHTMARES

BRETTANOMYCES (BRETT)

A spoilage yeast that causes barnyard aromas and flavors in wine. Often referred to as Brett, which means, statistically, it has a 90 percent likelihood to share either the name of your freshman year RA or that dick from high school who stole your girlfriend.

VOLATILE ACIDITY (VA)

An undesirable amount of acidity that gives a wine a sour, vinegary edge. The Brother Theodore of winemaking.

CORKED
When a tainted stopper causes wine to taste like Phil Spector has been rubbing it with his taint.

PHYLLOXERA
If vineyards were network TV shows, then the Phylloxera bug would be Matthew Perry. If it gets into your vineyard, it will inevitably kill it.

PIERCE'S DISEASE
If vineyards were L.A. comedy clubs, Pierce's disease would be Dane Cook. It just shows up sometimes out of the blue, it's incredibly hard to stop, and there's nothing funny about it.

BERRY ROT
This is what happens when the berries . . . you got this one, right?

OXIDIZED
When wine has been exposed too long to air and taken on a brownish color, lost its freshness, and begun to smell of rotten fruit. See also: David Lee Roth.

BOTTLE SHOCK
A condition that can occur just after bottling or due to bad handling. Also a forgettable 2008 flick about the time Alan Rickman saved America from the French. Thanks, Alan Rickman!

MERCAPTANS
Volatile sulfur compounds that can occur in wine. Imagine a skunk ate another skunk then took a dump in your wine. It's worse than that.

I NEEDED A BREATHER, SO I headed from western Illinois to Chicago. Hey, you know what's good in Chicago? Whiskey. I spent the better part of two days there hunkered down on a stool at Delilah's, arguably the finest no-frills whiskey wonderland in these United States. Delilah's boasts an amazing and expansive selection of single malts and bourbons, and owner Mike Miller is as knowledgeable a whiskey-phile as they come. If I hadn't had two more months and many thousands of miles' worth of wine research ahead of me, I'd likely still be at Delilah's sipping Highland Park Single Cask, making lists of things I was fucking up on this trip, and rocking out to Bad Brains. Don't judge me. I needed this.

Ultimately, however, duty called, and I couldn't let it go to voicemail anymore. If I really wanted to become the best there is at talking about learning to be the best there is, I had to keep popping corks and paying tolls across this Land of Freedom. So I said good-bye to Chi-town and pointed Carl Vehicle in the general direction of the Atlantic Ocean.

Do they make wine in Michigan? You bet your sweet bippy they do. They just don't make it from grapes. The foremost U.S. producers of nongrape wine, Michiganders make it from cranberries, apples, oranges. Basically whatever they can get their hands on that they can turn into booze. Because if they don't, that old bastard Winter wins.

The sour cherry wine produced at places such as Good Harbor Vineyards on the Leelanau Peninsula is said to be the best of its kind. Of course, the only people saying that are the ones who regularly consume wine made from cherries. It's like asking the Taco Bell Chihuahua where you might find a great burrito.

And of course they have grapes too. Now that I have finally explored the Wolverine State, I can attest with some authority that they make damn good ice wine in the Traverse City area. Ice wine is sweet wine made from grapes that freeze on the vine. Canada and Germany have long been the world's leading producers of this niche product, which is difficult and expensive to produce. But all of a sudden, Michigan winemakers be like, yo, we chillin'! A fact I include solely for the way it sounds when said in a Canadian-tinged midwestern accent.

Chateau Chantal and Brys Estate both make excellent ice wines. The Vidal Blanc from the Paw Paw region ain't too shabby either, with standouts like Warner Vineyards and Cody Kresta. The Vidal grape, incidentally, is a hybrid of Ugni Blanc and Rayon d'Or, both of which are commonly used to make ice wine.

See, I'm learning things! There's hope. Next I plan to move on to learning useful things.

I left pastoral northern Michigan for not-pastoral-in-the-least Detroit. Travel advisory: I firmly believe that a tribe of radical hipster communitarians will one day make Detroit over as a Utopia of free expression and social justice (and Robocops). Until then, I suggest you stay the fuck out of Detroit. If you stop for gas, directions, food, or human kindness, something terrible will happen to you, probably involving child gangs, wild dogs, or both. Take it from a guy who knows a thing or two about terrible things.

I DON'T KNOW HOW MUCH my mom made cutting hair at Olivieri's, but it can't have been much. Olivieri's was a no-frills place with a blue-collar clientele; a haircut couldn't have earned her more than a couple bucks. Every Wednesday we took the bus to the welfare office. I remember because I always got excited when it came time to pull the cord to let the driver know we wanted off at the next stop. Pulling the cord was important. You controlled the whole goddamn bus, if only for a minute or two. And let me tell you, I was *really* good at pulling that cord. Figured I might go pro one day. But that dream fizzled when my mom got an old beater of a station wagon and we stopped taking buses everywhere.

About three weeks after we got the station wagon, someone smashed out the rear windshield to get at the precious bounty inside—a carton of Kools. We had that car two more years, but my mother never replaced the rear window or stopped bitching about losing those cigarettes. But silver lining alert! By taking out our rear window, the Kools thief transformed our piece of shit wagon into a piece of shit winter wonderland. At least from January to March. Sure, Joey McGill said my mom was so poor she went to Kentucky Fried Chicken to lick other people's fingers and that little bastard Al Rossi said she married young just to get the free rice. But for me a little ridicule was a small price to pay for being able to build snowmen in the back of the car while rolling down I-95.

As I mentioned before, Nana's nickname was the General. She had a nickname for my mother and me as well. She called us "the wards of the state." Because that's the supportive thing to do when your daughter is on welfare and food stamps. She relentlessly chided my mother for "wasting" what little money we had on Catholic school rather than sending me to public school for free. But Charlene wasn't hearing it. The way she saw it, public schools were breeding grounds for degenerates and criminals. Catholic school meant I had a chance. A job that didn't involve mopping up floors or driving a truck like my bum of a father. Maybe even college. "Look at John F. Kennedy!" my mother always used to say. Because this is America, goddamnit, and no matter who you are, if you work hard, you've got a chance to become successful enough that someone wants to splat your brains all over the back of a Lincoln convertible. For years she harbored a dream that I would pursue a career as a mortician. When I asked why, she said, "Because people never stop dying."

Practical woman, my mother.

As poor as we were back then, somehow we wound up having an old-fashioned player piano in our apartment for a while. One day I came home from school and there it was, a big wooden thing standing in the small windowless space that passed for a living room. When I asked where it came from, my mom said it was a gift in a tone that told me to drop it. Charlene has never been a big fan of prolonged lines of questioning. A lot of people came and went at our apartment in those days, most of them men, many of them with gifts. Best I can figure, one of them must have really liked my mother and just so happened to have a piano in his pocket (in addition to being happy to see her).

It wasn't anything fancy and it had a few broken keys, but it was in tune and the player mechanism worked fine. We only had the piano roll that was already inside it, of course, which meant we were stuck with just this one song. For months we had no idea what song it even was. One day though, Joe Ferrand, a neighborhood old-timer who used to look after me, came over. He immediately IDed it as a Tin Pan Alley number called "Hard Hearted Hannah (the Vamp of Savannah)." He even taught me the lyrics . . .

> *Leather is tough, but Hannah's heart is tougher,*
> *She's a gal who loves to see men suffer.*

Those Tin Pan Alley guys didn't mess around.

Joe also taught me how to play "Chopsticks" and a simple version of "The Entertainer." In reality, my piano playing skills never progressed beyond rudimentary. But in my imagination, I was a virtuoso. Having a player piano at my disposal helped with this illusion. Now that my dreams of a career pulling the cord on the bus were dead, I was looking for a new career anyway. I was certain my lively, note-perfect rendition of "Hard Hearted Hannah" (nailed it . . . again!) was going to take me places. Maybe even one day, dare to dream, to Canada.

WHICH BRINGS ME TO THE most shameful episode in this book. Detroit shook me up pretty bad, left me doubting everything I ever knew . . . like the fact that Paul Masson would never ever sell a wine before its time. I was weak, America. So weak I . . . I cheated on you. With my Canadian girlfriend, Canada. The first time I entered her was right after leaving Detroit.

I swear it only lasted a day or two. I don't know what to tell you. She made me feel wanted. Seriously, I have never felt more like a walking mug shot than I have during my time among the sunny folk of Ontario. I was convinced that every hearty "Hello there!" would be followed by a swift call to the RCMP. Still, I never got arrested, or even hassled in the slightest while I was inside my Canadian girlfriend, Canada. And that means one of two things. Either I was wrong, and Canadians truly are the nicest people on the planet, or I managed to outwit the Mounties at the ice wine vineyards by cleverly blending in as a scarecrow.

If you're ever up that way, the booming wine region around the charming town of Niagara-on-the-Lake will make you wish you were nice enough to be Canadian. It doesn't hurt that Inniskillin, Trius, Stratus, and Kittling Ridge make the best ice wine in North America. Don't hold being Canadian against them. If you squint when you look at the map, you can convince yourself that Ontario is our fifty-first state. Plus you can see the Falls while you're up there. I can say with certainty that they're especially awe-inspiring when you're ripped to the tits on ice wine.

WHEN I REENTERED THE UNITED STATES in New York State, I was riddled with guilt. The United States gave me everything and I go parading around with some two-bit hussy with a prime minister and a funny accent? What kind of man was I? I stopped feeling bad almost immediately, however, once I realized I was headed through the toll-rich byways of the great Northeast. Drop some coin, apparently, and all is forgiven.

The only thing worse than the ridiculous amount of tolls up and down the East Coast is actually having to stop and pay at each one. Electronic tolling lets you roll through those things like a hot bowling ball through pins made of butter. I asked the guy at the first tollbooth I hit if he knew how I might go about getting an E-Z Pass transponder.

"No idea," the toll collector said. I got the sense he was being brutally honest with me.

"You have no idea how to get an E-Z Pass?" I said, with what I would characterize as an appropriate amount of incredulity.

"Nah," he said, his brow showing the ease of a man who has given his last shit.

"Any idea where I might find someone who would know?"

He wore an unmistakable moue of world weariness as he took a gander at the line of cars behind me. Then he heaved a sigh of exasperation before making a big production of searching for something beneath the register.

"Here," he sniffed, tossing an E-Z Pass brochure through my open window.

I guess I couldn't blame him. I'd basically pulled up and said, *Is there a way I could never, ever deal with someone like you again? Oh, and would you mind if I also put you out of a job?*

Then again, we were in New York. A state whose people

don't have the best reputation for being hospitable. At least where I come from, when you ask where something is, people have the decency to say "Up your ass!"

It dawns on me that on the *American Wino* book tour, I may have to do some damage control before paying visits to Ohio or New York. And basically every other state I visited. And Canada.

Some people believe that the wines being made near the Finger Lakes in New York rival the very best juice from Napa and Sonoma. Some people also believe the Jets will win the Super Bowl again one day and that paying $3,500 a month to live in a Manhattan closet is reasonable. Silly New Yorkers! Still, I go into everything with an open mind and to my delight discovered some truly lip-smacking Riesling produced around Seneca Lake, the so-called middle finger of the region. Standouts include the 2013 Reserve Dry Riesling from Hermann J. Wiemer, Wagner's 2012 Semi-Dry Riesling, and the 2012 Select Harvest Riesling from Glenora. They make delicious ice wine there too. Check out the Vidal Ice from Standing Stone Vineyards, produced at an exceptional vineyard site first planted by wine legends Charles Fournier and Guy Deveaux in 1975.

If you're looking to party hearty in Finger Lakes wine country, the place to be is Hazlitt 1852 Vineyards in Hector, New York, on the east side of Seneca Lake, where the rock and roll is played at high volume and twenty bucks gets you not one, but two bottles of Red Cat. Red Cat is the Red Bull and vodka of crushed grape juice. Not that there's actually vodka or energy drink in the wine, but it somehow effects the same delirious buzz, which goes a long way toward explaining why Hazlitt is one of the liveliest tasting rooms in the United States. Have dinner afterward down the street at Stonecat Café—what is it with the cats, guys?—for the best cornmeal-crusted catfish east of the Mississippi.

Should you decide to tour any New York State wineries,

you may want to put Manischewitz on your list. They've been making sweet concord wine in Canandaigua, New York, since 1927. Feel free to ask them about their famous kosher liquid, but know that any questions about the Dead Milkmen (whose song "I Dream of Jesus," from the album *Not Richard, But Dick,* tells the story of a family that finds Jesus Christ in a bottle of Manischewitz) may fall on deaf ears.

The state's other major kosher winemaker is Mogen David, known better by its initials, MD. As in MD 20/20. Though no longer sold in twenty-ounce bottles containing 20 percent alcohol (Fun fact? FUN FACT), it should be noted that at today's prices a bottle of Mad Dog costs more than that three buck chuck down at Trader Joe's. Guess it's time to recalibrate that Classy-O-Meter, friends. Alas, I was unable to convince anyone from the Wine Group (current owners of Mogen David, and producers of Cupcake Vodka among other tooth-rotting delights) to comment on the record about the fine art of selling $5 wine that tastes like Jolly Ranchers.

I'm actually pretty bummed I didn't get a chance to talk to them. No sense of adventure, these people! This is a book on American wine, and what's more American than someone saying "Sugar plus alcohol equals wine? Okay, fuck it! Here's sugar plus alcohol. It's wine, I swear. That'll be $5.95, please."

I can take a hint, New York. Besides, I got plenty of other states to talk to. The eastern seaboard is the geographical equivalent of a singles bar. Let's see, who's close? How *you* doing, Vermont?

Turns out rather well. Thanks to Ken Albert and other plucky sons of bitches like him.

Ken Albert is a problem solver. Before opening his winery in Shelburne, Ken worked for thirty-three years as an engineer at IBM. Which made him just the sort of man to figure out how to make high-quality wine in a cold region not particularly suited to doing so. One varietal in particular intrigued him—Marquette, a cousin of Frontenac and grandson of Pinot Noir that was developed at the University of Minnesota and introduced in 2006.

Shelburne Vineyard 2012 Marquette Reserve is not only the tastiest Vermont wine I sampled, it's the best wine I came across in all of New England. And while that may sound like the equivalent of being the toughest kid in glee club, these days you make fun of glee club at your peril. There is nothing quite so soul shattering as getting your ass kicked by a six-foot-two Sasquatch while he sings a pitch-perfect rendition of Queen's "Don't Stop Me Now" backed up in a five-part harmony by a squad of music savants who've seen *West Side Story* one too many times. And right now, California is cruising for a glee club bruising. Sure, it played underdog to Europe for decades, but ever since it was validated as a legitimate competitor in the 1970s, it's been shoving states like Vermont into lockers and taking their lunch money. A word to the wise, Napa: glee club never sleeps.

Shelburne's Marquette Reserve is medium bodied, with lots of vibrant fruit and a hint of spice, and it can hold its own against reds from the most prominent AVAs in America. Just another sign that we are living through the most important and transformative era in American winemaking. And that Americans, when their backs are against the wall, will find a way to make booze anywhere.

From Vermont it was on to Portland, Maine, where I attended Harvest on the Harbor, billed as the city's premier food and wine festival. I was excited to check out the many wines from Maine I assumed would be poured there, but failed to find even one. There was, however, plenty of delightful Maine-made craft beer on hand (Allagash Black!). And I would be remiss if I didn't single out the potato donuts (potato donuts!) from the Holy Donut as the single most appetizing gluten-free food that has ever been created. But locally produced wine, not so much. An old pal (and I mean, the guy is *ancient*) of mine lives in Portland, so I used the city as a brief respite from the road. Over the course of several days in Maine's most populous city, and numerous visits to its restaurants and wine bars, not a single one carried wine made in-state.

Come on, guys. I have a book premise to pay off. Can you pretend you're trying?

Still, I couldn't help thinking that given this is a state whose main exports are giant edible sea insects (lobster), an unshakable sense of creeping dread (Stephen King), and flinty resolve (every person who has survived a Maine winter), maybe it's for the best I didn't encounter any fruit of its native product. I don't want to end up in some story where a giant vengeful bottle of wine chases me across a craggy, unforgiving shoreline, hell-bent on using its "human key" on my head. My head's been through enough.

SPEAKING OF MY HEAD . . . I guess it's time to finish telling you about my attack in our apartment in Philly (I know you've been wondering). Like I said, I was in third grade. It must have been a particularly long day of slinging haircuts, because when my mother got home, she seemed more agitated than usual. I could usually gauge my mother's mood by the condition of her hair. The curlier her coif, the more flustered she tended to be. On this particular night, she was rocking some Robert-Plant-level frizz.

My mother was in the kitchen, and my back was to her. I heard her retrieve a pan from the cabinet beneath the sink, put it on the stove, and light the burner. I asked what we were having for dinner. We generally rotated between hot dogs, Kraft dinner, Elio's frozen pizza, and ground beef, rice, and gravy. On special occasions (or when my mother was just too beat down tired to cook), I got a Big Mac, fries, and chocolate shake from McDonald's. Those were good nights.

This being a regular night, though, in a regular year in my regular third grade, it was regular 7 P.M. and time for regular Jack Barry and *Joker's Wild,* along with regular ground beef, rice, and gravy. I had a complex, nuanced set of feelings about that night's gustatory fare, which I expressed with four well-chosen words. "Aw, come on . . . again?" before turning back to face the TV.

Then I woke up.

At first I couldn't figure out why I was on the floor. The chair I'd been sitting on was lying on its side next to me. Something hurt. A lot. And my hearing was all ringy and tinny and flanged-out like I was in a tunnel or a giant seashell. Then I saw my mom, a hazy silhouette hovering over me. As my vision cleared, her face came into focus. She was upset. Her lips were moving in slow motion, shouting. I couldn't tell if she was scared or hurt. Someone was in the apartment, no question. And they had snuck up and clobbered me? That must be why I was on the floor. Some uninvited asshole—my dad? Drunk? Probably—had shown up, angry and incoherent and laid into me without warning. She would have tried to protect me, but what could she do? The guy was bigger than her. She was probably just thinking about getting us out of there. Maybe it wasn't my dad. Maybe it was the guy with the long hair and the lazy eye who'd been hanging around lately. Ray. That was his name. Creepy goddamn Ray. He was a few years younger than my mother. Something wasn't right about him. I knew when I first saw him you couldn't trust that sidewinding fuck. What kind of sick lunatic would kill his girlfriend's kid and then torture her to death? A sick lunatic like Ray is who.

We needed to get out. Fast.

Still groggy, I lifted my head to look for Ray, but couldn't see him. Coward too. Come out, you scared piece of shit. My mom was still screaming, and my hearing was coming back now. She was repeating the same thing over and over again. I could just make it out through my confusion.

"Joker, joker, joker!" Jack Barry's signature line.

Jesus Christ, Ma, now? I mean I love Jackie B as much as the next guy, but . . .

"Joker, joker, joker, fucker . . ."

My head was clearing and I could make out the words now.

". . . motherfucker. You little motherfucker. You little . . ."

I looked at her again, her face trembling, contorted and grotesque. She looked like a Maurice Sendak Wild Thing, shaking the pan at me as tears soaked the front of her dark blouse. My mother always wore dark blouses to work. Said it hid the hair better.

Every bit of energy my mother had was going into screaming. And all I wanted, curled there in a ball on the floor, was for her to keep it up—whether "joker, joker, joker" or "you little motherfucker." As long as she was screaming like that, she couldn't swing the pan again.

It was the first moment in my entire life that I wished my dad would show up. Even drunk. That wouldn't matter, right? If he found Charlene beating his only son with a frying pan, he'd intervene. Grab her by the arms. Shake her. Make her calm down. Even drunk dads do that, right?

Of course at that moment my dad was probably holed up at P&Js Tavern trying to finally get Janice the "pretty" bartender to seal the deal in the men's room through the pungent odor of five-day-old piss. But it didn't end up mattering. My mother only hit me with the frying pan the once. Which is plenty when it's cast iron and in the head. Within a few minutes, everything was quiet again. The ringing in my ears settled and her sudden ferocity bottled itself up as quickly as it had exploded. She went back to the stove, put the pan on it, and made ground beef, rice, and gravy. Then she set it down in front of me and went straight into her bedroom and shut the door. She didn't come back out until the next morning. She took a look at the overripe eggplant that was the right side of my head and told me not to go to school. I got a whole day of Newhart, Mary Tyler Moore, and the king, Bob Motherfucking Barker, and I didn't even have to fake being sick. Score one for the millstone.

When she got home that night, Charlene's hair was straighter. She brought McDonald's. With an extralarge shake. She said that if anyone asked the next day why my ear was the size of a grapefruit, I should tell them I got hurt playing football with some kids back in our old neighborhood. It was a relief to have a story, for both of us. "Even though it was an accident," my mother said, "people could get the wrong idea."

She was right. Them getting the wrong idea would be awful. But so would them getting the right idea. Which was that she had acute bipolar disorder with psychotic features. Still, neither of us was ready for that information yet. And it's not like she killed me or anything. And if she had, well then, she probably would have had her reasons. Or at least the voices in her head would have.

In the end, though, the cover story didn't matter because I never told it. Nobody asked. The '70s were hilarious that way.

After my run-in with the business end of our frying pan, I told myself I would learn as many songs as there were to play on that old piano. Joe Ferrand didn't know very many, he confessed, but he said he knew a guy who would teach me for free if I promised to practice.

Then one day, about a week later I came home from school and the piano was gone. I asked my mother where it was, and she said, "They took it back." I knew better than to ask who "they" were. Accept these things. The piano is gone. You will not play your way out of that apartment, and you will not pull the cord for a living. You got a problem? Talk to Hard Hearted Hannah about it.

> *Start pourin' water on a drownin' man*
> *She's hard hearted Hannah*
> *The vamp of Savannah, GA*
> *Ooh! She's sweet as sour milk!*

The stranger who broke into our apartment and clocked me with a frying pan came back every so often. And no matter how many times she did, she never stopped being a stranger. Every time is as scary as the first. And every time I hold out hope I'll never see her again. Just like every year I hope the Eagles win the Super Bowl. It's what people do where I come from.

WHEN I MAPPED OUT THE trip, I made it a point to include a stop in Rhode Island because I am an idiot. Rhode Island isn't anything but adorable, mind, but Li'l Rhody is where Elizabeth is from. I think I planned it this way out of some kind of wishful thinking that by this point the two of us would be back together. It's like they always say: the first step to rekindling romance is to take off on a three-month wine-centric road trip across the country and only get in touch via hostile/creepy text messages. Where did my brilliant plan go wrong?

I kept telling myself I had two legitimate, nothing-to-do-with-Elizabeth reasons to be here. First off, I wanted to see Rich and Mia, two pals from Providence. Second, I thought, since I'm writing a wine book and all (See? Nothing to do with Elizabeth!), it'd be a good idea to drop by New England's largest grower of wine grapes, Newport Vineyards in Middletown.

Want to take a guess who grew up in Middletown? It rhymes with Belizabeth.

Total coincidence. (Is too. Shut up. God!)

The day started off fine. Rich came along to check out the juice with me and our first stop was Carolyn's Sakonnet Vineyard in Little Compton, Rhode Island.

Now I understand that visiting a winery in Compton might spook a lot of people. But I lived in L.A. for ten years. I knew what was up, yo (this "yo" is brought to you by the letter "white" and the number "asshole"). Turns out, however, that Little Compton is a far less intimidating place to visit than Big Motherfucking Compton back in L.A. As for the wines, well, there's no comparison. Seriously, do not ever, ever, EVER, compare the wines. You start throwing modifiers around, before you know it you got some kind of East Coast versus West Coast beef cooking—which would probably pair wonderfully with a 1977 Paul Masson Blush—and someone ends up getting drowned in a spit bucket.

We crossed the Sakonnet River Bridge from the mainland to Aquidneck, the largest island in Narragansett Bay and the flat-out weirdest name I saw on the entire trip. We drove south through Portsmouth to Middletown, whose only significance for me is the fact that it contains New England's biggest grape grower. (Lalalalalalalala. I can't hear you.)

A Tip for the Wise Wine Traveler: if your heart is on the mend following a devastating breakup, I strongly advise you to not visit a winery located in the hometown of the individual who was the cause of said heartbreak. Particularly not if you do not have a residence other than your car and are in the middle of some sort of infernal never-ending wine bender you can't even remember how you got yourself into and have no idea when it will end.

The publicist from Newport Vineyards was kind enough to set us up with a complimentary tasting. As we sipped our way through the portfolio, which included homegrown Chardonnay and Pinot Noir among other varietals, Rich must have sensed something was wrong. The profuse sweating and difficulty breathing might have been a giveaway.

He asked if he should get help, and I said no. He asked if maybe we just needed to leave.

"We should finish the tasting," I whispered. "I feel bad just splitting."

"What, you haven't drunk enough wine by this point?"

He had a point. "I just don't understand why I'm feeling this anxious," I said.

"Look," Rich said, "you and Elizabeth were together a long time. It's totally understandable that coming back to her hometown would be upsetting."

I reminded Rich that it was not a return visit.

"Okay, well, I'm sure there's a good reason she never brought you back here," he said.

There wasn't, I assured him.

"Maybe that's what's upsetting you. Maybe you're understanding that if you two never made it here during the many years the two of you were together, you can't have meant very much to her."

I thanked Rich for the finely crafted anvil he had dropped on my head. He signaled to the crane operator to start hoisting it up again ("Let's reset, people!").

"You're not going to get over this until you really understand why you broke up, you know."

Thanks, Oprah.

"You ever think maybe your relationship didn't go as deep as you thought it did?"

"You're saying I don't know how I actually feel about Elizabeth."

"I'm saying half of our lives are fantasy fucking island. You probably tell yourself five different lies just to get out of bed every morning."

That was probably an optimistic estimate. And lucky me, Rich was on a roll.

"Come on, man, you've had a lot of time to think about this. Is it really fair to lay all of this on Elizabeth? It's not like you grew up seeing a bunch of healthy relationships."

I didn't have anything approaching a valid response. It felt like Rich was one of those Maine wine monsters opening up my head and having a poke around.

"I've known you a long time. You weren't ready for something this heavy when you met her. You were writing for *Playboy* and fucking everything with a pulse. Being with someone for the long haul is a skill. It's something you have to learn. And, no offense, but you knew dick going into this one."

One thing. I wanted him to be wrong about just one, little thing. Just to take the edge off.

"You know how many times you told me your relationship was perfect?" he continued. "That is the number one sign you're deluding yourself. Perfect relationships don't exist. If you're not struggling, you're not really in it. And that means you're not giving her all of yourself. Until you do that, even if you're technically in a relationship, you're really just alone."

The tasting room manager taking us through the tasting

cleared her throat. "You guys okay? Because we can take a break if . . ."

"Which of these pairs best with a panic attack?" I asked feebly.

"Listen, it's none of my business," she replied, "but he's right."

Great. Rich had a therapy buddy.

"I was in four different long-term relationships before I met my husband," she went on. "It's his third marriage. Shit happens. All you can do is all you can do. The only way you really screw up is if you don't learn from it when things go wrong. Here, try the Gemini Red. I think you'll find it has a peppery finish and a hint of oak."

I've never been more grateful to someone for changing the conversation to wine. Luckily Rich was there to keep my head under water.

"Don't get the wrong idea here," Rich said. "I'm proud of you."

Could have fooled me.

"You came here. You faced your demons. This is the belly of the beast! It's actually really impressive."

I wondered aloud if he'd still feel proud if I puked all over the tasting room. It felt like my emotional upset was even affecting the way I experienced the wine. I'd had plenty of shit vino thus far on the trip, but this was different. It was like drinking misery. The wines we were sampling couldn't be that bad, I reasoned, forcing down a sip of Gewürztraminer. It was those stupid demons of mine wreaking havoc on my palate.

"It's not you," Rich said, placing his hand on my shoulder and giving it a gentle squeeze. "This wine sucks. Now let's get the hell outta here."

Sorry, Newport Vineyards, but it's not going to work out between us.

"FIRST, WE ICE THIS FUCK."

CHAPTER 9

NEW YORK CITY

"We're not in Kansas anymore," I mumbled, watching the endless New York City hordes stream past my perch atop a bar stool inside the Measure Lounge at Langham Place Fifth Avenue in Manhattan. Helluva wine list in that joint. They even carry a few bottles from places I'd visited along the way—Trefethen, Chalk Hill, and Bergstrom among them. But, like so many places in New York, the list was composed primarily of Old World wines.

"Did you visit Kansas on your way here?" asked the young man sitting across from me. He bore a resemblance to New England Patriots quarterback Tom Brady, only instead of tossing footballs for a living, Michael Smith slings high-priced hooch.

"I didn't go to Kansas, but I did meet a dog named Toto," I told Smith, who was twenty-seven and had been a food and beverage manager at Langham Place for three years. "Pretty sure his name was Toto. It was in Prosser, Washington. Big black

Labrador. Belonged to the ranch manager at a property owned by Precept Wines. When he was a puppy, poor Toto got into it with a badger and lost an eye and both his testicles. Badgers are nasty sons of bitches. This one bit Toto's balls right off. Not sure if he swallowed 'em or not—badgers are omnivores, right? Toto didn't seem too bothered by it, though."

Smith just shook his head. Either he hadn't spent much time pondering castration by badgers, or he was questioning whether the disheveled weirdo slugging back expensive Chardonnay in his joint was indeed the professional wine writer he claimed to be. He topped off my glass and excused himself. Said he had some urgent matter to attend to. I knew that look. Either he was calling hotel security or needed to take a wicked dump.

I was too tired to care anymore.

In the two-plus months since setting out from Southern California on a quest to become the leading authority on wine in America, I'd driven eight thousand miles, consumed approximately 177 gallons of wine, and squeegeed an incalculable number of dead bugs off the windshield of my Toyota SUV.

When I mentioned the latter to a winemaker in the Finger Lakes, he asked me if I knew what the last thing was that went through a bug's head when it hit the windshield.

"I don't know," I said, shrugging.

"His ass," he quipped.

I've told that joke sixteen times since. Seventeen counting this one.

I got a speeding ticket in Oregon, had a close encounter with a large bear in Colorado, and lost two credit cards, a pair of glasses, and some shoes. I'd *nearly* been in three fights, but had *actually* been in zero fights.

On the plus side, unlike Toto I had managed not to misplace my balls. Plus I hadn't seriously considered taking my own life since I was in Des Moines, Iowa—oh hell, what was it?—like, four weeks prior to that. And that didn't even count since virtually everyone thinks about killing themselves when they're in Des Moines.

NEEDLESS TO SAY, THERE AREN'T a lot of vineyards in New York City. But there are a lot of restaurants. Some of the best in the world, in fact. And, naturally, the wine lists maintained by these establishments are world class as well. To delve into this milieu I'd managed to wrangle a meet-up with Daniel Johnnes in Tribeca.

Johnnes is the James Beard Award–winning wine director for Daniel Boulud's Dinex restaurant group, and the founder and host of La Paulée de New York and La Paulée de San Francisco, which are inspired by the traditional Burgundian harvest celebration La Paulée de Meursault. He owns a successful wine-importing business and also runs a winemaking operation over in Burgundy. (What, Montana not good enough for you, Daniel?) In short, the guy has forgotten more about wine than I had even begun to learn on the trip.

There was no objective reason for a man of his viticultural stature to take time out of his busy schedule so a schmo like me could ply him with ridiculous questions for research. But after being connected through friends, he graciously agreed to meet anyway. Tellingly, he chose Racine's, a wine bar that boasts a list populated almost entirely with French selections.

Johnnes made no bones about it. He doesn't think American wine as a whole can hold a candle to the stuff the French produce. He also doesn't think holding candles next to *une bouteille du vin* is a good idea. I decided to keep my opinions on mulled wine to myself.

"But you've got to admit it's pretty cool that wine is being made in every state in the United States," I said.

He gave it some thought. "Sure," he said. "But that doesn't mean I want to drink any of it."

"Any of it?"

"There is certainly great wine being made in America, but you're not going to find it in Oklahoma or Florida," Johnnes said.

"Hey, you never know," I said.

"No," he said. "I do know."

Johnnes is a huge Burgundy fan and is considered one of the world's leading experts on wine produced in that celebrated region. He fell in love with Burgundy as a young man traveling around the countryside, eating and drinking with winemakers and immersing himself in the culture. In Burgundy he says he came to understand the essence of wine as an expression of the grape, the terroir, and, most of all, the people who make it.

"It's actually not dissimilar to what you're doing now," he said.

"Except no metric system. And my SUV is probably bigger."

"And the wine as a whole is *slightly* better over there," he added.

"You mentioned that," I said.

None of this is to say Johnnes is any kind of snob about this stuff. In fact, being a sort of walking wine encyclopedia seems to have made him far more open-minded than your garden-variety defensive wine hipster. He went out of his way to encourage me, actually. Said he appreciated the spirit of my cross-country trek, and he even admitted to being a bit envious that I was able to "just pick up and drive around for a while." He said that kind of freedom is "one of the perks of being young," which made me think that maybe his eyesight wasn't very good. Or maybe he recognized what a rickety mess I was and was simply being kind. Shit, I wish I *had* taken this trip when I was actually young. Back when I associated words like *chronic* and *intense* with getting high instead of lower back pain.

Johnnes asked if I'd spent much time in the winemaking regions in France, and I admitted I'd only been briefly a couple of times.

"French Wino. That needs to be your next book," he said. "Trust me on this. You may never come back."

"So if I'm reading between the lines correctly here, Daniel, you'd prefer Domaine de la Romanée-Conti over, say, a Pinot Noir from North Carolina."

"So you do know some Burgundian wines!" he said.

"Just that one. I Googled it before I came here tonight," I said.

And that's my story about the time I made Daniel Johnnes laugh.

Johnnes is not alone in his Francophilia, of course. I met with numerous authorities on wine in the Big Apple and every last one of them had a hard-on for Old World wines. Well, save for one, former adult film superstar-cum-winemaker Savanna Samson, who has a hard time getting it up these days on account of not being the owner of a penis. Not that it's held her back. On the contrary, if her filmography is to be believed, she's the one who's been holding all the penises. Regardless of who's holding whom, Savanna has been making critically acclaimed wine in Italy for over a decade and won't drink a drop produced anywhere else.

It makes you wonder what the hell this rampant Eurocentrism in the Manhattan wine scene is all about. I mean, New York is the greatest city in AMERICA, just ask any New Yorker. So why do so many of the movers and shakers in the NYC wine world prefer juice pressed across the pond? Daniel

Johnnes probably could have provided a reasoned explanation, but I'd only just started getting into telling him about
my wildlife encounters and dead bugs and porn star friends
when he received what appeared to be an urgent message.
He said he was terribly sorry, but he had a pressing matter to
attend to and had to go. I might have been being paranoid,
but I had an app on my phone that sends me prewritten messages when I want to get out of something (date gone wrong,
Jehovah's Witness visit, mugging). But it just wasn't probable
that a guy like Johnnes would have an app like that. It was an
absolute goddamn certainty. I guess I could kiss any possible
hookup at Boulud's restaurants good-bye. Can't say I blamed
him. Just being seen with me was probably draining his cred-
ibility by the second.

I've yet to encounter a wine wizard who has argued that
America doesn't produce at least some great juice. Indeed,
even Daniel Johnnes sang the praises of a number of stateside
producers and seemed genuinely interested in hearing about
some of the more off-the-beaten-path wineries I'd visited.
However, it's also true that most of the learned folks I've come
across are of the opinion that almost all the great domestic
stuff comes from one of three places—California, Oregon,
and Washington—with New York and Virginia occasionally
fielding a winner now and again. As for the rest of the wine,
well, they mostly think it's shit.

I wonder how many of them have actually ever tried Brianna from St. Paul, Nebraska; La Crescent made in Paw Paw,
Michigan; or the Bordeaux blend they make in Paonia, Colorado. I have, though, and I think it makes me see things
differently. When I see people making wine in far-flung spots
across America, I'm reminded of Toto, that irrepressible, ball-
less dog in Prosser.

The critics come at these winemakers like rabid badgers, intent on clawing out their eyes and chomping off their privates. And while these plucky pups harbor no illusions of supplanting Napa, Tuscany, or the Rhone any time soon, they're every bit as serious, hardworking, and innovative as the industry's heavy hitters. And after decades of relentless abuse (or utter disregard) they just don't give a shit what you think about them anymore.

Patrick Zimmerer opened his Table Mountain Vineyards and Winery in Huntley, Wyoming, right around the same time a naive, eager puppy in Washington State decided to get into it with a bitter old badger down the far side of the pond. And at the time, the cognoscente—had they taken notice—likely would have given Zimmerer less of a chance to survive than ol' Toto. Yet here they are ten years later, tails still wagging. Only somehow now their balls, far from getting bitten off, are actually several times bigger than they were back then.

That takes grit, a large helping of blind faith, and an unshakable belief in one's ability to endure in the face of near impossible odds.

I was starting to identify with my subjects just a wee bit. Stockholm Syndrome I think they call it.

IT WAS A GOOD THING there are no vineyards in New York City because I was bone tired. Unfortunately, the City That Never Sleeps is a terrible place to be when sleep is the thing you need most. It's the central paradox of the place: doing nothing in New York actually takes a fair amount of work.

Complicating matters, the fine folks at Langham Place had comped me a spacious one-bedroom suite with a fantastic view of glittering Manhattan. Ah, the perks that come with being a ~~shameless media whore~~ member in good standing of the international travel and leisure press. I had my own washer and dryer, a full kitchen, an oversized closet. The bathroom was huge, with a double vanity, a deep soaking tub, and separate rainfall shower. On top of that they'd set me up with not one, but two complimentary bottles of fine wine. If there was ever a hotel room to impress a date with, this was it. So naturally I went into a sort of date acquisition mania.

I sent texts to a few women in the city with whom I had been intimately acquainted at various points. Hadn't seen any of them in years, though. Still someone must be interested in . . . No? No one? Is this thing on?

Actually one of them did write me back, which was comforting. Her thoughtful note read: "Who is this?" Good question.

When you're in a long-term committed relationship you stop thinking about certain things. Like maintaining a healthy set of fuck buddies. It's like a garden. You could work on it every day for decades, but take your eyes off it for six months and you're back to square one. As I scrolled through my iPhone contacts looking for past flings, I realized I'd been so damn happy with Elizabeth the last few years that I'd forgotten entirely about Suzy (Swedish girl @ Gramercy Tavern), Lucy (Hot/Asian/drugstore), and Jo (Chrissy's friend superfun). And they, clearly, had forgotten about me. Which is only fair. I made a vow right then and there to never be so selfish again.

It was clear that to take advantage of the room's aphrodisiacal value, I would need to venture out into the night. Expend what few fumes I had left in the tank, and most likely endure a miserable drive to Philadelphia the next morning. But it also meant possibilities. Lots of possibilities. New York is a magical place, after all. Various scenarios started playing out in my head, as did—inexplicably—the Glenn Frey tune "You

Belong to the City" from the original *Miami Vice* soundtrack. Goddamn, all the time alone on the road really was making me loopy. But you try getting that hook out of your head.

It was only 8 P.M. now, though. Hours away from Manhattan go-time. I figured I'd relax a little bit, gather myself. I opened a Cabernet Franc from Browne Family Vineyards in Washington's Yakima Valley. Between gifts and purchases, I had about three cases of the stuff in my truck. I climbed into bed, turned on the TV, flipped through the channels, and immediately found *Taken*. Just started too. The bad guys hadn't even snatched Liam Neeson's daughter yet. Possibilities and Glenn Frey be damned, I wasn't going anywhere for a while.

In my time so far on the planet I've uncovered two key coping mechanisms for dealing with life's topsy-turvy twists and turns: strong drink and Liam Neeson, preferably in combination. There's a steadiness and predictability to Liam Neeson's oeuvre that's not unlike a favorite bottle of whiskey. If I devote a few hours to it, I know I'll wind up feeling warm and fuzzy and ever so slightly brain-dead. In fact I have made it my mission to see every movie the man has ever made. Including *Krull* and *Ethan Frome*. And *Battleship*. Especially *Battleship*.

The most important thing about Liam Neeson movies is the deadlines. Almost every Neeson film contains two. The first is a prescribed time frame thrust upon Liam by the bad guys. It typically calls for him to pull off the impossible to save himself and/or others from some terrible fate. For instance, in the film *Non-Stop*, Neeson plays an air marshal on board a transatlantic flight that has been hijacked by villains who are threatening to kill a passenger every twenty minutes unless their demands for a $150 million ransom are met. Spoiler: the bad guys ain't gettin' a dime. Not if Liam Neeson's signature throat chops have anything to say about it. Spoiler number 2: they totally do!

The second deadline is the cutoff point Neeson gives his antagonists to either surrender or have their asses seriously effed up. Like when he says "I'm going to start beating the shit out of you in the next five seconds" in *The Grey*. I'll give you no guesses what happens five seconds later.

The other important aspect of Liam Neeson movies is their consistency. While there are subtle variations from film to film, for the most part you have a pretty good idea going in of what you're going to get. Of course, there's the occasional treacly piece of crap like *Love Actually*, where not only are there no deadlines, but Neeson inexplicably plays a giant wuss you want to smack in the face the whole time. But for every one of those aberrations there are ten *Takens*, where Liam throat-chops the shit out of everyone who gets in his grill.

I'm not exaggerating. There are literally ten *Takens*—the three that have already been released, the one they're shooting now, the five more in various stages of preproduction, and the one I'm writing, where the climactic scene revolves around Liam Neeson tracking down a boozed-up writer because he found out the guy is writing a *terrible* screenplay for *Taken 11*. When Neeson busts in, *Michael Collins* is playing on a TV in the background and the writer has been playing some sort of drinking game with Montana wine while crying.

I would like to share the details of this game with you now. To play, you will need a case of wine, various bottles of Irish whiskey, a Netflix account, and several friends. On no account should you play this game alone. Liam Neeson has a very particular set of skills, skills he has acquired over a very long career. And if you play this game alone, he will hunt you down and get completely schnockered with you. And there's nothing more dangerous than a drunk Liam Neeson in your house.

THE LIAM NEESON DRINKING GAME

- Every time Liam Neeson fixes someone with a flinty glare, take a shot of Powers.
- Every time Liam Neeson fixes someone with a steely glare, take a shot of Johnnie Walker Black.
- Every time Liam Neeson fixes someone with a steely, flinty glare, slam a Rusty Nail, and then turn to the person next to you and say "I'm going to start beating the shit out of you in the next five seconds."
- If the person next to you threatens to start beating the shit out of *you* in the next five seconds, the only way to avoid said beating is to give the full name of a character Neeson has played besides Zeus and Oskar Schindler. Be forewarned, this is perhaps the most difficult challenge in the entire game, as almost everyone is under the impression that with the exception of *Love Actually,* Liam Neeson has simply been playing himself for the past thirty-five years. If you do miraculously manage to recall another Neeson character name, however, the person who threatened to beat you must drink two more Rusty Nails. By the way, did you know Neeson's character in *Taken* is named Bryan? Not Slade or Jake or Greer or Rex. Bryan . . . with a Y, no less. I think they should have gone with Carl.
- Every time Liam Neeson points out that he has "a particular set of skills," everyone in the game in turn has three seconds or less to name one of those skills. Acceptable answers include but are not limited to glaring (both flintily and steelily), the ability to remain preternaturally calm in situations that would cause 99.9 percent of the human population to shit themselves, catlike reflexes, throat-chopping, extreme

tallness, horse testicles, an uncanny knack for obtaining cell phones with unlimited battery life, *Narnia* breath, George Lucas's home phone number, sexyvoice times infinity, telepathy, and the ability to not let steaming piles of crap like *Battleship* tarnish his career (his character's name in that is Admiral Shane. I'm here to help). First person to draw a blank must drink a Rob Roy. (And don't forget that name, by the way. It could come in handy at some point during the game.)

• Every minute Liam Neeson is on-screen in *Battleship*, everyone must be drinking wine from the bottle. Their own bottle. Assuming an average tolerance for alcohol, you are all likely to pass out within the first fifteen minutes of the movie. Everybody wins.

• Every time you catch a hint of Liam's Irish brogue in *Schindler's List*, take a shot of Jameson and shout "Top o' the mornin' to ya, Hitler!"

• Finally, every time Liam Neeson makes you laugh hysterically, take a shot of Croizet Cuvée Léonie cognac (the most expensive in the world at $157,000 per bottle). It may seem steep, but I believe a special occasion deserves something special.

....

SHIT. WHERE WAS I? HOTEL. TV. Bed. I had this crazy dream where I was driving across the country drinking wine. Then I'd gone back to my real life where every day I go to school naked, but my backpack is full of wooden nickels. I hand them out to everyone, but no one will accept them. "What's the big deal?" I shout at them. "I made these myself! At home! Because I love you guys!" Then my mom shows up in a ball gown and asks me if I want to ride the Cyclone.

The truth slowly coalesced around me . . . I'd fallen asleep during *Taken* (please don't neck-chop me, Liam) and it was now nearly midnight. I checked my phone. One message!

Ooh, another text from Lucy (Hot/Asian/drugstore) . . . "Hey, seriously, who is this?"

I walked over to the bar, poured a glass of wine, plugged my laptop into the speaker system, and dialed up the *Miami Vice* soundtrack on Spotify. I'd forgotten what a great collection of tunes that is—Jan Hammer's scintillating theme song; Tina Turner at the height of her vocal puissance with "Better Be Good to Me"; the '80s sax appeal of "Smuggler's Blues"; and of course, la pièce de la résistance, Phil Collins's—Phil Motherfucking Collins!—"In the Air Tonight."

Well, I remember!

I remember, don't worry (worry worry worry worry) seeing Phil Collins play that song live in Philly in front of a hundred thousand people at the U.S. Live Aid concert on July 13, 1985. How could I ever forget? It was the first time and the last time we ever met (met met met). Collins was the only musician to play at both the London and Philly concerts. Dude played, then got on a plane and made it across the Atlantic in time to play again. And everyone in JFK Stadium simulated the climactic drum fill of "In the Air Tonight" at the top of their lungs.

> *You can wipe off that grin*
> *I know where you've been*
> *It's all been a pack of lies*

Seriously, I'm sorry. In case you can't tell, I'm not really driving this bus.

> Hey ;) It's Dan Dunn. Writer. From *Playboy*. We met at Duane Reade.

WOW <

Just wow. No punctuation. No emojis. No context. Could only mean about a hundred thousand different things. I tried to recall exactly what had gone down with Lucy. I knew we met at a drugstore. Wintertime. She was in front of me in line buying toilet paper. I made a poop joke (the ladies looove the poop jokes) and she laughed. I liked her short bob hairdo and soft features and willingness to laugh when I said something dumb. Japanese? Korean? We ended up meeting for happy hour somewhere in the West Village. Shit, how many years ago was that? Had to be a few, at least. Before Elizabeth. We got drunk. Had fun, I think. Where did we leave things?

> Wow good or wow bad?

Just wow <

I waited for her to elaborate, but she didn't. *Drop it,* I thought. *You cast the reel and this fish ain't biting.* But then again, maybe a "just wow" was a "good wow." (Nope.) It was midnight, after all. Prime booty-texting time. I wrote:

> How are you? What are you
up to tonight?

Several minutes passed before she wrote back:

why do you want to know? <

Ah. A question served over ice with a dash of bitter. My instincts told me it was time to abort.

Instead I wrote:

> Do you mean "why do I want to
know how you are?" or "why do I
want to know what you're up to?"

An old tactic—play dumb and hope she finds it charming.

Both. <

> I'm in town somewhat randomly.
> Thought we might get together. I could
> tell you more poop jokes ;)

Why would you think that? <

Okay, this really wasn't going well. Though she hadn't gotten truly nasty yet. Quick, what would Phil Collins do? Easy. He'd hold on. (Hold on.) But no. I could feel it coming in the air. It was time to cut and run.

> Sorry. Let's just forget about it.
> Take care ;)

You're good at that apparently. <

> Huh?

Forgetting. <

> I'm not sure I know what
> you mean.

You obviously forget what you did. <
Though I'm impressed you
remember my name.

Oh boy. I had myself a roiling Krakatoa on my hands, and she was about to blow.

> Look, I'm sorry if I've upset you.

Oh really? <

> Yes.

I find that hard to believe. <

I had nothing. So I texted her a confused-face emoji.

How's your girlfriend? <
You remember her. Dirty blonde?
Supercute? Pixie cut?

It all started to make horrible sense. I remembered when I met Lucy.

Knowing with every fiber of my being that I was doing something earth-shatteringly stupid, I wrote:

> We're not together.

REALLY?! Did she break up <
with you?

> I don't see how that's any
of your business.

You wouldn't, would you? <
Just like you didn't think it was
my business when we met and you
told me you were single when
you actually had a girlfriend
so you could fuck me.

> Look, this is my bad. I'm sorry
I texted you.

Are you sorry you fucked me? <
And told me I should come visit
you in L.A.? And then fucking
disappeared?

I started to type a reply, then . . .

Are you sorry that after you blew <
me off, I went and looked you up on
Facebook and saw all the pictures of you
with the girlfriend you told me you didn't
have because you wanted to fuck me?
Are you sorry for that?

> I'm sorry for all of it.

I considered sending her a note, <
you know. Letting her know what an
awful cheating coward she was dating.

> Thank you for not doing that.
I should probably say good night.

Fuck you asshole! <

I sent her an "expressionless" emoji and switched the phone to silent mode. Because I'm supergood at dealing with conflict.

Elizabeth and I had been dating a year when we moved in together. Her into my place. And for another year and change after that everything was wonderful. Then, for a host of reasons, things started to fall apart. On the very last day of 2012, she moved out. Happy New Year! A couple of weeks later I visited New York City. While I was there I met Lucy in a drugstore. Hot, Asian, we've been over this. When I told Lucy I didn't have a girlfriend, I was not lying. I was also not entirely forthright about just how newly single I was. Which is forgivable, I think. In addition, I was less than honest about the fact that I was still very much in love with my ex. This is less forgivable. Does it help that I was also lying to myself? Didn't think so. But while withholding that information might make me an asshole, or an un-self-actualized dickhead, it didn't make me a cheating coward. Just a coward. Garden variety. It made me a guy who wanted to feel wanted. And who hadn't gotten laid in a while. After that, though, things got a mite more complex.

Lucy and I texted a little after I headed back to L.A. A couple weeks later she said she was coming out to the West Coast for work. Would I be interested in hanging out? Hell yes I would. I picked her up at the airport, and we had a great lunch at a bistro on the water in Marina Del Rey. Then we went back to my place and fucked the rest of the afternoon. It was supremely relaxing.

Around 5 P.M. I got a text from Elizabeth. She wanted to know if it was okay to swing by after work to pick up the beach cruiser she'd left in the storage closet downstairs. I said I was going out for the evening, which I was, and that I'd leave the storage unit unlocked. No need, she said. She still had her keys.

I glanced over at Lucy, who was sitting across from me on the sofa in her underwear, checking e-mail on a laptop. She was a showstopper. With a mind to match. I thought, *I'm a lucky motherfucker.* She looked up and saw me watching her and she smiled.

"What?"

"Just taking it all in."

"Oh yeah? How's it looking?"

"Like Jesus and Victoria's Secret had a baby and named it Lucy."

She leaned over and kissed me. The phone buzzed, another text. I slid my hand into my pocket and switched it to silent. More kissing. This could be going somewhere. I squeezed her breast.

"You really did miss me, huh?"

"Uh-huh," I said.

"How about we save round three for after dinner," she said. "It was a long flight. I really need to take a shower."

When she left the room, I checked my phone. Another text from Elizabeth. Since she was going to be at the apartment picking up the bike anyway, would it be okay if she let herself in to see the dog for a few minutes? I didn't see any harm in it, so I typed "ok" and hit send. And almost instantly shit my pants. Metaphorically. Though I have been incontinent on several occasions, this was not one of them.

What had I done? There was Lucy's laptop on the coffee table. And her bag over by the fireplace. Her shirt was draped across a bar stool. Her water bottle was on the kitchen counter. If Elizabeth came into the apartment, she would see all of it. It would be alarmingly fucking clear that another woman had come to stay with me.

Rational Me chimed in. "She dumped you, dude. You're not doing anything wrong."

Which is when Pathetic Elizabeth-Whipped Me and his controlling best friend Loco Me were all, *who the fuck are you?*

"Oh, I'm Rational Me. Hey, guys! You know I've got a lot of good ideas for ways we can—"

"Haven't seen you around here before," Pathetic Elizabeth-Whipped Me said.

"Fellas, come on! I used to live here . . . Like, forever," Rational Me replied.

"Not anymore, esse," Loco Me chortled, shoving Rational Me in the chest.

Rational Me picked himself up off the floor. "Listen, I think if we can all just calm down, there's definitely a way to—"

"If I wanted to hear from an asshole I would have farted!" said Loco Me. His grin suddenly fading to grim.

"What's the plan?" Pathetic Elizabeth-Whipped Me asked. "She's coming in less than an hour!"

"First we ice this fuck," Loco Me seethed.

"Whoa, whoa, fellas, let's hold up just one second. I think it was Emerson who said—"

BOOOM! Loco Me had pulled out a .44 and shot Rational Me in the gut. Guy was alive, but not for long.

"Thank you!" Whipped Me said. "I couldn't think at all with him yapping. Now what are we going to do?"

"I got this," Loco Me said. "We'll call Beau and explain the situation. He can come over here *after* Dan and Lucy leave but *before* Elizabeth gets here."

"And do what?" Whipped Me asked.

"He'll hide Lucy's things in the closet so Elizabeth won't see them," Loco Me explained. "Easy."

"Uh, fellas?" Rational Me wheezed. "If either of you has a cell phone, it would be great if you could uh . . . call a uh . . . a uh . . ."

"Can you shut up for one second?" Whipped Me said. "That's not a bad idea, Loco. But what happens when Lucy returns and finds all her stuff in the closet?"

Loco Me thought for a second. "Maybe someone broke in?"

"And instead of stealing anything, they tidied up?"

"Good point," Loco Me said. "That's stupid."

"I got it," Whipped Me said. "Beau can come back after Elizabeth leaves but before Dan and Lucy get home and put all the stuff back where it originally was."

"Holy shit," Loco Me said. "That's the best idea I've ever heard." He listened for the sound of the shower running. "Quick, let's call Beau!"

Beau is an old friend, so he was kind enough not to laugh. He even offered me a loan so I could seek professional psychiatric care. Loco Me and Whipped Me were undaunted, though. Beau not only shut them down, he called an ambulance for Rational Me, who looked like he might make it after all.

Beau's counsel was simple and, in retrospect, brilliant. Do nothing. Take Lucy to dinner as planned. Let Elizabeth come and see what's going on. See another woman's things in my place. See me not missing her. This is what moving on looks like.

"Bravo, chaps," Rational Me cheered weakly from his gurney.

Which was when Loco Me showed up in a paramedic uniform, horror movie style, and said, "There, there, you've had a long day. It's time for your medication," as he lowered a pillow over helpless Rational Me's face.

"If you'll just give it the merest second I'm sure you mmmmmph glrrrrrrgh hmmmmmmmmffffl," Rational Me opined, before getting the shit murdered out of him.

Which is when I lied to my friend. I told Beau I was serious about moving on, and that the only reason I'd asked him to hide Lucy's things was out of concern for Elizabeth. Yes, she had dumped me, but she seemed really conflicted about doing so. Plus, it had only been a few weeks. A few measly weeks after everything we'd been through over so many years. Elizabeth, more than anyone, helped get me through the nightmare of losing Brian. And sure, she understood there would be other women eventually, but there was no need to shove it in her face so soon. It didn't benefit anyone for her to see another woman's undies on the bed we used to share.

"Perfect!" Loco Me cackled.

"Masterful!" Whipped Me agreed.

Beau was skeptical, to say the least. It took a lot of convincing, but eventually he grudgingly said that if sparing Elizabeth pain truly was my intent, he'd help me out. After we split, Beau came by and tossed all of Lucy's stuff in the closets.

Elizabeth came by and got her bike. She also let herself in to spend a little time with Buna. And it must have been a long day at work because she fell asleep on the couch with Buna's head in her lap.

Meanwhile, Lucy and I were having one of those early courtship dates where neither of you knows the other's awesome stories and you drink a ton of wine and you both feel like rock stars because both of you are incredibly impressed and turned on by the other. On the way home we could hardly keep our hands off each other, practically spilling through my doorway, already tugging at belts and bra straps.

"Oh . . . hey."

"Oh. Fuck."

It wasn't any kind of Armageddon or catfight or even any drama at all. To both of their incredible credit, they managed the situation with a minimum of rancor. It was awkward, sure, but isn't most of life?

It made me cringe to see Elizabeth realize I was with someone new. And so soon.

But for her part, Lucy seemed to get it. Elizabeth used to live here. She had come by for her bike. And to see the dog for a minute. This is hard for her, give the girl a break. So what? She fell asleep. And everything was good. Elizabeth left and Lucy and I retired to my bedroom, Feeling vaguely naughty, like we had shared a secret. Until . . .

"Hey, where's my stuff?"

"Huh?"

"My things. My bag was here. And my clothes were over there and . . ."

"Oh, they're in here!" I said cheerfully, beckoning her toward the closet.

"What the fuck are they doing there?" she asked.

"Funny story," I began. But she didn't stick around for the ending.

The great thing was I did get laid that night. Just not how I thought I would. In fact, I ended up having a three-way, with Loco Me and Whipped Me double-teaming me for a good two weeks straight.

And while I didn't enjoy it one bit, I have to hand it to them. What they lack in common sense, they more than make up for in stamina.

CHAPTER 10

THE NEW JERSEY TURNPIKE

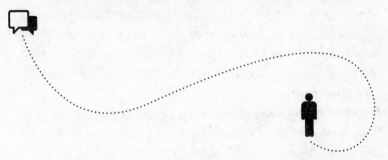

"EVERYONE SUCKS BUT US."

New York City to Philly is only a two-hour drive. Compared to the distances I'd been averaging on this trip, it barely qualified as going anywhere. To make up for this unconscionable lack of hardship, as I crossed the Verrazano Bridge into Staten Island, the cranky-looking sky opened up and unleashed a rainstorm of biblical proportions. By the time I got to Jersey it was so bad, I could barely see ten feet in front of me.

Philly and NYC have been rivals ever since Ben Franklin called Manhattan's whorehouses "substandard" and "unfit for even the vilest strumpet," but as far as I can tell, the bad blood is primarily fueled by the fact that the two cities are shockingly similar to each other in temperament. Which is to say, both are populated by a high percentage of balls-out maniacs. Case in point: the New Jersey Turnpike between New York City and

Philadelphia, where this goddamn monsoon had cut the speed on the packed highway from eighty to seventy.

L.A. people say they don't need weather because they have traffic. But at the risk of bursting my friends' bubbles, it's worth noting that—and stick with me on this—other places have traffic also. And get this: they have weather too! Also seasons, wrinkles, anger, and shame. This is not to say that I remain unwarped by L.A.'s peculiar delusions. My first instinct when the storm started was to compliment the special effects guy. I swear, at one point on the drive I thought about taking a break and stepping out of my car, where I'd find a green screen and a second AD handing me a chai tea latte and a hot towel.

This was no CG guy's weather porn, though. The storm was down low and furious, the 11 A.M. darkness broken by lightning strikes followed instantly by Carl-rattling thunderclaps. There was probably an inch of running water on the highway. Glances at my fellow road surfers revealed a white-knuckled crew, eyes wide, unnerved, and kicking themselves for not springing the extra fifty bucks for brand-name rain-tread tires. There was a palpable sense that something was about to go horribly, horribly wrong out there, the only question being how many of us were going to go down. That of course is the usual feeling you get on the ribbon that connects our nation's two most pugnacious cities, but this storm wasn't doing anything to calm people's nerves. It felt supernatural. Like at any second, Thor might get jealous of Zeus's light show and slam down his hammer, splitting the Jersey Turnpike wide open. The thought of being swallowed up, interred forever like a turncoat mobster in the bowels of the Garden State, was almost comforting. It sure would beat driving in this shit, anyway.

None of this was helped, of course, by the acute wine-induced hangover I was enjoying. Despite it being cold outside, the increased levels of acetaldehyde in my system were causing me to sweat profusely. My central nervous system was operating with the approximate efficiency of the 113th Congress, only my organs were being a little nastier to one another. I'd been this banged up behind the wheel on the trip before—Wyoming, for instance—but out there it was all blue skies and open spaces. If you can stay awake and avoid suicidal wildlife, you'll be okay. Here, though, I was surrounded by minivans piloted by panicky soccer moms, windowless beat-to-shit construction vans, and SUVs that plainly gave no fucks about you or your silly ideas about what constitutes a "lane."

The key to surviving a particularly acute hangover—say, one precipitated by excessive consumption of Damiani Syrah from the Finger Lakes—is to remain calm and ride it out. If parts of your body claim temporary independence, know that their glorious revolution will be short-lived. Your right eye has its reasons for not opening. Your left hand will almost certainly be able to grasp things tomorrow. In rare instances your guts may go rogue. If so, pray that it is in an upward direction. With luck you might just reach a proper receptacle. If it's headed south, however, just pray you're in a hotel room with enough cash in your wallet to properly apologize to housekeeping ($200 is a good place to start), and chalk it up as fodder for your future AA testimonials.

As these thoughts stumbled around my wounded brain, somewhere far away an alarm began to sound. There had been an audible rise in the engine RPM. *What the hell would cause that when I'm moving at a steady . . .* and slowly, like a sunrise that never seems to arrive and then suddenly blinds you, I knew. Hydroplaning. It explained a lot. Not just the noise, but the gentle rotational movement Carl Vehicle had begun to take on. The world had downshifted into ultraslow motion with infinite space inside of every moment, allowing me to savor every facet of the experience. I told myself to stay calm, but it didn't work. So I screamed at myself to stay calm. That always works. Then I screamed back at myself to stop goddamn yelling, unless I wanted to die right now. In New Jersey.

That shut me up pretty good. No one wants to die in New Jersey. Even those *Jersey Shore* knuckleheads. They all want to die in Miami. The hair on my body was standing on end, like a million teenage boners. I opened my mouth because somehow it felt like I should say something, but either I didn't have anything to say, or I couldn't hear myself over the rain. Or the radio, which was blasting "Bohemian Rhapsody."

Who's going to take care of my dog? I'm gonna miss you, Buna. Then I remembered the things on my pretrip to-do list I had biffed. One stood out: make a will. You can do it all online now. Only takes a few minutes. I would have given Buna to Brian.

"I'm dead, asshole," Brian noted from his cup holder. "Besides, I'm already taking care of your last dog. Piglet says hi, by the way."

Shit, that's right. Brian's dead. Okay, my brother John should get Buna. Brian would get my record collection.

"Still dead!" Brian cackled.

Shit. Okay, then Elizabeth should get the records. We might not be together anymore, but at least she knew how to take care of them.

"You want to give your record collection to your *ex*?" Brian sputtered, incredulous.

"Sure. It's not like I'm going to be listening to them."

"Yeah, but you want her to die in a fire, don't you?"

"Can you cut me just the tiniest speck of slack, Bri? I have a couple small things on my mind at the moment, not the least of which is the fact that I'm sliding, helplessly, into the lane next to mine."

Man, people make some funny faces when you lose control of your car next to them in a thunderstorm. I see you shouting, sir, but unfortunately there's not much I can do about this. My steering wheel is no longer a steering wheel, you see. Just a giant round hunk of metal and plastic that's about to explode an airbag all over me. You want to talk to someone in charge? Talk to Carl Vehicle. But you can take it from me. No matter how much you shout at him, Carl doesn't answer. Stoic motherfucker.

"Being dead's pretty sweet," Brian interjected, helpfully. "You'll like it."

"Why, because you get to come back and annoy the shit out of family members while they're at their worst?"

"That is one of the perks, yeah," he replied.

Thunderbolt and lightning very, very frightening me

"Little on the nose, don't you think?" Brian said.

"I don't control the playlist, dick. It's the radio," I shot back. I was now fully in the next lane over, with no sign of stopping, my lazy fishtail starting to swing back the other way.

"Sure, but you're the one listening to *Classic Rewind* all day. This wouldn't have happened if you'd been listening to *The Message*."

"The fucking Christian pop channel? You're seriously saying that my choice of radio stations is why I'm about to get into a massive traffic pileup on the Jersey Turnpike?"

"Naw, dude. I just like the way your face gets all scrunched up when I say something stupid."

"Fuck you, Brian. Seriously. Fuck you. I have to deal with this."

"Deal with what? It's out of your hands. Just sit back and enjoy the ride. How often do you get to slide across two lanes of traffic at seventy miles an hour?"

"That attitude is exactly what pisses me off about you dead fuckers. You don't have to deal with anything! Well, guess what? Back here we're all picking up your shit for you and trying to get over your stupid ass."

"But that's what's so awesome about being dead," Brian replied. "No responsibilities, no expectations, no bills. Oh, and no spam. We don't even have phones. It's awesome."

Oh shit. When I die, they're going to clean out my bedroom. That means they're going to find the Viagra and the butt plugs. Those aren't even mine! What was that Bill Hicks bit about his parents finding his porn after he died? At least the VCR era is over so I don't have a bunch of giant tapes hanging around.

"You also don't have a fuckin' bedroom," Brian reminded me.

Okay, notch another point for the smart-ass. He was right. I had moved to Nowhere. The closest thing I had to a bedroom now was Carl Vehicle. Okay, so they'd find fewer butt plugs and more dashboard hula girls. Still mortifying. And now I was clearing the second lane. How's the shoulder looking? Nice and wide actually, but then it was Guardrail City. America's second shittiest town, right behind Skokie, Illinois.

"Cheer up, man! Just think of the look on Elizabeth's face when she hears you're gone."

I pictured Elizabeth at my funeral. Jack with his arm around her as she wept behind her sunglasses. Classic L.A. sun streaming down on the . . . but wait, fuck. I was going to die in *Jersey*. They'd probably have the funeral in Philly, where the family is. Doubtful she'd come out east to bury her ex-boyfriend. Shame. She looked amazing in black.

"Don't worry, man. You can *Ghost* her," Brian offered.

"You mean haunt her?"

"Naw, man, *Ghost* her! Hang around her house and look longingly at her face and do pottery and shit. Like Kurt Russell!"

"That was Swayze. Kurt doesn't do that sentimental shit."

"Yeah, but you do."

"I do what?"

"That sentimental shit."

If you'd asked me three months prior what my ideal after-life was, it might have resembled that 1990 cinematic shitsterpiece *Ghost*. The wistful looks, the flowy shirts, the pottery, "Unchained Melody." But now, in the super slow-mo realm of pure reaction and total consciousness, it hit me. I didn't want that stupid sad-sack can't-move-on crap. Not for Elizabeth. Hell, not for anyone.

I had my life. She had hers. She might have been a dummy for breaking up with me, but that was on her, not me. Or maybe she was smart for breaking up with me. Either way, I was done feeling shitty about her.

"Good! You can finally start feeling shitty about me," Brian mumbled. "Dick."

All this talk of shit got me thinking of whether I'd shit myself in the wreckage. Didn't people do that? Was I even wearing underwear today? Just my luck, they're going to pull me out of the pileup with a giant stain down my back. And some asshole will pull out his phone and film it because that's what people do now, and then my final, shitty act on this planet would end up going viral. And that would be what everyone remembered about me. Not the writing. Not the dogs I rescued. Not the radio show, or the time I was on Conan. Not the women I almost married or the kids I never had. Not the charity work I always talked about wanting to do.

"Jesus Christ, let me get a fuckin' box of tissues," Brian said.

"You know what, Brian, I didn't make fun of you while you were dying."

"Oh, I know. You didn't do anything. Except sleep, of course. You're good at that."

"What's that supposed to mean?"

"You don't think I'd still be alive if you'd come out with me that night?"

"I didn't want to encourage you. You were drunk."

"You should have protected me. I was drunk."

"Is this really the time for us to discuss this? I'm trying to die here."

"Not hard enough, apparently."

I must have instinctively eased off the accelerator or hit a dry patch or appeased Thor or Patrick Swayze because just as Carl Vehicle was entering the outskirts of Guardrail City, his wheels found traction on the asphalt again. And whaddya know? He was facing approximately the same direction as he was traveling. Life snapped back to normal speed again and Brian shut up. I had threaded a needle through the gaps between four or five different cars to the far right lane and I could feel the drivers of each of those cars screaming as a wall of adrenaline slammed into my body, making all my muscles contract at once, my thighs aching with flight hormone. Which is why, on the shortest trip of my entire journey, I stopped halfway for a breather. Breathing seemed like a pretty awesome, if undeserved, thing to be doing at that moment.

RAIN RAIN GO AWAY

You know it as a nursery rhyme, but it also serves as a rallying cry for grape growers, who dread precipitation and moisture the way cops fear cell-phone cameras. Grapevines are essentially weeds, after all. They flourish in the gravelly soil and dry conditions that tend to be ruinous for other crops. Of course, zero rain isn't an option, but too much can be just as disastrous.

If you've ever spent any summers in the southern Pennsylvania/New Jersey region, you know they're right out of Dante: hot and humid with frequent thunderstorms (and occasional appearances by Joe Piscopo). According to South Jersey–born winemaker Daniel Brennan, "that's not good," particularly when grapes are plump and soft and not quite ready to harvest.

"If the humidity breaks and you get a huge downpour, the vines might soak up all that water and either dilute the berries or, even worse, cause them to burst," says Brennan, who moved to New Zealand several years ago to start Decibel Wines.

These days Brennan says places like Jersey have more success with grape growing due to new viticulture techniques. One such practice is to open the canopy (i.e., remove the leaves) around the fruit zone to allow greater airflow (i.e., quicker drying) after rains.

"Then the breeze can blow away all that disease pressure like a moldy fart in the wind," says Brennan, whose wine tastes far better than his metaphors.

Still, choosing the correct varietals, clones, and rootstock are essential in the unforgiving, humid summers of the Jerz. Growers there have had the most success with thick-skinned varietals such as Cabernet Franc and Viognier.

Brennan is also a big proponent of organically grown grapes, which he says are more resistant to disease pressure caused by rain and humidity. Spraying with pesticides and weed sprays can apparently cause vine health to diminish over time, while robbing free-draining soils of the essential nutrients vines need. Going organic makes it tough to establish a vineyard, but supposedly if you can make it to your second or third year, it's smoother sailing.

But while Brennan doesn't miss much about making wine in his home state, he hasn't gone entirely native in the antipodes. "What I miss most about making wine in Jersey," says Brennan, "is grabbing some hoagies and a case of beer after work on Friday and heading down the Shore." I didn't have the heart to tell him what the Shore was like these days.

....

The Molly Pitcher Service Area in Middlesex County, New Jersey, offers a fantastic panoply of choices. If, that is, you don't mind choosing from nineteen varieties of ridiculously inexpensive glop (An entire meal. For a dollar. What's the catch?) designed to inflict more damage to the human body than Guardrail City. Having already cheated death once that day and therefore having nothing to lose, I went all-in at an establishment I was both delighted and surprised to discover still existed (sorry Nathan's Hot Dogs and Cinnabon).

When I was a kid, Arthur Treacher's Fish & Chips was a regular part of my weekly diet. It's worth remembering that this was also a period when I regularly ate my own boogers. Every item on the Arthur Treacher's menu was deep-fried and batter "dip't." Even the soda (or at least it tasted that way). Every once in a while you would get a speck of actual fish in your batter. Those were good days. The average meal had an equivalent nutritional value that hovered somewhere between Elmer's Glue and Play-Doh (the other staples of my diet back then).

After retrieving a "meal" equal parts nostalgic and disgusting, I looked for a seat in Molly Pitcher's communal dining area. Apparently I wasn't the only one taking refuge from the End Times weather going on outside. The place looked like I'd lifted an enormous rock and peered underneath to find an ocean of half-formed organisms, wriggling and fishbelly white. I found a spot across from a hairy and spectacularly obese man draped in a tattered Philadelphia Eagles poncho that could double as a four-man tent. He wore a resigned, hangdog look on his face as he polished off a Roy Rogers double cheeseburger and a gallon of fries with the grim efficiency of the back end of a garbage truck. It was clear he did not derive pleasure from the experience. He looked numb, somnambulant, like he might drift off to sleep midchew. A bead of ketchup and melted cheese dripped from the burger onto the poncho/tent, landing just below the eagle's eye. Either the man didn't notice or it didn't bother him. It just sat there, dripping in slow motion, a fast-food tear wept by a once-proud symbol mourning its former glory.

Then, as will happen when you stare at someone for an inappropriately long time, he noticed me. The attention seemed to energize him. He gave a sort of scowl, then his face twitched in what might have been a smile, then the scowl was back again. A moment later, he pointed at me and flashed a thumbs-up. He smiled again, wide, affording me a clear view of neglected teeth and masticated food slop. I quickly averted my gaze, finding sudden fascination in the half-eaten "boat" of deep-fried batter-dip't fishlike substance in front of me.

I should have known this was coming. Swayze and the Traction Gods didn't spare anyone for free. Tribute must be paid. I should have just gotten a latte and a protein bar. A wave of nausea swept over me. I could *feel* my own arteries hardening. I looked up, and the mastodon man gave me another thumbs-up. Why did he keep doing that? He didn't know me. He couldn't know me, could he? I did used to live around here, though. Maybe I went to school with him? Or we had beers after a game. It would not be the first time that age and poor food choices had transformed my childhood peers. But come on, man. You gotta keep the ketchup off your tent-poncho. You're making the eagle cry.

I was suffocating. I wanted to jump up and sprint straight out the doors of the Molly Pitcher Service Area and into the cold, cleansing rain (the secret of New Jersey's cleansing rain? It's packed with detergent!), get back on the turnpike and take my chances with the elements, become one with the rain and thunder, offer myself as a sacrifice to Almighty Swayze who would deliver me from the evil of fried "food" and tent ponchos and into a new life of penance and humility and vegan kale smoothies.

Just then, the mastodon hoisted his hulking mass up out of his seat—if I come back as anything in the next life please oh please oh please, let it not be a seat at the Molly Pitcher Service Area—and began waddling toward me. *This is it,* I thought. This quivering profusion of hirsute flesh and weary bones was coming for me. Coming to squash me for some reason that would probably never be clear to me. Oh, but I knew the reason, didn't I? There are rules. Staring at someone in a rest stop in Jersey is grounds for assault. Pure and simple. No jury would ever convict. In my defense, it was practically impossible to be in that room and not stare at him. He was just that astronomically ample. Still, my mother always said it's not nice to stare. Why couldn't I be nice? Surely this fellow human being deserved better than to be ogled at disparagingly all day long. Hell, there could be any number of reasonable contributing factors to his hippopotamus-like appearance. Genetics. Poor parenting. Maybe he couldn't afford to eat right. Or maybe he just didn't give a fat fuck. Whatever. I had no right to judge. And now he was coming for me.

As he got within striking distance his mammoth arm shot out and I recoiled. I also noticed something strange. He had tiny hands. Pink and devoid of any hair. A baby's hands. They were so incongruous to his galactic proportions that for an instant I forgot I was about to get throttled or shot or at the very least punched in the face. Only one thought was thrumming through my brain, blotting out everything else: it must be really difficult for this guy to wipe his own ass.

Which is when he reached out and touched my head with one of those diminutive digits. Or rather, he touched the brim of the thing I was wearing on my head: a Philadelphia Eagles cap. Until that moment, I'd forgotten it was there. I looked up at him and realized he wasn't enraged at all. On the contrary, he was smiling. A smile without a trace of burger or fries. He pointed at my cap, then jabbed a thumb at the poncho-tent. Right on the glob of ketchup and cheese, smearing it across the eagle's eye.

"Go, Birds!" he said. And then he shuffled away.

Indeed, good sir. Go, Birds, go.

PLAIN SPEAKING

Historically, as is true of so many of the places I visited in the middle of the country, the wines of southern New Jersey have traditionally been syrupy, sweet, and so-so. But in recent years folks like Lou Caracciolo of Amalthea Cellars in Atco, have been trying to change the state's candy-apple reputation by making dry, European-style wines in a place where people tend to pair local wines with cheesecake rather than chateaubriand. Hearteningly, Amalthea's wines scored nearly as well as Mouton Rothschild and Haut-Brion in a competition held back in 2012 called, without a trace of irony, the Judgment of Princeton.

Unfortunately, as it turns out, the biggest impediment to selling South Jersey wine is not its quality. Rather, it's the fact that it's from South Jersey. The notion that South Jersey's only exports are pollution and sorrow, while demonstrably untrue, has proven a remarkably resilient idea in the popular consciousness.

So Caracciolo's wines don't come from South Jersey. Instead, they come from "The Outer Coastal Plain," an appellation Caracciolo and a coalition of nearby winemakers came up with in 2009 to rebrand and rehabilitate their growing region. The plan seems to have worked a treat. Sales are up and wine tourism is on the rise. The Outer Coastal Plain sounds like a lovely place for planting vines. South Jersey, on the other hand, sounds like a place where they plant evidence. Allegedly, some say. Probably nothing. Actually, upon further review, forget I said anything. I don't know nothing about South Jersey. All I know is that I prefer my kneecaps right where they are, thank you very much.

....

HAVING NARROWLY MISSED TWO CALLS to the great beyond, I emerged from the Molly Pitcher Service Area's food court to find the storm had passed through, leaving a cool, breezy, sunny day in its wake. Carl Vehicle, though he still wasn't talking, looked relieved. When I got back in, I realized that in my beflusterment on arrival, I'd left my phone in the car. I missed a call from my cousin Dennis, whom I'd made plans to meet up with that night in Philly. He left a voice mail saying he'd be around for another thirty minutes or so, but after that he "had to run." I couldn't tell if his joke was intentional or not, but I laughed anyway, just to be on the safe side.

It never really surprised me that Dennis "lost" his foot, along with a good chunk of his leg. Dennis had been losing things all his life, including things that were larger and more expensive. What was surprising to me, however, was the way he lost it.

If you'd told me it came off in a knife fight, I wouldn't have batted an eye. Same if it was a motorcycle accident. Or a drunken fall from an electrical tower. Antibiotic-resistant syphilis? Par for the course. Retribution for an unpaid gambling debt, a drug deal gone wrong, or a roll in the hay with another man's old lady? Vacation in South Jersey? Any one of these things would have been a reasonable, predictable explanation for why Dennis suddenly found himself, at age forty-five, a leg down. Like most of the degenerates we came up with in Philly, throughout his adolescence Dennis had courted disaster like she was the hottest chick in school. Only Dennis married her, had kids, then got caught cheating with Disaster's sister during a family reunion. Disaster kind of has it in for him at this point.

Still, though. A Christmas tree ornament? It's just goddamn embarrassing. But there it is. A Christmas tree ornament took my cousin's leg.

He stepped on it on December 26, 2013. Reilly, the frisky family kitten, had batted the harmless thing off the Christmas tree and it rolled out onto the living room floor to meet its untimely end beneath, as shit luck would have it, Dennis's bare left foot. It was the one literal misstep in a life full of figurative ones. Dennis, I should note, is a type 2 diabetic, which makes him more susceptible to infections than those of us with normal blood-sugar regulation. Diabetes also inhibits blood flow, which results in decreased sensitivity in the extremities. Decreased sensitivity blocks the body's primary warning system, pain. So when the bulb broke under his foot, he didn't feel much of anything. He didn't much feel the resulting infection, either. It being on the bottom of his heel, he didn't even see it. It wasn't long, though, before the smell became hard to ignore. He went to the emergency room and was diagnosed with gangrene with one sniff. Three weeks into the New Year, twenty-seven days after stepping on a sparkly fetish item meant to induce a nostalgia-driven retail orgy, the doctors took Dennis's left leg, just below the knee.

Dennis doesn't remember a damn thing about the offending Christmas ornament. When I asked him what it looked like, he barked, "How the fuck would I know?" Which illustrates a clear difference between Dennis and myself. If it were me, and I'd lost a foot to an ornament, I'd know that Christmas ball inside and out. I'd know its date of manufacture and would have memorized its model number. I'd call the company that made it weekly and harangue their poor innocent receptionist, demanding to speak to an ever escalating series of managers and vice presidents. But if you think that Christmas ball haunts Dennis's dreams, well, then you don't know Dennis.

Dennis's apathy is a thing of terrible beauty, a dogged lack of determination exceeded only by his lack of luck. He's a Rodney Dangerfield joke as told by Mitch Hedberg. A guy who wears his indifference like mirrored sunglasses, a reflective barrier between him and this least of best-possible worlds.

And I understand that these may seem like awfully harsh things to say about a one-legged diabetic cousin, but I assure you, Dennis doesn't give a shit. Plus, I'm going to leave out the part about how, at the time of his unfortunate Christmas ornament accident, Dennis was also unemployed and sleeping on his mother's living room sofa, because that would be kicking a man when he's down. And we're talking about a man who can't even kick you back. At least not unless he's sitting down. Harsh? Again, only if Dennis gave a shit. And I assure you he doesn't.

Throughout his podectomy, Dennis remained surprisingly upbeat. I should note that Dennis is not in most senses a "downer" kind of guy. Indeed, his defiance is unmatched outside the world of third-party presidential candidates. When I asked him what they did with his foot after they lopped it off, he said they probably put it through a wood chipper to prevent it from reanimating. I'll admit, I found this ridiculous. Because if the foot is infected, then all those individual, atomized pieces are infected, and all you're doing messing around with a wood chipper is creating a bigger problem. Soon the conversation had moved to a more productive place with our idea for *Attack of the Zombie Legs,* the movie Dennis says he's going to write, that's PERFECT for Richard Grieco. "Someone get that asshole on the phone," Dennis shouted. "Tell 'im it's comeback time!" In other news, Dennis doesn't have a computer, and the last time he wrote anything was in Sister Mary Flanagan's eighth-grade English class. A trenchant treatise, titled "Everyone Sucks But Us," about his beloved Philadelphia Flyers.

When we were trying to build "how I lost my leg" cover stories for use in various social settings, we agreed that under no circumstance should Dennis reveal the humiliating truth about his injury to strangers. Especially in Philly. He'd paid his pound of flesh—with the bone and tendons included it was probably more like ten to twelve pounds—and bought himself some bullshit rights. If history has taught us anything—and by history, I'm referring here specifically to the most memorable scene from *Jaws*—it's that few things in life are more compelling than a well-told scar story.

In the end, we settled on a few go-to fabrications:

1. He's a professional stuntman and lost his leg wrestling an alligator for an upcoming George Clooney film. He doesn't remember what it's called.
2. He got stung by a very, very large bee.
3. He tried to jump Snake River Canyon on a rocket-powered cycle.
4. Cancer. (Bonus: also explains his baldness.)
5. Cut himself shaving.
6. He was on the USS *Indianapolis*. Eleven hundred men went into the water. Ship went down in twelve minutes. Didn't see the first shark for half an hour. Tiger. Thirteen-footer.
7. He was wounded trying to save a kitten from a bear. Stupid kittens.
8. Lost it in a poker game. Trip-ace boat to four twos. Ouch.
9. Stepped on a Saint Patrick's Day ornament. When they point out that there is no such thing, he says, "Oh, now you tell me!"

Often he tries to scratch his missing foot. Like many recent amputees, Dennis gets phantom feelings in his not-there-no-more limb (the wood-chipper treatment notwithstanding). He compared the sensation to waking up in the morning to go to the office, only to realize it's Saturday, and you're like, "Oh, never mind. I don't have work today."

Now for a moment I want you to set aside the fact that

this is a guy who's never had an office job or gotten out of bed before 10 A.M., because Dennis's analogy speaks volumes about his Panglossian outlook on misfortune. Equating the loss of your leg to forgetting that you're allowed to sleep in is like comparing getting punched in the mouth to being given free orthodontia. Dick that I am, I pressed him on this, and Dennis conceded that he'd rather have the leg than the luxury of not needing to scratch it. But his reflex answer reveals why, despite all the drama and surgery and lack-of-leggedness, he's probably going to be just fine. Wake up one day and you're an amputee? That's one less shoe to worry about. And $10 worth of socks is actually $20 worth of socks if you only have one leg. Score.

Turns out he's also grown fond of Reilly, the kitty that got the ball rolling toward his leglessness. Just another lesson from The Book of Dennis. To me, that cat would be destined for a burlap sack and a river. But Dennis doesn't see it that way.

"I don't know," he said. Just that. If the Buddha came from Ireland, I know what his name would be.

It's tempting to think of Nietzsche: what doesn't kill you makes you stronger. Now Friedrich wasn't typically one to sugarcoat things, but I'm pretty sure that's bullshit. Sometimes life kicks you in the balls and instead of making you stronger, the shock makes you sterile, and then you never have kids to pass your misinformed bullshit onto. Allow me to propose a slight edit, mister *Ubermensch*: what you don't put behind you makes you its bitch.

No one gets in Dennis's head but Dennis. Not a gambling debt. Not a jealous husband. Not a drunken fall off an electrical tower. Not a kitten and a Christmas ornament that teamed up to steal his leg. Dennis is not going to solve the unified field theory and he's not going to fix world hunger. But he honestly doesn't give a shit about doing those things. Honest being the key word.

Not giving a shit is a skill I've never been able to master. For example, I know I'm not Tom Wolfe or Jack Kerouac or any of those genius fuckfaces that changed the world every time they put pen to paper. But instead of not giving a shit, like I should, I take up time and energy being envious instead of working away at things I'm good at, which is to say being an adorable, half-drunk nongenius. Heroes aren't all in text-books or on TV imploring us to sweat to the oldies. Some-times they're sleeping on their mother's couch, snuggled up with the cat that took their leg, without a trace of bitterness in their soul.

I was looking forward to seeing Dennis precisely because I knew he didn't give a shit. He would not be impressed that I was driving around the country, or writing a wine book, or about anything else. I offered to let him read this chapter before publication, so he could see if there was anything in here he wouldn't want to see in print and he said "sure." And then he never read a word of it.

THE CITY OF PHILADELPHIA LOOKED like Carl Vehicle fresh from the car wash I hadn't given him in months. The rain had washed away the grime and you could imagine old Ben Franklin himself promenading with his favorite prostitute before retiring to the Hellfire Club for a restorative orgy. What the rain couldn't wash away, though, was the potholes. You get used to navigating them once you've been in Philly awhile, thanks to the city's spectacularly shitty infrastructure program. The trick is to accept that you are powerless to keep yourself from driving over a pothole. But you do have some small agency over which one. All potholes are not created equal, after all, and keeping your suspension intact while navigating the streets of Philadelphia depends on being able to estimate a given pothole's depth. However, when the streets are covered in water, all bets are off. Every pothole looks the same. Could be a half-inch deep, could be a sinkhole leading to the center of the earth. Or worse, Danny Bonaduce's basement.

After rattling my coccyx a few dozen times, the buildings started getting shittier and I started to recognize some landmarks. I was in Northeast Philly. It may not have been home (I am a proud resident of Nowhere after all. Go Nothings!), but it's where I'm from.

"BE CAREFUL OR YOU'LL BE
WEARING NIGHTGOWNS LIKE ME!"

CHAPTER 11

PHILADELPHIA

My dad and my brother were both thirty-one when they jumped. Neither was trying to kill themselves, but they both almost died. Then after almost dying, Brian went ahead and died all the way. That's what you get for being a perfectionist. But while my dad held onto his life, his jump still cost him.

Dad was driving a cement truck at the time—one of those giant bastards they call an "in transit mixer"—for Liberty Concrete. Growing up, he'd wanted to drive for a living, but his aspirations leaned more toward the Daytona 500 than hauling ready-mix. Still, driving a cement truck was an honest living, at least compared to what he'd been doing for money over the previous decade. But let's be clear, this was a Teamsters gig in the rough end of Philly in the 1970s. Getting that job is like finding a Twinkie on a dive bar toilet seat. You'll take it if you're hungry enough, but it will permanently recalibrate your threshold for what is and isn't acceptable behavior. My dad's bedtime stories all started with "once upon a time and a half." His favorite joke? "How many Teamsters does it take to fill a pothole?" (Answer: None of your fucking business.)

Like everyone he worked with, my pops took a few liberties on the job from time to time, but he swears it was all penny-ante stuff: overreporting hours worked, underreporting hours spent in bars during lunch break, or breakfast break, or fuck-it-let's-get-a-drink break.

It was October 25, 1977. A Tuesday, just before noon. Dad was in Northeast Philly driving a truck full of concrete, headed west toward Willow Grove, Pennsylvania. To do that, he needed to cross the Rhawn Street Bridge. That day, however, a crew from Bell Telephone had blocked off the eastbound lane about fifty yards ahead of the bridge. As he trundled past them, he looked up to see, of all things, another cement truck. It's worth mentioning that stopping and starting a cement truck is a colossal pain in the ass that takes a lot of effort and can seriously cut into the time you're allotted to drink your lunch. Suffice to say, once you're rolling you want to keep rolling. And in the '70s people didn't buy into today's nanny-state adherence to trifles such as crosswalks, traffic lights, and actually looking before you blindly pull into the oncoming lane.

In any event, my dad suddenly found himself in a game of chicken. And man, if you thought chicken was fun to play on motorcycles, wait till you try it with both drivers piloting thirty tons of concrete at fifty miles an hour in a residential neighborhood. When concrete trucks crash into things, usually it's the things that get flattened, not the concrete trucks. However, the pink fleshy humans strapped to the front of the concrete trucks almost always come out of it poorly. On the bright side, their funerals tend to be very economical as their remains can typically fit into an infant-sized casket.

Acting on instinct, my dad cut his wheel to the right and somehow managed to avoid the other truck. Unfortunately he was now in danger of missing the bridge entirely and taking a one-way trip to the bottom of Pennypack Creek. A sharp swerve toward the center of the road put him back on the bridge, but at the losing end of the world's shittiest physics problem. He was driving a thirty-thousand-pound vehicle that had another thirty thousand pounds of liquid concrete sloshing around inside it. Add in a few vectors, some angular momentum, and a little fluid dynamics, and you've got yourself a truck tilting toward the guardrail that no amount of steering, praying, or pants-shitting will stop.

A moment later the truck was on its side, midway across the bridge, wheels spinning, fuel and concrete spilling out all over the road. The Bell Telephone crew sprinted over to help. In the wreckage they saw a rubber glove sticking out from beneath the mixer. They assumed it was attached to a hand, and that that hand was attached to a flattened corpse, whose former owner had been operating the truck. Then one of them took a look over the guardrail.

To avoid being crushed, at the last minute my dad had jumped out of the cab and, unintentionally, off the bridge. Now he was eighty feet below the roadway, crumpled on the dirt and rocks. Both his legs were broken, along with all his ribs. His lungs had collapsed, he'd lost several teeth, and blood was pooling from a gash on his head. Then there was his right arm. Or rather, there wasn't his right arm. The appendage was nearly severed, mangled beyond repair. He says it looked like a sausage that had exploded inside a microwave. Who wants another bedtime story!

Luckily, Dad's a lefty. Amazing what passes for good luck when you're looking up at the Rhawn Street Bridge from the banks of scenic Pennypack Creek.

"There's absolutely no reasonable explanation for how I survived," my dad told me. "I don't believe in miracles, but that was a friggin' miracle."

To be fair, the friggin' miracle had a little help. The Bell Telephone guy who spotted him immediately dashed across the bridge, scrambled down a steep embankment into the woods below, and then waded across the creek to reach the smear of the human lying there. He would later tell investigators that he was amazed to find my dad was still breathing, albeit barely. He recalled it sounding like my dad was choking to death. Or gargling. The clinical term is terminal respiratory secretions. In common parlance, we call it the death rattle.

The guy tore off his shirt and used it as a tourniquet to tie off my dad's arm at the shoulder. Then he rolled him over on his side so he wouldn't choke on his own blood. And that's how he saved my father's life. A few more seconds of confusion, a moment's hesitation, or an unwillingness to get wet, naked, or bloody in public and my dad would have been dead. They've been friends ever since. Now I call him Uncle Tommy and his family comes over for Thanksgiving every year.

Just kidding. My dad never saw him again, and can't even remember the guy's name.

It's possible my dad not keeping in touch with the heroic stranger who saved his life had to do with the trauma of the accident or of the three-month hospital stay that followed. Or perhaps it's related to the fact that during his hospital stay, the doctors waived their usual no-alcohol policy for him, putting him on a strict six-pack-per-day drinking allowance. They were worried that in his condition, drying out could put enough stress on his body to kill him. Basically they were saying, "We're a rehab center, not a 'rehab' center." So they gave him enough booze to keep him functioning, but not enough for a proper drunk.

Naturally on the day he got out of the hospital from getting fucked up beyond all recognition, he celebrated his new lease on life by getting fucked up beyond all recognition. As if to prove to the world that his arm was all he lost in the accident, that same week he knocked up my stepmom. Nine months later I met my brother Brian for the first time. He couldn't talk and kept shitting himself (a tradition he revived decades later on a few of our gnarlier benders).

So I lost a dad arm but gained a baby brother (technically a half brother, but we never used that word). Not a bad trade. I remember seeing him for the first time at my dad's house in Juniata and thinking, *Holy shit, kid. You have no idea what you're in for.*

The wheels on the cement truck go round and round . . . round and round . . .

I didn't connect the fact that Dad and Brian were both the same age when they jumped until I started writing this book. After checking and rechecking my math, I gave my head a second to stop spinning, then called my dad. Which is when I discovered one other similarity.

"Hey, Dad, did alcohol play a role in your accident?"

"Nah," he said, without hesitation. "I'd only had a couple of beers that morning."

I CROSSED THE RHAWN STREET Bridge on the way to my mother's house. It wasn't the most direct route, but after all the time I'd spent living in Nowhere, I'd gotten caught up in the spirit of nostalgia. Which was a little weird, since I've never had much of an emotional connection to the spot where Dad almost died. It was just another bloodstained landmark in a landscape dotted with them. Maybe it's because the accident didn't really change him much. He was the same hot-tempered absentee alcoholic deadbeat dad he'd been before it happened. The main difference was that on those rare occasions when he did come around, having just the one wing made him a lot less intimidating.

If there's a place that really speaks to me about my dad, it's Marworth, the rehab center where he finally got sober. Thirty years ago (eight years after losing his arm) his twin brother, my uncle Dennis, sat him down and told him he needed to be done with booze. That if he didn't stop drinking he was going to die. And to his credit, my dad listened. An entirely different guy walked out of Marworth, a guy who hasn't touched a drop of alcohol since. And I love that sonofabitch more than anything. I'd say he deserves a hand, but he already has the one, and frankly he lost the other one fair and square. I'd love to tell you I visited Marworth to pay my respects, but it's in Waverly, a good two hours from my mom's house, and the wine selection there is atrocious.

The main reason I chose to detour by way of Rhawn Street is because of Datillo's Deli. Datillo's sits at the corner of Rhawn and Horrocks, a block away from that apartment on Bustleton Avenue where the Intruder clocked me with a frying pan. I practically lived at Datillo's when I was a kid. I was their mascot. The latchkey kid with the hot mom from down the street. I'd go there after school, and they'd let me hang out for a few hours until Mom got off work. She'd come down to fetch me, and all the Italian guys who worked there would fall all over themselves peacocking for her attention. I loved it. I really did. And so did Mom.

But despite the warm familial feel and the wealth of Italian cuss words I learned, there was at least one drawback to spending so much time in a deli—unlimited food. Around third grade I began to plump up a bit. By the time I was ten, I looked like Dom DeLuise in Toughskins. And being obese in a tough neighborhood is no fun. What I endured from the fifth to ninth grade makes Piggy's traumatic experiences in *The Lord of the Flies* look like *Malcolm in the Middle*. The kids were savages, chief among them being Joe McGill, the merciless little fuck who nicknamed me "Titman." I've changed a lot of names in this book to protect real people. But I didn't change Joe McGill's name because as far as I'm concerned he is not a real person. Rather, he is a despicable pinheaded fuckwit who deserves to have his testicles stapled to his left leg. Not that I'm still carrying a grudge around or anything.

The Titman nickname followed me everywhere. It was irresistible to kids once they heard it. Because, yeah, I had a pretty decent pair. I was probably a B cup, maybe creeping up on a C. Put me in a pushup bra and I could have hit the burlesque scene. And turns out when you live in Northeast Philly and your mom watches soap operas and drinks wine coolers and calls you a worthless piece of shit and your dad smacks you around even when you do everything he tells you to, nothing's more fun than having a fat kid around to fuck with.

During the summer following eighth grade, though, two things happened. First, John showed up. John was a fireman, a scrappy little sonofabitch with a mustache and a temper and a marriage certificate to my mom. John took an immediate interest in me (or at least in not being the fireman with the morbidly obese stepson) and put me on an exercise regimen that was heavy on the cardio and heavier on the fat shaming. My other discovery that summer was a bottle of diet pills in a medicine cabinet at a friend's house. I had just ducked in there to whack off real quick—when you're twelve, you're always whacking off, and it's always real quick—and was looking for some Vaseline, when there it was. Honest to God full freight of 1970s prescription diet pills. I had no idea what they really were, all I knew is the label on the bottle said, "For weight loss. Take one by mouth twice a day." Man, did I have a lot of energy that summer. And I never felt like eating. The guys at Datillo's would wave as I rolled by on a jog, "When we gonna see you again, Danny?" The pills were gone in a few weeks, but they'd given me a jump start. I could still get Dexatrim over the counter, and back then it was basically legal speed. By the time the fall rolled around and it was time to start high school, I was a different kid. People literally didn't recognize me. And if they did— "Holy shit, *you're* Titman?"—without my B cups the name just didn't stick.

What did stick were girls. To me. Midway through my freshman year I got to second base for the first time. And with Erin O'Shea, one of the prettiest girls in the neighborhood. Even now I consider it one of the seminal experiences of my life, and not just because of the fluid I released when her bra came off. On top of my first interactive ejaculation (albeit premature, albeit none of her conscious doing) I received something much more meaningful and far longer overdue.

Because I'd spent weeks getting close to Erin despite the fact that she had a boyfriend. And despite the fact that he was a known badass who would, without question, pound me to dust if he ever found out. Which he did because Erin dumped him and started seeing me and I got to see a lot more of second base (sometimes without spontaneously ejaculating!). And so yes, I took a beating. I had it coming. And it was worth every bruise and both black eyes. Because Erin's boyfriend was none other than that *figlio di puttana* Joe McGill.

Like Zero, Datillo's manager, always told me: a little violence never hurt anyone. That and *Non c'è megghiu sarsa di la fami.* Hunger is the best sauce.

DATILLO'S DELI STILL MAKES THE tastiest Italian hoagies in Philly. Some people (read: fuckwit assholes) may argue this point, but trust me, they are incorrect. Datillo's cheesesteaks are similarly phenomenal. So I got in touch with my inner fat kid and ordered one of each. Then I drove to Burholme Park, a beautiful wooded area between Jeanes Hospital and the Fox Chase Cancer Center. It's the highest point in Northeast Philly and had it been eight hours later I would have been disturbing some serious teenage action. Local high schoolers have been getting it on in the backseats of their cars at Burholme Park for at least fifty years, maybe since before there were cars. It felt almost gauche bringing Carl Vehicle up there. When I thought about the times I'd had in my '77 Nova, it was easy to think that the reason I was only lasting around 120 seconds or so during those encounters was the lack of space. I could sense Carl getting uneasy with this line of thinking, so I focused on my hot threesome with those sandwiches. After about 120 seconds I was on my way to my mom's.

For months, I'd fretted over going to see her. It'd been a long time, and I feared she might not be able to handle it. My visits have triggered breakdowns in the past, starting a year or so after I moved away. It only got worse as time went on, to the point where I stopped going altogether.

"You look good. A little older and grayer, but good." For the first time in almost a decade, I was stepping into the house where I spent the bulk of my formative years. John's house.

"You look good too, Mom," I said. "I see you're wearing your best nightgown for the occasion."

"Oh stop!" she guffawed. "All I wear is nightgowns. I'm so fat, I can't fit into anything else!"

It was a fair cop. My mother had put on a little weight. Still, not nearly enough to warrant a wholesale wardrobe shift to bedclothes. Still, if I lived alone and left the house as infrequently as she had over the past decade, I'd have probably gone Full Lebowski too.

"You want something to eat?" she asked.

"No. I'm stuffed."

"You never eat a thing. Are you still taking those pills? Here, why don't I get you a soft pretzel? I got some in the freezer. I can defrost them in the microwave and melt some Cheez Whiz."

"I'm good, Ma. I ate a hoagie from Datillo's earlier."

"Oh, what kinda hoagie?"

"Italian. Extra oil and hot peppers."

"I always get the cheesesteak at Datillo's," she said.

"Yeah, I had one of those too," I said.

"You ate a hoagie AND a cheesesteak?! Jesus, Danny! Be careful or you'll be wearing nightgowns like me!"

"We'll be like two peas in a pod," I said. It just came out. But man did it make Mom smile. *Shit*, I thought to myself, *is this all it's going to take? Just serve up some clichés and she's all peaches and . . .* shit. I wasn't affecting her, she was affecting me.

She asked how the trip had been so far. I told her I'd been having the time of my life. The truth, as you know, was a tad more complicated. Best not to burden her with it.

"That's good," she said. "Are you dating anyone?"

The truth on this one: "Not right now, Ma."

"What happened to that girl you were living with? Jessica, was it?"

"Elizabeth," I corrected. "It didn't work out."

"You were with her a while, right?"

"About three and a half years," I said.

"Oh, okay," she said. That was her two cents and not a penny more.

We got onto some other topics where she had a little more to say. Family. The Phillies. Pajamas. Whether or not she should continue going to bingo night down at the senior center (My vote: yes. Her vote: looking at old people is depressing. My reply: withheld). To be honest, my mom acted like such a normal person I found it unsettling. I wasn't used to seeing her that way. Granted, I hadn't seen her in a long time, but the last time I did she'd been out of her tree. Hanging from the opposite end of the sanity pole, so to speak. Making calls to Congress and the local police.

"C'mon, let me fix you a soft pretzel," Mom said.

"Sure, Mom. Why not."

She went to the kitchen to nuke some soft pretzels. I sat in the living room sucking on a Yuengling Lager and taking stock of my surroundings. I was surprised how familiar it all felt after so much time. The place was almost exactly as I remembered it, only smaller.

I noticed the display case on the mantel that held a neatly folded American flag. John's. I remember my mom had called me once and told me a story about him. About them. About a great night they'd had. It was August. My brother and sister were both out for the evening and John popped opened a bottle of wine. No big deal for most people, but for most of her adult life Mom wasn't a drinker. She'd never had a problem or anything, she just didn't like it much. In fact, she hadn't had a drop in years. But on this night, when John offered her a glass, for whatever reason, she said, why not? And then she and her husband of twenty-three years proceeded to tie one on. They listened to old records. Danced. Ordered pizza. Went skinny-dipping in the aboveground pool in the backyard. She said it was the most fun she'd had in years. Maybe her whole life.

Three nights later—August 20, 2004—Captain John D. Taylor Jr. of the Philadelphia Fire Department and his crew answered a call at a basement fire in a row house in Port Richmond. Same drill as the innumerable fires he'd worked over his thirty-three-year career. Guy had been growing weed down there. Cat knocked over a light, something shorted out, I don't even know. It was a tight, dark space, though, and one of John's men got his equipment tangled up in some wiring. He was trapped. So Captain John D. Taylor Jr. of the Philadelphia Fire Department did what fire captains do. He went to get his man out of there. Neither of them made it. John was fifty-three years old.

At his funeral, John got the same treatment dead soldiers do—buried the way heroes are buried: honor guard, badge shrouds, bagpipes, and a bugler playing "Taps." Instead of a hearse, the flag-draped casket topped with his helmet was transported on the engine that took him to Port Richmond that fateful night.

For the first year or so, my mom held up remarkably well. But when she did lose it, she lost it bad. Bipolar bad. Talking to people who aren't there bad. Without John to help keep her shit together, the shit went everywhere and hit everyone. My brother and sister, aunts and uncles. Me.

No wonder Elizabeth bailed. Living with me must have felt like being trapped inside the most histrionic Lifetime movie ever, written by a hack screenwriter who hasn't yet learned that the answer to good drama isn't just adding sad things until it's over. (Everyone knows the answer to bad drama is to hire Ian Ziering and tell him you need more intensity.) I was a lot. Broken home on the wrong side of the tracks; alcoholic father; bipolar mother; drowned brother; burned-alive step-father; multiple lost limbs; rogue cement trucks; dead dog. You know that saying, you can't make this shit up? You totally could make it up. It's just no one would ever believe you.

I should be thankful Elizabeth stayed with me for as long as she did. Hell, most women would have walked as soon as they grasped the sheer probability of winding up in either an amputee ward, an insane asylum, or a graveyard. Statistics may lie, but history is a remarkably good predictor. And the fact is almost everyone who ever got close to me has been blindsided by booze, stupidity, insanity, or a goddamn house fire. (But check out my Tinder profile. Maybe we'll match!)

"Here ya go," my mom said, handing me a soft pretzel smothered in melted cheese. Another culinary homecoming. I was feeling vulnerable, and when I feel vulnerable, I get cynical. Given my oenological odyssey of the last several months, my thoughts immediately went to how the pretzel would pair with fine wine. In lieu of making a twist-off-cap joke she'd never get, I give you this . . .

....

GOOD WINE, SHITTY FOOD

A lot of ink and hot air has been spilled over the act of "pairing." That is, combining food and drink effectively to create a taste that is greater than the sum of its parts. What no one ever seems to talk about, however, is that you can add good wine to shitty white trash meals to make them not only slide down your gullet more quickly, but to get you a little buzzed so you forget about the fact that you're eating Kraft dinner for the third time this week.

Which is to say, this is my attempt to reconcile my past with my present. Bon appetit, motherfuckers.

Fried baloney sandwich with Gloria Ferrer Carneros Chardonnay: The intensely unctuous baloney calls for a well-rounded wine that strikes a delicate balance between fragility and belligerence. Don't forget to add mustard.

Bucket of KFC Original Recipe with Geyser Peak Sauvignon Blanc: Because the colonel's fried chicken begs for a wine with bright acidity and herbaceous flavors to temper the spontaneous coronary artery dissection you just suffered.

Hamburger Helper with Conundrum California Red: Why do they call it Hamburger Helper when we all know it's the pasta getting the help? It's quite the conundrum. See where I'm going with this?

Chef Boyardee Beefaroni with Boone's Strawberry Hill: Aw hell, if you're going to surrender, you might as well surrender completely.

....

"I'm only having half of one," Mom said. "I gotta lose weight."

"It looks delicious. Thanks, Ma."

We sat there for a few minutes, chewing. The silence was actually comforting. She had always seemed to need to fill this kind of space with words, most of them incoherent.

"The place looks good," I said finally.

"Thanks," she said. "I got a new cleaning girl that comes every other week. I had to fire the old one."

"Well, it's very clean."

"She was stealing."

"Who?"

"The old cleaning girl."

"Oh yeah?" I said. A lifetime of looking for these turns told me our chat might be headed down the rabbit hole.

"Yep. A few months ago, she stole all my Charlie Brown figurines from the family room. I went down there and they were all gone from the shelves. Then, the next time she came, she put them all back."

And there it was. As far back as I can remember, my mother has been convinced that there is a significant cohort of people who exist solely to torture her. As far as I could tell they were doing a pretty awful job. To hear her tell it, they were putting a terrific amount of time and effort into messing with her possessions. Come on, guys, you never heard of the IRS? The banks? You don't have hackers? That's how you mess with someone.

During the more acute manic episodes, my mom's been known to throw out garbage bags full of family heirlooms, food, or clothing. Then she'll call the police to make a report. Burglars had broken in, stolen everything in her house, and replaced it with exact replicas. These extremely meticulous burglars were probably halfway to the Bahamas right now with her blocks of Velveeta and Precious Moments dolls while she was stuck with poisoned food and Chinese knockoffs only she was sharp enough to recognize. Out of respect for John, the cops came to the house for a while, longer than they would have for any garden variety loony. Eventually, though, you just can't keep feeding someone's delusion. Police man-hours cost money. It was actually pretty amazing someone hadn't gotten sick of her shit and pulled the trigger on an involuntary psych ward stay. If it weren't for John's pension and death benefit, all of which we'd set up to automatically pay her mortgage, utilities, allowance, and so on, I had no doubt she would have been roughing it down on Bustleton Avenue again. One of us, me or one of the two kids she and John had, would have had to step in and either institutionalize her or effectively destroy our own lives by letting her live with us.

She didn't appear manic now, but I still needed to proceed delicately. Acknowledge the imaginary crime and put it in the rearview as fast as possible. Pedal to the metal toward a more consensual reality.

"Well thank God she brought the Bugs Bunny dolls—"

"Charlie Brown figurines!" she said, her voice rising. "Bugs Bunny is a rat."

"I'm pretty sure he's a bunny, Ma. Okay, so Charlie Brown. She brought them back, right? No harm no foul."

"He's not nice."

"Who's not nice?"

"Bugs Bunny!"

"Well, people are shooting at him all the time; I probably wouldn't be too nice either."

"He gives Lucy all those ideas."

"Ma, I'm not sure if . . ."

"She's a nice person. Deep down. But Bugs is always whispering. Whispering, whispering, whispering."

"Wait, who now?"

"Lucy. You think she'd pull that football away on her own? Every time?"

"From Charlie Brown?"

"Yes from Charlie Brown! It's obvious Bugs Bunny behavior!"

I should have felt it earlier. The old familiar click under my foot. I had stepped on a land mine. I'd forgotten I was even in a minefield. All these traps laid for an imaginary enemy who would never come. More of us coming back limbless by the day.

The button was pushed now. I was still standing on it, though. Not dead yet, but I might as well be. Events had been set in motion, destruction was an inevitability. I saw my mom staring into the middle distance, dangling out there with the old spark in her eyes, the toxic certainty of her delusions. The patterns only she could see.

I felt myself begin to panic. I wanted to toss the soft pretzel at her as a distraction, pull down the cabinet full of stolen-and-replaced figurines, and make a dash for Carl Vehicle and drive. Drive anywhere. Off the Rhawn Street Bridge if I needed to. I didn't run, though. Instead I did something just as risky. Something I'd never done before. I told myself that if I willed myself to jump high enough off that mine, the explosion would propel me away, just like Tom Cruise at the end of the movie. Then I'd just sprout wings and fly home.

"I want to tell you about my ex-girlfriend, Mom," I said. "About what happened."

"You don't have to tell me. I'm sure it wasn't your fault," she said.

Hold the wheel. Steer into the skid.

"No, I *want* to tell you. Really."

Deep breaths. Calm mind.

"Okay, honey, sure."

And then, for the first time since I was eight and my wrist was broken in three places, I spoke openly and honestly to my mother about what I was going through emotionally.

I told her about how horrible and alone I felt after Elizabeth moved out. About the craziness with Lucy. About getting back with Elizabeth and the thirteen-month downward spiral that ended with her leaving and me hating myself.

I told her that it felt like I'd been incapable of rational

thought for over a year. She said I should start to worry if it lasted fifty. It was a joke. A pretty decent one too. I told her I felt like my emotions were cross-wired, that I couldn't see things that were plainly in front of me. That I had wanted everything to stay the way it was even though it wasn't that way anymore. That it felt like someone had crept in during the night and replaced Elizabeth with . . . an exact replica of her. And only I could see the difference. But I didn't want to know it, so I decided not to know it. And the harder I tried to see the idealized version of the way things were, the worse I felt and the further apart we grew. I was consumed with this frenzied desire to make it work, she with trying to blow it up, but without having the guts to take her foot off the land mine. And then I had to find out about it all on Facebook.

"What's Facebook?" my mom interjected.

"It's how people communicate now," I said. "It's on the Internet."

"Oh no," she said disapprovingly. "Noreen's boy got that Internet. Says he just sits in his room now looking at girls doing the most terrible things. This Elizabeth . . . she's an Internet girl then?"

"It's not like that, Mom. Facebook is . . ." I was at a loss how to put it into words she'd understand. "It's like a church social. Everyone's there and you can see all your friends."

"And everyone's naked," she confirmed.

"No, Ma, it's not a sex thing."

"Sounds like it was for her."

"You gotta trust me, it's pretty innocent stuff."

"Until someone steals your girlfriend."

"You never saw something like that happen at a church social?" This appeared to get through to her.

"All right, well, that's that then, huh?" This was her cue

that she was done talking about something. Normally I'd let it go, pull the ripcord on the conversation, but something made me keep going.

"I didn't come here to explain Facebook to you, Ma."

"I would hope not! Talking about that filth to your own mother. Who would do that?"

So I explained that the day I found out about Elizabeth and Jack was July 5, 2014, when a friend told me he'd seen them together the night before, and that they were making out at a local bar. And how it was four years to the day when my brother jumped into the Pacific Ocean and died.

"That's really not a funny thing," my mom observed.

"When you're right you're right, Ma."

"So what are you going to do?" my mom asked, after I'd finished putting it all out there.

"There's nothing to do," I said. "It's over between me and her."

"No," she said. "I mean, about this clown Jack. You just going to let that slide?"

And with that, I knew the Intruder had hightailed it out of there. Was probably off investigating the Freemason outpost on Pluto by now. This woman in front of me was Charlene, the Philly-tough no-diploma hairdresser who had worked a double shift so she could afford Kraft dinner for her kid. The one who knew if you started taking shit from people, they wouldn't stop giving it to you.

"You remember what I always used to tell you?"

"You told me a lot of things, Mom."

"About what to do when someone does you wrong," she explained.

"An eye for an eye?"

"That's a good one, but what else?"

"What goes around comes around?"

"That too. I was thinking more along the lines of 'pay-back's a bitch,'" she said.

Mom and I went on to have one of our most enjoyable conversations in years, spitballing increasingly fiendish ideas for retaliating against Jack. Her tactics focused on his car, mainly flat tires. My ideas ranged from online shaming, to using his real name in this book, to just kicking his ass one hot Venice summer night the way Joe McGill had done to me because I got to second base with Erin O'Shea.

Then I remembered the perverse way I'd enjoyed that ass kicking. How it meant that I had won. And I realized I was done fighting. I was done retaliating. Stop struggling and you'll float.

My mom seemed to sense the shift. Her eyes got red and she started blinking. Then she stood up, came over to me, and said, "Give me a hug." When she couldn't control her sobs, I heard her mutter "Aw, Christ." Then she held me tight awhile and told me she loved me. When she finally let go, she put her glasses back on and glared, assessing me like a figurine she'd finally determined was genuine.

"You didn't fail, Dan," she said finally. "With whatsername. You did the best you could. And you're a good person. And nothing else matters."

And that's a load of horseshit. But when your mother says it to you, you get to believe it. And that matters a whole fucking lot.

I PACKED SOME THINGS I found in the garage in a box to take with me. Among the keepsakes was a framed image of Led Zeppelin's "ZOSO" symbol that I'd won at a carnival when I was fifteen, a pulp novel titled *Dan Dunn, Secret Operative No. 48*, and a bedsheet that used to hang on the wall of a house my friends and I rented one summer in Ocean City, New Jersey.

Someone had spray painted "Welcome to the Jungle" on it, and it was signed by every young fuckup, delinquent, and miscreant who'd passed through that summer. None of us were young anymore. Three of the signees, I noted, were no longer alive. Probably because they met me.

My mom packed some soft pretzels and a six-pack of Yuengling and made me promise I wouldn't drink the beer while I was driving. It was time for the leg of the trip I'd been alternately dreading and anticipating the entire time. It was time to head for the Deep South.

"I'M PARTIAL TO 'PUSH IT' MYSELF."

CHAPTER 12

VIRGINIA AND NORTH CAROLINA

Winemaking in the South is like institutionalized racism. It's definitely there; we just like to pretend it doesn't exist. It's actually bizarre that winemaking isn't one of the first things we think of when we contemplate the southeastern United States, given both the rich historic wine heritage of the region and the preponderance of wineries there (there are more than 240 in Virginia alone). Still, though, wine hasn't joined the pantheon of southern culture exports along with triple-A baseball, deep-fried everything, and racial strife.

Virginia was home to the first commercial winemaking venture in the United States, which started two years before it was even called the United States. The Virginia Winemaking Company was founded by a thirty-one-year-old whippersnapper you might have heard of, one Thomas Jefferson. A sophisticated man with international tastes, Jefferson enjoyed three things beyond all others: American liberty, French wine, and

African women, often, one assumes, at the same time. Since this is a book about wine, though, I won't get into Sally Hemings (something Jefferson, who fathered six children with her, seemed incapable of doing) or political ideology.

In 1760, a seventeen-year-old Jefferson matriculated at William & Mary in Williamsburg. College kids back then liked to drink just as much as they do today, and over the next few years, TJ fell in with two of the most notable vinophiles in the colonies—Francis Fauquier (which I choose to pronounce "fuck-yeah"), the royal governor of Virginia; and George Wythe, Jefferson's law tutor. Both men had expansive cellars and introduced young Thomas to the pleasures of the finest Old World wines. I like to imagine Jefferson's "aha moment" with wine was similar to my experience drinking those incredible Bordeaux vintages with Charles Smith in Walla Walla. The parallels are eerie. For instance, after his wine awakening, Jefferson wrote the Declaration of Independence and helped found America. After my awakening, I wrote a bunch of dick jokes and binge-watched *Veep*. It's like we're the same person. Except that I have never had sex with a slave. I think we know who has the moral high ground here.

Over the next decade, Jefferson's interest in wine intensified and he built an impressive collection of his own. Then on a fateful day in 1773, one of his wine brokers swung by Monticello with an Italian winemaker named Philip Mazzei. Mazzei had spent eighteen years selling wine in London and had come to the New World with the intention of cultivating Old World grapes (i.e., vinifera). Indeed, he was on his way to a parcel of land in Augusta, Georgia, that had been promised to him by the Brits. When he saw the land at Monticello, however, he immediately recognized it as a primo grape-growing location. With a hearty "*fottere Georgia!*" he and Jefferson struck up a partnership.

Mazzei got some land and the assistance of Jefferson's, ahem, "uncompensated workforce," in exchange for planting and maintaining vineyards at Monticello. He was also very taken with the American cause, which was cooking along underground at the time, and endeared himself to many of the founding fathers. A year later, in 1774, when the Virginia Wine Company was born, Jefferson, George Washington, and several other prominent colonists were among its financial backers. But while their ideals may have been unassailable, their timing was for shit. Two years after the VWC was founded, Jefferson wrote the Declaration of Independence, forcing George to spend an inordinate amount of time on the road and making life more than a little dicey for area winemakers.

By 1778 the plucky ~~land stealers~~ colonists found themselves in dire financial straits. Eventually it got so bad that they sent Mazzei, their bestest *paisano* (who had become quite the American patriot), back to Italy to rustle up some more money for the war effort from his rich Italian friends. Rather than let his estate lie fallow during this time, Mazzei rented his place out to Heinrich Riedesel, a Hessian general captured by the Americans and being held as a prisoner of war. The fact that a POW was allowed to rent out a plush Virginia plantation is just another example of how civilized war was back then. Wait, that's wrong. Sorry, got confused. War is never civilized. This is an example of the fact that when you're rich, you get to do whatever the fuck you want.

In a development only everyone could have seen coming, it turns out Mazzei Airbnb-ing his place to an opposition general was not the best idea. Riedesel, in a truly impressive dick move, pastured his horses in the baby vineyards Mazzei had so lovingly cared for over the previous four years, utterly destroying them. Jefferson later wrote that the "horses in one week destroyed the whole labour of three or four years, and thus ended an experiment, which, from every appearance, would in a year or two more have established the practicability of that branch of culture in America." Which imparts an important lesson. Always check that "no pets" box.

The Virginia Wine Company would never produce a single bottle of wine, setting a new standard of productivity government officials have been trying to live up to ever since. On the plus side, the Americans won the war, paving the way for Jefferson to succeed Ben Franklin as French minister. His friends thought the change in scenery would do him good after the death of his wife, and he ended up staying for five years. During that time he took two major wine expeditions, producing important historical documentation of that period's winemaking customs along with copious tasting notes. Apparently I'm not the first person to think of using a wine road-trip to mend a broken heart. I'd say he's a better man than I, if not for the fact that he sent for Sally Hemings three years into his trip. Phew, thought I was losing my moral high ground there for a sec.

While Jefferson's cultivation efforts failed, he was enormously influential on American taste in wine, pushing toward the drier, lower alcohol wines favored by the French and Italians as opposed to the syrupy high-test plonk the British liked to throw back. He was instrumental in establishing European-style wines as a staple at White House dinners, starting with the George Washington administration. If Mazzei had been given a few more years to get Monticello's grapes in shape before they were trampled by Teutonic demon horses, who knows how much faster we might have started catching up with Europe on wine quality.

The important thing, of course, is that we got there. It just took two centuries. Almost exactly two centuries, actually. In 1976, the bicentennial of the Declaration of Independence, another Italian came to Virginia with almost exactly the same dream as Philip Mazzei—make wine from vinifera in Virginia. Gabriele Rausse, however, had the good sense not to start a vineyard during the birth trauma of modern democracy.

As a vigneron for hire, Rausse spent the late 1970s and early 1980s establishing some of Virginia's oldest and most distinguished wineries. He played a pivotal role in the development of fourteen of the state's most prominent producers, among them Barboursville, Kluge Estate, and Jefferson Vineyards (now with 100 percent fewer slaves!). Nearly forty years later, the 240-plus wineries operating in Virginia owe a lot to Rausse, the man who finally realized Jefferson's and Mazzei's vision.

Fittingly, Rausse is now director of the gardens and grounds at Monticello. He agreed to show me around, and I spent two hours touring the grounds, marveling at the sheer amount of wine-related knowledge the man carries around in his head. Rausse's mind is an almanac of names, dates, locations—he's got the inside dope on virtually every significant development in the history of the Virginia wine industry. I gave him a nickname, Winipedia, but he didn't seem to like it too much. In fact I got the distinct impression he would gut me like a hog if I continued using it.

Another thing about Rausse, the man has no filter, and no compunction about letting you know who he believes has wronged him. The list is impressive and includes Virginia State officials, several well-respected Virginia vintners, and the Enology Department at Virginia Tech, which Rausse claims conspired many years ago to have him deported for "poisoning the minds of local farmers" by preaching the gospel of vinifera and encouraging them to grow Sangiovese and Cabernet Franc.

"I tell them, you can no throw me out of this country. I know my rights. I have a right to grow these grapes," he said, getting excited. "Thomas Jefferson himself grew these grapes! Would they throw Thomas Jefferson out of the country? No, they would not. It's not possible."

I did some research on this last claim, and I believe he is correct. No way are you kicking Thomas Jefferson out of this joint now. Dude is OG (Originalist Gangster). I inquired as to who, in particular, had threatened to send him back to Italy over his agricultural ambitions, so I could get their side of the story, but Gabriele demurred. "Is better you don't talk with these people," he said with a dismissive wave of his hand. "It's over now. I won." Then he took me to Jefferson's grave and told me which Virginia winemakers have their heads up their asses. Lest you think he's just an embittered old man, Rausse also said lots of nice things about his fellow winemakers. But that's far less entertaining, isn't it?

Talking to Rausse was incredibly eye opening about how far the Virginia wine industry has come, a fact that was driven home as I pulled out of Monticello and looked down the hill where two more successful wineries sit side by side on some of the most pristine land in the United States. Both are owned by scrappy upstarts who epitomize American ingenuity. One of them rocks out for screaming, hairy fans in stadiums. The other rocks a screamingly odious hairpiece in the shape of a stadium. I'm talking, of course, about Dave Matthews and Donald Trump.

The Donald, who claims he doesn't drink (except "when

I drink my little wine and eat my little cracker" in church), got into the wine game in 2011 when he bought Kluge's spectacular 776-acre vineyard. As Trump told the *Washington Post* at the time, "I'm really interested in good real estate, not so much in wine."

The winery was founded in 1999 by a socialite named Patricia Kluge, on the site of Mazzei's old residence, Albermarle House, where he'd quartered the Hessians and their asshole horses. Kluge built a lavish new Albermarle residence and poured piles of money into planting vineyards (hiring Gabriele Rausse for the work, natch). For a while, her gambit appeared to be paying off, as Kluge wines pulled down a clutch of awards and quickly gained a reputation as one of the state's premier producers. Then Kluge went all-in on a major expansion, just as the economy nosedived in 2008. The ill-timed investment ended up costing her the vineyard. With her hand forced, Kluge put the house and land on the market for $100 million, but got no offers. The bank foreclosed. It was a miserable situation.

And as we all know, where there is misery, there is Trump.

The land was auctioned off in parcels, much of it at fire-sale rates. However, the bank held out for big bucks for the plantation house itself. So Trump bought the relatively cheap parcel of land that included the house's front lawn. At that sale, Trump's general counsel commented on the house's $16 million asking price, asking, "Who's going to pay that for a house with no front yard?" They ended up picking up the house for $6.5 million after the bank apparently realized they'd been Trumped. Great job ruining everything, Bank of America. Oh, and great job letting Donald Trump into the wine game. This is why we can't have nice things.

The tycoon's first order of business was to change the name

of the winery from one that carried a great deal of cachet in those parts, to one that has come to represent tacky, self-indulgent buffoonery. And you'd think that would be the end of the story. Another low-quality, overpriced product for Trump to stick his name on. Not so. In a shockingly cogent move for someone whose idea of business acumen is bragging about the size of his cock, Donald installed his son Eric as head of operations at Trump Winery and got the hell out of his way. The younger Trump brought on a team of sharp wine professionals, who started producing great wine right out of the gate. Remember when I said Gabriele Rausse said nice things about people too? Many of them were about Trump winemaker Jonathan Wheeler. In Rausse's opinion, he's one of the bright young stars of Virginia winemaking. Which means there is now a Trump product on the market that *doesn't* make you feel like you just bought a refrigerator in Antarctica. Some would call that a step in the right direction. I say call me when he shaves his head and starts doing charity work in Calcutta.

In a wonderfully jarring juxtaposition, directly across the road from Trump and up the street from Jefferson's old home, is Blenheim Vineyards, owned by David John "Dave" Matthews. Maybe you've heard of him. He's a musician.

Matthews built Blenheim, which opened in 2000, on a site listed in the National Register of Historic Places. As you might expect from a rock star who played his first public gig on Earth Day, the winery is a model of environmental friendliness. The building was constructed from reclaimed wood and is lined with south-facing windows and skylights, which let the space operate without electric light during the summer. In winter, the tasting room benefits from passive solar heating throughout the day. I felt like I was doing my part to save the planet just by drinking there. Well, that, and not giving money to Donald Trump.

Now I know what you're asking yourself. Did I prefer the wine of the guy who played campaign fund-raisers for Obama, or the juice made by the guy who raised questions about his birth certificate? Honestly, it's a toss-up. Each has a high-quality Bordeaux blend in its portfolio, some lively Rosé, and the crisp, floral Viognier that's a staple at virtually every Virginia winery. When you factor in the socially conscious rock star and all-around good guy factor versus the raging narcissistic megalomaniac nutjob factor, it's tempting to give Blenheim the nod. Then again, if I learned anything on this trip, it's that the only common ground required between winemaker and wine lover is the stuff in the glass. Then *again* again, one of these two vintners is on record as saying "I have a great relationship with the blacks" and defended his decision not to share his "surefire secret plan" for defeating Islamic terrorists by telling the interviewer "Because I don't want to!"

Sorry, Dave, I gotta give it to Trump here. He's just that gifted of an entertainer.

MIDDLEBURG IS AN AFFLUENT ENCLAVE located fifty miles west of Washington, D.C., in Loudoun County. Many rich and famous people have called Middleburg home, including John and Jackie Kennedy, Liz Taylor, Paul Mellon, Robert Duvall, Willard Scott, and Sheila Johnson, the billionaire founder of BET. I stayed at Johnson's place, actually. Not her home, but the 340-acre resort she owns in the foothills of the Blue Ridge Mountains called Salamander. In truth, Sheila Johnson has no idea who I am. Indeed, she is one of a number of billionaires—that number being the sum total of *all* the billionaires—to whom I am a stranger.

My first stop in Middleburg was Boxwood Winery, a marvel of modernist design. Rachel Martin, Boxwood's executive vice president, tasted me through a delightful array of

Bordeaux-style reds. My favorite among them was Topiary, a blend of Cabernet Franc and Merlot that would hold its own against almost any of the standout wines I'd had in Northern California and Oregon.

Later, we had dinner in the Gold Cup Wine Bar at Salamander with another unflinching iconoclast, Jennifer McCloud of Chrysalis Vineyards. Jenni delivered a lively and comprehensive sermon on the history and merits of wine made from Virginia's most successful grape, Norton, of which Chrysalis is the world's leading purveyor. Norton is a hybrid created in 1821 by amateur horticulturist Dr. Daniel Norton, which became a vineyard staple across the East Coast and throughout the Midwest in the nineteenth century. By 1930, Norton had all but disappeared, done in by the twin demons of the California wine industry and Prohibition. Still, the hardy Norton—most likely the oldest native grape now being widely cultivated in America—has made a comeback in its old stomping grounds, thanks in large part to the unstoppable Jenni McCloud.

After our dinner I retired to my room at the Salamander and surfed to its website, looking for local color. Did I ever luck out. The site contains copious passages from *The Visitor's Guide to Middleburg, Virginia and the Surrounding John Singleton Mosby Heritage Area* by the late Audrey Windsor Bergner. And it's fascinating stuff. For instance, I learned that "long before the advent of Englishmen on the shores of Virginia, Algonquin, Iroquois and Cherokee tribes roamed, farmed and hunted this land." And that these Native Americans "left behind a legacy" of trails along Goose Creek and Little River, before they "decided to move westward" as a result of "pressure from white settlers."

I imagine the situation was similar to the time when thousands of Japanese Americans "decided to go camping" as a result of "gentle prodding" from the U.S. government during World War II. Or that time Hitler threw that going-away party for all the Jews in Europe.

Being in the middle of a cross-country attempt to spray cologne on my own past's stank, I couldn't really quibble about the way some deceased southern matron had tried to polish one of history's foulest turds, though. In an effort to forget all about both, I made the brilliant decision to see what was up on Tinder. And Middleburg's online dating scene did not disappoint. Of the first ten swipe-rights I got six matches. The most promising was Bobbi, thirty-four, a Yale grad who had her own "wellness business" and was a self-proclaimed "badass." Ah, but she was also "looking for the real deal only. NO HOOKUPS!" Unfortunately, my real deal was that I was only in town for the night. Oh well.

Lyssa, thirty-three, had potential. She looked like Eva Mendes with blond hair, down to the same cute mole on her left cheek. According to her profile, Lyssa wants a man she can sing Salt-n-Pepa's "Whatta Man" to and mean it. I wondered if she'd settle for "Push It." Personally, I've always wanted to meet a woman I can sing A Tribe Called Quest's "I Left My Wallet in El Segundo" to. Because I mean it.

Lyssa wrote that she wanted to "die with memories, not dreams," which I interpreted to mean she hopes she doesn't pass away in her sleep. In general, I think death is a topic best left out of a dating profile, along with STD outbreak schedules, your criminal record, and photos of your ex.

A notification popped up—Bobbi, the Yale grad wellness badass, had sent me a message.

Hey! <

> Hey!

You're very handsome. <

> That's very nice of you to say.
  You're very pretty.

Thx ;) <

> I'll also have you know I'm a mighty
  good man. A mighty mighty good man.

(If a lady wants some Salt-n-Pepa, I bring the Salt-n-Pepa.)
A good five minutes went by with no response.

> That was from the Salt-n-Pepa
  song you like.

Five more minutes and still nothing from Bobbi. Maybe I
wasn't Whatta Man-worthy, after all.

After five more minutes, I realized I'd crossed Bobbi with
Lyssa. Shit. Rookie mistake. I attempted a Hail Mary play.

> Ha! I meant to say the Salt-n-Pepa
  song I like. It was on the radio while I
  was messaging you and . . . oh god,
  I just admitted to being a Salt-n-Pepa
  fan, didn't I?

After several minutes of radio silence from Bobbi, I turned
my attention to Lyssa who had yet to respond. Desperate
much, Danny?

I'm partial to "Push It" myself <

It was Bobbi. And bringing the innuendo!

> That's a classic. And let's talk about
  sex . . . the song, I mean ;)

Haha <

> Ha!

Where do you live? <

The truth was probably a deal breaker, but I went with it anyway. I was really growing as a person.

> Nowhere currently, I'm on a
cross-country drive.

So you're looking for a hookup? <
Lovely. Did you read my profile?

> I did. But I assure you I am the
REAL DEAL. I just don't live here.

Four minutes. Tick, tick.

> Plus, you're too damn pretty
to swipe left. It just felt wrong ;)

Five minutes. Tick tick tock. Apparently I would be getting neither Salt nor Pepa.

I went to the bathroom and took two 5-milligram Ambien pills. Normally one does the trick, but I was feeling antsy and had a long drive the next day. I really needed a good night's rest. I plopped on the bed and turned on the TV. *Dateline* was on, the perfect thing to slowly stop caring about. They were investigating the disappearance of an attractive young mother from Georgia. Isn't that what every episode of *Dateline* is about? The murders of pretty white women? I didn't even need to watch to know that the husband did it. For the money. It's always for the money. Zurr zurr talking head zurr . . .

DING! A notification on my phone. Another message from Bobbi!

How long are you in town? <

> Jus t onigh, unfornaly.

Where are you staying? <

I told her the name of my hotel. As I felt the Ambien kick into gear, I began worrying if this might be some sort of con. "Sure! Maybe! Who cares!" my brain replied. This was the first time on the trip I'd gone beyond the "just looking" stage on Tinder and I was on prescription meds. Coincidence? Who cares! I was on autopilot now.

There's a bar just down the street <
from your hotel. I'll meet you there
for a drink in half an hour.

> Ok, sure.

And that, ladies and gentlemen, is some sparkling repartee. Great job, Dan. Really excellent work.

Did you know it's possible to forget you took Ambien? It's true! Any guess when that is most likely to happen? When you're on a high dose of Ambien. The thrill of man-lady interaction had roused me to burst through my oncoming stupor, and that same stupor convinced me it was perfectly normal for me to be heading out at 11 P.M. in a strange town to meet a total stranger in a place I'd never been before. I feel dumb even writing this down, because adults are supposed to be responsible with the drugs our doctors prescribe to us. "I'm sorry, Dr. Johnson," I thought to myself as I pulled the hotel door open and tottered out into the night.

I WOKE UP WITH A start. It took me a second to get my bearings. I was in the hotel room. Phew. The clock on the nightstand said 6:30 . . . That's A.M., right? Had to be A.M. Otherwise, I would have lost a whole day. I couldn't have lost a whole day, could I?

Could I?

Okay, let's take a look around and . . . WELL NOW. There's a lady in my bed. A no-clothes-type lady. Asleep, thankfully. I peered around to get a look at her face. It was Bobbi. The one who didn't do hookups. And an easy match to her Tinder photos. On the minus side, I had no idea what the hell had transpired. On the plus side, hear-hear for accurate Tinder profile photos.

I strained my mind back to the previous night. I remembered leaving the hotel. I remembered taking a cab. I remembered arriving at the bar. I remembered meeting her. I remembered thinking she was prettier in person and didn't appear to be either a prostitute or serial killer. I remembered ordering a drink. I remembered confessing that I'd taken the Ambien. I remembered her thinking that was hilarious. I remembered her suggestion I stick to cola or water. After that I remember nothing.

We were both naked. Had we had sex? No idea. I looked around for signs—used condom, condom wrapper, trashed sheets, tearstained cheeks. I didn't see anything conclusive. My wallet was on the dresser. Everything was in order. But what about my . . .

The clock now said 8:30. Bobbi was gone.

The clock now said 11:30. Not good. And now I had enough of my brain working to start making sense of the world. I grabbed my phone to text Bobbi, only to find I had somehow never gotten her number. Or her last name. I sent her a message via Tinder.

> Had a great time last night (I think).
> I'll be in Barboursville tonight. Not sure
> how far that is, but maybe you want to
> come meet me down there? This time
> no Ambien!

Five minutes.

Ten minutes.

Twenty-four hours.

Bobbi, if you end up reading this somehow, please get in touch. I am genuinely curious how our night went, no matter how humiliating it might be. Okay, strike that. If it involves farm animals or Donald Trump, please don't tell me what I did.

I swore off Tinder for the remainder of the journey. I'd like to think I went out with a bang, but truthfully, I have no idea. When I mentioned this to Brian during the drive to Charlottesville the next day, the only response was, "Dude, seriously?"

When Brian is criticizing your behavior, you have done something truly odious. Speaking of which . . .

....

WINE AROMAS EXPLAINED

OLD SADDLE LEATHER
Or, as Maureen O'Hara used to say, smells like John Wayne's ass.

BABY DIAPER
A scent common to Chardonnay from Burgundy, where the delicate poo of French infants is often added to oak barrels during aging.

GRUMPY CAT PEE
It's got forty-five zillion YouTube views!
Hay!
Whassup girl?

BOILED CABBAGE
Or, as John Wayne used to say, smells like Maureen O'Hara's ass.

DIESEL
A petrol-like aroma often found in Rieslings from Australia and American street racing movie franchises. Also known as Le Vin Diesel.

PENCIL LEAD
Commonly associated with the red wines of Bordeaux, it's the No. 2 most familiar wine scent in the world.

MUSK
Think Pete Rose doused in Aqua Velva . . . it smells like man.

ROTTEN EGG
Redolent of that goddamn low-life brother-in-law of yours.

DIRTY DISHCLOTH
Next time try using a clean glass.

WET CARDBOARD
The UPS guy dropped the box with your wine club delivery again.

WET DOG
. . . on top of your poor shih tzu.

SWEATY SOCKS
Scent commonly associated with now-defunct brand Pete Rose's Sparkling Rosé.

BISCUITY
Like the treats you used to give your poor dead wine-crushed shih tzu.

I'M NOT SURE WHAT IT is, but something about Virginia seems to bring out the oversize personality. Of all the winemakers I met along my oenophilic odyssey, Rutger de Vink of RdV Vineyards in Delaplane, Virginia, is the one most likely to inspire a character in a romance novel. Tall, rugged, handsome. Dutch. Came to the United States in high school, then joined the Marines. Served in a recon unit in Somalia, where it's entirely possible he took down hordes of terrorists with his bare hands (de Vink, always the gentleman, had no comment). After the military, he earned an MBA from Northwestern and started making gobs of money in the financial sector. Then one day he decided he'd had enough of that soul-killing bullshit, quit his job, and devoted his life to working the land. He fell in love with winemaking. Seriously, if you're looking for someone who could hold his own in a cage match between Thomas Jefferson, Philip Mazzei, Dave Matthews, and Donald Trump, I gotta say, it's de Vink all de vay.

In the early 2000s, de Vink studied under the godfather of Virginia winemaking, Jim Law of Linden Vineyards. He then bought a perfect plot of vine land overlooking the Blue Ridge Mountains where he lives to this day in an Airstream.

I say again. *In an Airstream.*

De Vink wisely recruited two of the world's top consultants, Eric Boissenot and fellow Dutchman Kees Van Leeuwen, to help him realize his dream of producing world-class Bordeaux varieties in Virginia. RdV Vineyards's first release was 2008. And today it is producing, in my humble opinion, the best wine in Virginia. I would drink these wines every day of the week and twice on Sunday. In fact, I drank two bottles of Rendezvous last Sunday before church. After which, like every week, I skipped church. In fact, you could classify almost every alcoholic beverage I've ever had as "before church." I'm going to go one day, I swear. I hear it's just like Tinder when you're in your seventies.

Did I mention that Rutger de Vink's dog has been on the cover of *GQ Magazine*? It's true. And Rutger wrestles bears for charity. Then he rehabilitates the vanquished bears and teaches them how to harvest grapes. And then get MBAs. He's a remarkable man.

De Vink found a mentor in Jim Law, who played a major role in bringing Virginia wine to the national stage. Law moved to Virginia in 1983 and purchased an abandoned farm off Route 638, transforming a hardscrabble plot into one of the East Coast's finest vineyards. The man knows how to make wine as well as anyone who's ever done it down there, and he went ahead and laid some technical explanations of key vineyard-related language on me. I've translated them here as best I can.

....

VOCABULARY OF THE VINEYARD

TERROIR
The supercilious asshole word for "dirt."

DOWNY MILDEW
A highly destructive disease that attacks all parts of the vine and can result in severe crop loss. As mildews go, it's the quicker picker upper.

ASPERSION
Technique in which water sprinklers are used to protect budding vines from late-spring frosts. Centuries ago, the French—who pioneered this technique—would, in fact, hurl insults at the grapes to toughen them up, which is where the phrases "thick skin," "cast aspersions," and "the French are dicks" originated.

BUSH TRAINING

A term that sounds like the punch line to an off-color joke, but in actuality is a growing system where vines are kept individually and not supported by trellises.

EMASCULATION

The removal of the male parts of a hermaphroditic grapevine flower in order to prevent self-pollination. As a daily self-pollinator, this is yet another reason I'm glad I'm not a grapevine.

LEACHING

A process of barrel production during which tannins are deliberately removed from the wood by steaming. Also, a process of taking advantage of wine producers across America by promising them glowing coverage in your book in exchange for first-class lodging, expensive meals, and an endless supply of strong drink.

PHYLLOXERA

A minuscule insect capable of bringing the wine industry to its knees.

VERAISON

The onset of ripening.

VERIZON

The iPhone autocorrect for the wine term for the onset of ripening.

VINTAGE

Wine made from grapes that were all, or primarily, grown and harvested in a single specified year. Also, my fourth favorite porn category (behind emasculation, bush training, and downy mildew).

I WAS RELUCTANT TO LEAVE Virginia and its outsize characters, but it was time to move on (also Bobbi had not responded to any of my messages). Next stop was Shelton Vineyards, which sits twenty miles south of the Virginia border and forty-five miles northwest of Winston-Salem. I didn't know what to expect when I visited North Carolina's largest family-owned winery. All I knew was that it becomes increasingly difficult to cultivate vinifera the farther south you travel down the eastern seaboard.

Casey Hough of Visit Winston-Salem was waiting for me at Shelton. Casey's a stand-up guy and native North Carolinian who would act as my wingman/tour guide over the next several days. Over lunch at the Harvest Grill, Casey provided me with plenty of useful information about the region he represents, while I filled him in on the various parts of my body that were no longer functioning properly as a result of riding the road so hard for so long.

Casey told me that Winston-Salem is often referred to as the gateway to the Yadkin Valley, an area that was once synonymous with tobacco growing, but that in recent years has become a hotbed for the wine industry. I informed him that since pulling out of Boston, I'd had no feeling whatsoever in my right ass cheek. Also, I was pretty sure I'd sprained my liver back in Michigan. Goddamn ice wine. According to Casey, the Yadkin Valley AVA is comparable to Italy in climate and soil types. He was surprised to learn that "ball throbbiness" is an actual condition that can result from a combination of dehydration and spending too much time behind the wheel of a Toyota SUV.

After lunch we met up with Gill Giese, the head winemaker at Shelton. We started out talking about Shelton's wines, but ended up ranting about this country's confounding shipping laws. In case you didn't know, booze-shipping laws vary from state to state. Which is superconvenient when you want to, for example, ship a goddamn bottle of wine to one of the forty-nine states you're not currently in. In Florida it's legal to get shipments directly from a winery, but not from a retailer. In Louisiana, the opposite is the case. Some states, such as Pennsylvania, Utah, and Mississippi, don't allow any direct shipping. California is essentially a free-for-all.

But there is one thing that's true across the board. No one gives a shit about the rules.

"Far as I know, nobody's been prosecuted for illegally receiving wine for their own personal consumption in this country since Prohibition," Gill said. "But you might want to look it up."

I did, and he's correct. I also discovered that the knot of rules that stymied wine commerce for decades was largely untangled in 2005 when the U.S. Supreme Court ruled that states could no longer ban out-of-state wineries from shipping wine directly to consumers while allowing in-state wine producers to do so. The court voted to level the playing field, paving the way for a future in which anyone will be able to obtain wine from anywhere. This, in conjunction with the recent swell of high-quality regional producers, might be just the catalyst America needs to get its great regional wines into the glasses of consumers who might otherwise dismiss them out of hand. The revolution is coming, people. Via UPS.

FOR ALMOST A CENTURY, THE site where RayLen Vineyards is located was home to a working dairy farm. In 1989, however, a merciless hurricane called Hugo paid a visit, and the dairy farm was reduced to ground beef. The land sat vacant for a decade until Joe and Joyce Neely bought the place and planted some vines. In 2001, RayLen became the fifth bonded winery in the Yadkin Valley AVA. Today, there are more than four times that many in the area.

When vintner Steve Shepard started making wines for RayLen in 2000, they produced about twenty-five hundred cases of mostly Chardonnay, Merlot, and Shiraz. RayLen now has forty-five acres planted with a variety of grapes such as Viognier, Cabernet, and Vidal Blanc, and they do eight to ten thousand cases a year.

When Casey took me to meet Erin Doby of RayLen Vineyards & Winery, the first thing I said was "How y'all doin', darlin'?" because I am an asshole. I chewed on a piece of straw for added effect because I also dabble in being a dick. Erin, a model of professionalism, was unfazed, simply saying "How y'all doin'" right back and proceeding to pour me a sample of every wine in the tasting room—nearly twenty in all. Thank goodness I had Casey to chauffeur me around. Even better, he refused both tips and sexual favors in lieu of tips (my old standby).

RayLen's most popular wine is a $20 Bordeaux-style blend called "Category 5," a nod to the intensity of the storm that cleared the way for the vineyards. But while I appreciate the twisted homage, my personal favorite bottle was the 2013 Carolinius, a medium-bodied Cabernet blend with bright fruit and unobtrusive tannins. As for the whites, the crisp Pinot Grigio and the elegant Viognier were standouts.

Casey whisked me down to Divine Llama, a small winery owned and operated by a couple of old college buddies, Michael West and Thomas Hughes. They're both architects with a mutual appreciation of fermented grape juice. In 2006 they purchased seventy-seven acres in East Bend and planted five acres of vines that yield about twelve hundred cases a year. The rest of the property is reserved for llamas. Yes, llamas. Because, you know, we are talking about North Carolina. That's llama country.

"In a Heartbeat" is a semidry red blend named after an Appaloosa llama that took third place overall in a national competition a few years back, according to tasting room manager Dana Dalton.

"Wow, that's impressive," I said. "How many other wines were in the competition?"

"Oh, I'm not talking about the wine," she replied. "I'm talking about the llama."

And if that's not already a punch line to a Jeff Foxworthy joke, it should be.

The final place Casey took me to was Sanders Ridge, a farm that's been in the Shore family for 170 years. Neil Shore, who's been farming the land all his life, started planting vines back in 2000, mostly French varietals that today produce around twenty-five hundred cases a year. Neil told me that Sanders Ridge is the only winery to win "Best in Show" in two categories in the same year at the North Carolina State Fair—in 2009 their Muscat Canelli bested all white wines and their Muscadine was picked as the best native grape. Right before the judges took on their ultimate challenge: deciding whether deep-fried, bacon-wrapped peanut butter cups were better than the legendary Twinx. If you're wondering, a Twinx is not, in fact, a category of porn, but rather a deep-fried, bacon-wrapped Twinkie with a Twix bar inside it. Like I said, it's not a category of porn. It's the physical form of porn.

Neil built the tasting room and restaurant himself, everything from the structure to the tables and chairs. The place is filled with old photos chronicling the Shore family's rich history. Neil is especially fond of his aunt Beatrice, who was born in 1898 and lived to be 106 years old.

"She lived in three different centuries," Neil said, shaking his head. "Not many folks can say that."

I resisted the urge to say, "Including Aunt Beatrice." It's all about the moral high ground.

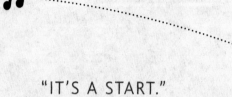

"IT'S A START."

CHAPTER 13

GEORGIA, LOUISIANA

It was one of those roadside antique shops you find in places that are just far enough from a city to be considered the country. This one happened to be in northern Georgia, right at the beginning of the Appalachian foothills. It was a good little spot. And for reasons I'm not entirely clear on, I purchased a thirty-pound bronze ram's head there.

Of all the items I could have bought at White County's largest consignment store, why did I choose a giant metal effigy of a farm animal? I'm not sure, but I'm fairly confident it has something to do with my budding case of *Viopsychostrictia arbiosa*. This is the technical term for what happens to your brain when you expose it for too long to a combination of fatigue, stress, the interminable flatness of the Great Plains, and a diet rich in donuts and Arby's, then combine that with running over the occasional small house pet. Hey, someone has to keep Arby's in business.

Basically when humans spend too much time behind the wheel, shit gets real weird. It's been documented. Sal Paradise didn't split for Mexico because it was prudent. Hell, he nearly died of dysentery down there and it would have served him right. But see, all that time on the road drove him to it. That and he was still pretty busted up over losing Terry and her kid. Plus, Dean Moriarty was this vortex of duende. He says let's go to Mexico, you go to Mexico. You just do it. State of grace. Muskrat love. Excalibur, man.

Originally, I named the ram's head Sautee-Nacoochee after the village I thought I bought it in. It was only after I got home that I discovered the Nacoochee Village Antique Mall is actually located about three miles northwest of Sautee-Nacoochee in a tiny town called Helen. Now, I couldn't very well change the ram's head's name to Helen, not unless I wanted him to get teased incessantly by all my other weird collectibles. Pancho Sansabelt (a shellacked, dead frog from Mexico who has been made to appear like he's playing the congas) can be especially vicious. So after much deliberation (a.k.a. three glasses of wine), I decided to call him Michael Stipe. This, of course, is also the name of the lead singer of the greatest rock-and-roll band Georgia has ever produced (if you don't count Reptar, who are, pound for pound, one of the best bands on offer in today's kaleidoscopic indie landscape; thankfully Reptar didn't start up until R.E.M. was done, though, so the two never had to throw down). Plus, Pancho Sansabelt is a huge *Fables of the Reconstruction* fan.

R.E.M. is responsible for one of the three songs that never fail to make me think of Brian. According to R.E.M. bassist Mike Mills, "Nightswimming" is about the times in the early 1980s when the band and their friends used to go skinny-dipping after the clubs would close in their hometown of Athens. As nostalgia triggers go, I realize it's a bit on the nose. But I've found these things often are. For instance, every time I hear "Leaving on a Jet Plane" I'm reminded of my aunt Louise, the one who died on the Pan Am flight that terrorists blew up over Lockerbie, Scotland, in 1988. Even now, I get sad just recalling my story about Aunt Louise and how she lost her imaginary life just so that I could get out of taking a difficult art history final. In those days, I was a virtual serial killer with a focus on the family. Hell, by sophomore year I'd killed off at least four grandmothers, a cousin or two, an uncle in a Fort Meade helicopter accident, and, of course, poor Louise. I now realize that the only reason these tales were remotely credible was that the actual rubble and destruction in my life made them look in proportion. It's hard to tell when a kid's lying about his dead aunt when his real family is dropping like flies.

But so the ram's head. It was a cold, sunny morning in November. I parked alongside the Chattahoochee River near Helen. I found a beautiful spot filled with lots of tall trees. My guess is they were pine trees, but I'm not sure. Dendrology is not my thing (yes, I Googled it). The river was running strong, though. I listened to "Nightswimming" and, surprisingly, didn't cry. Not a single tear. It's usually automatic. So I listened to it again, only this time I went and grabbed the mason jar with Brian's ashes in it out of Carl Vehicle's center console and brought it down so he could see it too. That did it. I wept like a Best Actress winner.

> *And what if there were two*
> *Side by side in orbit around the fairest sun?*

I had pulled off the road to shoot up on raw sentimentality, a risky proposition for neurotics like me. Reminiscing makes me uncomfortable. It's a gateway drug to self-loathing. On an intellectual level I understand that grief is a perfectly normal and natural response to loss in the same way that I recognize indictment and arrest are perfectly normal and natural responses to crime. Still, I find myself ashamed or uncertain about the way I process pain in the same way no one in their right mind thinks the law enforcement system in the United States is a universally (or even occasionally) impartial instrument. And no amount of good cops you put on the street will change that. So I hope you'll pardon me for rolling my eyes when I pull myself over for driving while emotional. I look back at losing my brother, my girlfriend, or my dog and alternately scold myself for taking so long to get over them and revile myself for being some kind of zombie robot sociopath for not being more broken up about them.

Agonizing over whether or not I'm agonizing properly.

It's a well-worn rabbit hole for me, given my ill-starred existence thus far. Half the time I worry that people are going to look at me and think I'm so full of shit my eyes have turned brown. (This would be easier to disprove if my eyes were not, in fact, brown.) Half the time, I want to punch those same people for even entertaining the possibility. Luckily, the one thing that doesn't scare me is *actually* being full of shit. I've known that I'm full of shit for a very long time. It's pretty much the one thing I'm comfortable with in life.

I'm grateful for the fact that on the occasions I've had uncontrollable crying jags when listening to the three songs that remind me of my dead brother, no one else has been around. Next to that river in North Georgia, I just let it go and bawled. When "Nightswimming" was over, I switched to another R.E.M. song, "It's the End of the World As We Know It (and I Feel Fine)." I played that twice too. Sang along both times. I feel fine. I feel fine. I feel fine. After a while I actually kind of did.

Then I opened the mason jar and dumped approximately two tablespoons of ashes into my hand and clenched it tight. It's the end of the world as we know it. I feel fine.

I waited. Holding on for just a minute. Be here for this. Don't rush.

Now.

I threw the ashes up high, ready to watch Brian atomize and float away on the breeze. The breeze, however, had other plans and blew about half of Brian back into my hair and face. Oh, hey buddy. You smell like an ashtray. The mason jar was about half full now. Or half empty. Or twice as big as it needed to be (rest in peace, George Carlin).

....

R.E.M.'S TEN BEST ALBUMS PAIRED WITH VINTAGE AMERICAN WINE

"Nightswimming" is on *Automatic for the People,* which I regard as R.E.M.'s best album, just ahead of *Document* and *Murmur.* Some purists will tell you that's blasphemy, but I've never given much of half a shit about purity. Also, I'm aware that not everyone is an R.E.M. fan, but even if you don't like the music, I think we can at least agree they have a knack for album titles. If I didn't know a single thing about the band and someone said to me, hey, would you like to listen to *Life's Rich Pageant* or *Monster* or *New Adventures in Hi-Fi,* I would listen to it, just to see if they were as awesome as they sound (they are). Given that one of this band's songs is about my dead brother, I think I speak as a completely impartial unbiased bystander in this.

Over the three decades that R.E.M. was making sensational music, American vintners were producing exquisite wines. I invited a few sommelier friends—because I have sommelier friends now—to weigh in on oenological treasures that share birthdays—okay, fine, birth years—with R.E.M.'s finest offerings. Here are their pairing suggestions with select comments. While I have not personally tried all these wines, as always, I stand by my sources. Unless they're wrong.

10. *Fables of the Reconstruction* (1985) — Robert Mondavi, Reserve Cabernet Sauvignon

> "Kickass album from a kickass year for California Cabernet. Alas, the album still holds up but the wine is probably past its time."
>
> —Ian Blackburn, founder, Learnaboutwine

9. *New Adventures in Hi-Fi* (1996) — Araujo Estate Cabernet Sauvignon, Eisele Vineyard

> "I'd love to pop the cork on this bottle to celebrate Hi-Fi's 20th anniversary. Or to celebrate anything, for that matter."
>
> —Greg Van Wagner, Jimmy's, Aspen

8. *Monster* (1994) — DeLoach Cabernet Sauvignon, Russian River Valley

> "'Strange Currencies' is on *Monster,* right? This wine is as awesome as 'Strange Currencies.'"
>
> —Anthony Lerner, Mastro's Steakhouse, Beverly Hills

7. *Out of Time* (1991) — Far Niente Cabernet Sauvignon, Napa Valley Cave Collection

> "It was drinking great as recently as 2013, but it's definitely running out of time. Get it? Get it?"
>
> —Rosalina Pong, The 21 Club, New York City

6. *Green* (1988) — Silver Oak Cellars Cabernet Sauvignon, Napa Valley

> "A wine as sumptuous as Michael Stipe's voice, which has aged just as gracefully."
>
> —Mary Thompson, The LINE Hotel, Los Angeles

5. *Reckoning* (1984) — Opus One, Napa Valley

"I don't know much about R.E.M. Are they into wine?"

—Greg Van Wagner

4. *Life's Rich Pageant* (1986) — Dunn Vineyards Cabernet Sauvignon, Howell Mountain

"This was one of the vintages that made me want to be a wine professional. And 'Fall on Me' inspired me to try and save the world."

—Ian Blackburn

3. *Murmur* (1983) — Joseph Phelps Vineyards "Insignia"

"I'm a big fan of everything by both this band and this winery."

—Massimo Aronne, Michael's on Naples, Long Beach

2. *Document* (1987) — Beringer Private Reserve Cabernet Sauvignon

"Dan Dunn is writing a wine book. It's the end of the world as we know it."

—Anthony Lerner

1. *Automatic for the People* (1992) — Dalla Valle Vineyards "Maya" Cabernet Sauvignon

"If I do this, can you get me a bottle for free?"

—Rosalina Pong

....

I VISITED A HOST OF vineyards in North Georgia, and tasted some surprisingly delicious juice. I say surprisingly because I was in friggin' Georgia. Anyone who claims to have gone to Georgia *expecting* to find great locally produced wine is either lying or out of their mind or both (a combination, by the way, that has served Georgia politicians well for decades).

And I'm not talking Muscadine, either, although the

supermarket shelves in Georgia are filthy with the stuff. According to the folks I spoke with, wine is still a relatively new concept to a lot of southerners, many of whom have only known vino that tastes like fermented Dr Pepper. In a bad way. But, like the Bible says, it's okay to kill people if they don't believe the exact same things as you. So I went ahead and kept my views on wine to myself during my visits to the supermarkets of Georgia.

The way I see it, if a Jeff Foxworthy acolyte sipping Autumn Blush over ice on his front porch means there's one less Bud Light drinker in this world, I say Muscadine winemakers are doing the world a service.

A PRIMER ON MUSCADINE

WHAT IS IT?

Muscadine is a native North American grape grown mainly in the South. It's well adapted to warm and humid climates, thrives on summer heat, and needs far fewer chilling hours than better-known varieties.

HOW LONG HAS MUSCADINE WINE BEEN AROUND?

Muscadine has been used for commercial wines and port since the sixteenth century. So about five hundred years too long.

WHAT DOES IT TASTE LIKE?

Fermented Dr Pepper. In a bad way. C'mon now, try and keep up!

WHO DRINKS IT?

People for whom chiggers are a major hygiene concern. Also, anyone who has a homemade fur coat.

WHAT TYPE OF FOOD GOES WELL
WITH MUSCADINE WINE?

Whatever you run over with your pickup truck.

WHERE CAN I PURCHASE IT?

Walking distance of a Waffle House. And, most likely,
at Waffle House.

HAS THE MUSCADINE GRAPE BEEN
IMMORTALIZED IN SONG?

As a matter of fact it has. Muscadine is used in the production
of Ripple, which is included in the lyrics of numerous tracks of
the album *Banned from the Planet* by the Nasty Niggas. Most
notably, "By the way, where's my Ripple? I seen this bitch with
tha big ass nipples." Now that is a good question, my friend. A
good question indeed.

....

The general population's tastes notwithstanding, there are
some serious producers coming up in the Peach State these
days. They grow *Vitis vinifera*—the vine species that produces
over 99 percent of the world's wines today—and French-
American hybrids all over North Georgia, and they grow it
well. Because of the higher altitudes, the vines are less likely
to succumb to Pierce's disease, the number one threat facing
lowland southern grape growers.

My first stop was Tiger Mountain Vineyards on Old South
Highway in Tiger, Georgia, where sweet tea has long been the
drink of choice. Tiger Mountain sits on one hundred acres
of impossibly picturesque country, ten of them planted with
vines. They produce about twenty-five hundred cases per year,
85 percent of which is sold straight out of the tasting room.

The rest is available in select shops and restaurants throughout the state.

They make a Petit Manseng at Tiger Mountain that's won a slew of awards. It's a white wine grape grown primarily in the Languedoc in southern France. If you like Viognier, you'll probably dig Manseng. And if that doesn't do it for you, they make some pretty killer Cabernet Franc as well.

The small group of folks who work there are representative of two traits I noticed in the majority of southerners I met on my travels: friendly and passionate. Martha Ezzard, who owns Tiger Mountain along with her physician husband, John, is a lawyer, political activist, mother, grandmother, winemaker, writer, and unbelievably gracious host. As we like to say where I'm from, she's a friggin' badass. Her daughter Lisa works at the winery, as does Lisa's daughter Georgia. I sort of fell in love with all of them. It's impossible not to. They're a great family, with a long and storied history. To be honest, I probably could have written a whole book just about the Ezzards and their wine odyssey. If Martha hadn't already done so.

The Second Bud: Deserting the City for a Farm Winery is a story about saving a fifth-generation family farm—her husband's—and she tells it beautifully. She chronicles the arduous work required to birth and maintain a vineyard, digging holes, hammering wooden posts, stringing trellis wire, and, of course, pulling weeds. It's a far cry from her law practice, where blisters, bee stings, and chigger bites were not a routine part of the job. Martha also writes of the majesty of sighting a giant blue heron in the mist by a pond, and the sound of geese honking as they pass overhead.

Martha laughed in disbelief when John first suggested they leave Atlanta to have a go at winemaking on the family farm in the Blue Ridge Mountains of Georgia. It is the Bible Belt, after all, and their parents on both sides are avowed teeto-talers. She reminded John of her mother scolding her dad every year for having a single glass of wine at the office hol-iday party. Eventually, though, Martha warmed to the idea.

"I still have to pinch myself when I look at our lush green vines, the seventy-five-year-old barn wearing its new coat of red paint, and the roses blooming madly at the end of each row of grapes," she writes in *The Second Bud*. ". . . both of us resolved to cultivate something that will reflect our particular passion: we want to save a piece of the earth, not just any piece of earth, but the hundred acres at Tiger Mountain that are part of John's soul."

Hey, easy on being great at writing about wine, lady. Some of us don't have law degrees to fall back on!

The next day I met with Emily DeFoor at Habersham Vine-yards & Winery in Helen. Emily had been the bookkeeper at Habersham for many years before owner Tom Slick promoted her to GM in January of 2014. Slick also owns the antique shop next door to the winery—the one where I bought Michael Stipe the ram's head. The building has been there since 1876, a former brothel. Emily told me it's haunted by the ghost of a nineteenth-century prostitute who was murdered there by a miner. Do any significant amount of traveling throughout the South, and you come to learn that hauntings are a fairly com-mon thing. As are former brothels.

They make a succulent Chambourcin-based dessert wine at Habersham. I highly recommend it, but see here's where I ran into something of a dilemma. I can sit here all day and sing the praises of the wines at Tiger Mountain and Habersham. I can also attest that Yonah Mountain Vineyards in Cleveland, Georgia, makes Cabernet Sauvignon that is as delicious as just about anything you'll find in the Napa Valley. Of course,

Yonah Mountain buys their fruit from California. But that's okay because the Bible also says that quibbling about grape sources is grounds for a good martyring.

The problem is, unless you're planning to actually physically visit Georgia, you're going to have a hell of a time procuring any of the wine they make there. They're just not making enough of it. Their supply is overmatched by the demand. Which is great news for the local Georgia wine industry, not to mention the farm-to-table movement and the carbon footprint Nazis. (I kid the carbon footprint Nazis. But seriously, you guys should really find something else to pair with your environmental agenda than the genocide of the Jewish people.)

For the time being, though, the most reliable way to get some Georgia juice in your belly is to get your ass to Georgia. You can drive, like I did, but I've also heard there's a midnight train that goes there as well. There are certainly far worse places you can go. Take Mexico City, for instance. I mean, look what happened to Sal Paradise when he visited.

Plus Georgia has more than wine and bronze ram heads. They've got peaches and soon-to-be reality TV stars and a very liberal interpretation of the words *65 mile per hour speed limit*. And there's a Waffle House within walking distance of every other Waffle House. It's a luminous network that drapes itself across the state like so many glistening globs of trans fat. (Who's the wordsmith now, Martha Ezzard?)

Then there's Georgia's most plentiful natural resource, soul. Ray Charles knew how to name a record. Or, at least, his labels did. Nothing complicated. No esoteric bullshit. Don't get crazy. Just keep it simple and underscore the fact that Ray was a genius: *The Genius of Ray Charles, The Genius Hits the Road, The Genius Sings the Blues, Genius Loves Company, The Genius Develops Severe Drug Problem and Fathers Twelve Children with Ten Different Women.* You know, the classics.

What I'm getting at is this, I need to go back to the Nacoochee Village Antique Mall, buy another bronze ram's head, and name it Ray Charles, Genius at Large. Maybe even pick up a James Brown and an Otis Redding while I'm at it. In other words: Damn, Georgia. You fine.

I DROVE THE NEARLY SIX hundred miles from Helen to New Orleans in one day. Took me thirteen hours and change. I'd considered breaking the trip up with a stopover in Alabama, but when I called my buddy Surcouf—a native New Orleanian—and inquired about the merits of Birmingham versus Montgomery, he said "that's like choosing between getting kicked in the head and kicked in the ear" and advised me to push straight on through to the Big Easy. It should be noted that only days earlier, Alabama's football team had defeated Surcouf's beloved LSU Tigers in overtime, thus eliminating LSU from national title contention, so it's possible he was a little bitter.

In retrospect, I regret skipping Alabama. I'd had it in my sights while planning the trip. There's just so much history (some of it none too pretty) and of course a tremendously rich literary tradition (which seems to collocate with things that are none too pretty). But I was relatively certain the juice was going to be unremarkable, if not downright gross. There was the fact that I was born a Yankee and had been out in California for long enough to get my moonbeam green card. But in my experience, people don't care anywhere near as much about that stuff as they used to. Don't be an asshole and you'll be fine.

The real reason I skipped 'Bammy is that by the time I reached the Heart of Dixie I was running on fumes. As much as I'd enjoyed discovering new places and meeting new people, my soul was in need of something that felt familiar. Birmingham and Montgomery would have to wait. My old friend the Big Easy was calling. I'll say this much, I enjoyed the drive through Alabama. It's quite scenic. Especially the part that's Mississippi.

Remember when I said don't act like an asshole? I've never been very good at that.

YOU DON'T HAVE TO STUDY the drinking habits of the American public for a living to know that millions of people flock to Bourbon Street annually for the sole purpose of getting blotto on jet-fuel cocktails. The Big Easy is a famously sot-friendly city, particularly during the annual festival of excess that is Mardi Gras. This is not a city that "gets its drink on" for the same reason that nudist camp residents don't specify "casual dress" on their dinner invitations. These people never really sober up, and it's one of the few places on earth where your bartender will almost always ask if you want one more for the road. Plus it's legal to walk around with your drink, and there are drive-through frozen daiquiri shops.

Wait. How is New Orleans still legal again?

There are no wineries or vineyards located within New Orleans, but wine has become a booming business there. Over the past decade, the number of wine shops in the city has nearly doubled, many of which are located in sections of town not traditionally frequented by what you'd call "uptown" oenophiles.

Take Catherine Markel, for instance. Her "friendly and fearless" wine shop, Faubourg, opened for business on Claude Street in Marigny—a stark old neighborhood in the Bywater just walking distance from the French Quarter.

It was a Friday afternoon when I stopped by, and the small but well-stocked shop was doing brisk business. Faubourg (an ancient French term that loosely translates to "suburb," a reference to the Marigny being the first neighborhood to extend New Orleans proper) specializes in small producers and reasonably priced wines. It's a favorite local hangout, and Markel said she'd developed a following from all over the city.

"There's a growing number of New Orleanians who are very passionate about wine," Markel said. "And I think the reason the shop has been successful is that people appreciate the fact that we tend to eschew the big names and focus instead on the little guys who are making fantastic wines."

Markel's right; the shelves at Faubourg Wines were filled with an impressive array of cult favorites, both New and Old World alike. One thing I didn't find there, however, was a single bottle of wine produced in Louisiana with locally grown grapes. Markel shrugged and smiled sheepishly when asked about the home state being shut out. "I don't know. I guess Louisiana wines aren't quite there yet."

We'll see about that, I said.

ANOTHER *DUCK DYNASTY* CONTROVERSY BREWING . . . ER, FERMENTING

I can't very well report on Louisiana wine without mentioning Duck Commander, a line of low-cost wine that trades on the success of A&E's Bayou-based reality show, *Duck Dynasty*.

As of this writing, Napa Valley–based Trinchero Family Estates, which produces Duck Commander, was being sued by Napa Valley–based Duckhorn Vineyards for alleged trademark violations. A classic case of one duck too many.

Now I'm not at all sure how the court will or may have already ruled on this, nor do I care all that much. Like many of you, I've still got a hangover from that other *Duck Dynasty* uproar. You know, the one where A&E edited out their gratuitous references to Jesus. Now they want to shove this wine junk down our throats? How would Phil Robertson feel if I tried to shove my junk down his throat?

Still, I worry that a ruling in Duckhorn's favor could set a legal precedent that would give rise to similar lawsuits. Once a judge decrees that Duck Commander is too similar to Duckhorn, next thing you know Ravenswood will be suing the Baltimore Ravens over their branded wineglasses and J. Rochioli will be hauling J. Crew into court over, say, a spiced wine taffeta dress.

My guess is Duck Commander will prevail, and I suspect they'll sell a ton of the stuff. In recent years, wineries have made a killing pairing vino with popular TV shows, movies, and bands such as *Downton Abbey, Fifty Shades of Grey,* and the Rolling Stones (which I hear ages well for the first fifteen years, then goes right off a cliff).

But you know what? As tacky as they may be, I'm fine with these pop cultural phenomenon-themed wines. This is America, after all. Opportunistic branding is our birthright! In fact, if I have a problem with anything, it's that the booze industry isn't taking this trend far enough. Here are just a few no-brainers I've come up with. Diageo, I hope you're taking notes.

PROCTER & GAMBLE PRESENTS . . . HONEY BOO BOO'S OLD-FASHIONED AFTER-DINNER CORDIAL

The show may have gone the way of a pedophile doing life in prison, but the party must go on. Five parts Scope, three parts Red Bull, two parts Everclear, one part delicious McIntyre, Georgia, creek water, and a bunch of Pixy Stix powder. Just one sip will have you smiling so wide, people can see all six teeth.

AMERICA'S NEXT TOP BOTTLE

For the weight-conscious booze lover, this beguiling combination of Clenbuterol, Adderall, valium, caffeine, and laxatives is dissolved in a vodka base then filtered through a $9,000 Hermès silk scarf. Each bottle comes with a pack of cigarettes and a bottle of ipecac. Pairs well with cotton balls.

12 YEARS A SLAVE RUM

Now, I know what you're thinking. You're thinking, man, that is an incredibly offensive booze to try to bring to market. And that's the whole point. This rum, like the movie, is purposely designed to increase awareness about the evils of slavery. Would it be a bad thing if it also increased profits? I think that makes this the feel-good rum of the year. Two thumbs way up!

LORDE'S "WE'LL NEVER BE (CROWN) ROYAL" BLENDED WHISKY

This ain't your grandfather's whisky, and whatever you do don't let him try it, because that guy likes Crown Royal and this will never be that. He'll just bitch about how shitty it tastes. Because, man, this stuff tastes shitty. But that's not the point. The point is to make a statement about our culture of conspicuous consumption and to confront the ever-widening gap between the haves and have-nots. Which is why this sells for $500 a bottle. Is irony powerful or what?

RIESLING GOSLING

The picture on this bottle: a shirtless Ryan Gosling. The text on this bottle: "Hey girl. I heard you like white wine, so I made you some. Let's drink it together and go buy you some shoes." If someone puts this into production they will make all of the money. All of it.

TRUMP WINE

Oh. Wait.

AT TWENTY-FOUR MILES LONG, THE Lake Pontchartrain Causeway is the longest bridge over water in the world. I drove another thirty miles outside of New Orleans to get to Pontchartrain Vineyards, which has been producing wine in southeast Louisiana since 1993 with both grapes grown on-site as well as some sourced from vineyards along the West Coast.

It's a gorgeous property. At the end of a windy road lined with southern live oaks, I arrived at a cozy French provincial-style tasting room. It was a Saturday around noon, and while the weather wasn't particularly pleasant, the place was jammed. I mean, like, Napa Valley tasting room, tour-bus-popular crowded, mostly with young people looking to have some fun and learn about wine. But it isn't Stag's Leap, y'all. It's Bush, Louisiana. And, oh, does it warm my heart to know that such a place exists.

I sampled all of the wines made with estate-grown grapes at Pontchartrain Vineyards and found at least two that Catherine Markel ought to seriously consider carrying at Faubourg. The Zydeco Rosato is crisp and pleasantly tart, made with estate-grown Blanc du Bois and Norton and a scooch of Syrah from California. It's a really nice summer sipper. The Le Trolley Reserve is as fine an expression of the Blanc Du Bois grape as I'd come across on my long journey (and believe me, I came across plenty in the South). Blanc Du Bois—a hybrid developed in Florida—yields fruity wines, to be sure, but the Le Trolley has ample acidity in there as well. It would pair nicely with the savory dishes of South Louisiana—oysters and freshly caught fish prepared with rich but not overly spiced sauces.

Still, despite the region's French roots and culinary chops, Louisiana wines can't really compete with the stuff being made in more grape-friendly climes. Not yet anyway.

Maybe the wizards in Minnesota will figure something out. Or maybe some good old boy is cultivating a swamp grape that will change everything. For now, though, the bayou is an extremely difficult place to cultivate any grape varietal. Pontchartrain Vineyards has been at it for two decades, but most of the producers in Louisiana are still relatively new and figuring things out. Fact is, they're doing it. They're there. It's a start.

Six months after I returned from my trip, I heard from Catherine Markel at Faubourg Wines. She wanted to let me know that shortly after my visit she started carrying a Blanc du Bois from Pontchartrain Vineyards called Roux St. Louis. She said I was right, a Louisiana wine shop ought to carry some native juice.

"That's fantastic!" I said. "How much have you sold so far?"

"Not a single bottle," she said.

"Oh."

"It'll happen," she said. "It's a start."

Not unlike the advice Rich gave me in Rhode Island. Damn you, you thematically cohesive continent!

"FUCK YOU, MOLECULES."

CHAPTER 14

TEXAS

Texas is vast and intimidating, like a fire-breathing dragon tattooed across North America's back (Florida, by contrast, is the "your stupid" tattoo on the continent's ankle). It contains multitudes; it's a ten-gallon hat full of contradictions. For decades there have been disgruntled Texans petitioning the U.S. government to allow the state to secede from the Union. What they don't seem to grasp is that the Lone Star State has always existed in a universe all its own.

Texas is home to Austin, one of the country's most progressive cities, which is, naturally, the capital, because the rest of the state is just like Austin. It's also home to some of the most barefacedly corrupt politicians, as well as its most hilarious. You might think I'm talking about Rick "Oops" Perry or George W. "Sorry About Your Country There, Buddy" Bush. I'm talking about Clay Henry, the beer-drinking goat that was mayor of Lajitas for several years in the 1970s. I'm definitely not talking about Kelvin Cletus Green, the teenaged mayor of Archer City. That kid's going places.

Texas has executed more prisoners than any other state in the Union and boasts the city with the highest percentage of gay and lesbian parents in the United States—San Antonio. Some of the greatest entertainers the world has ever known are Texans. As is Chuck Norris. The Dallas Cowboys are known as "America's Team," even though every football fan in America seems to despise them. Texas has two Major League Baseball teams in Texas, neither of which has ever won the World Series.

And while you might have Texas pegged as a haven for beer-swilling good ol' boys, in truth it is home to far more wineries than breweries. The state ranks second behind California in wine tourism in the United States.

There are over forty wineries scattered throughout the Texas Hill Country, from Austin to Fredericksburg and Lampasas to New Braunfels. Bending Branch, in Comfort, is one of the better ones and is home to the country's first fully automated flash détente machine. Proof positive that the past few governors have given the state a bad name—not everyone in Texas is afraid of science.

Bending Branch's first vintage was 2008 and produced eight hundred cases, according to founder and VP of operations John Rivenburgh. In 2015 they're on track to do fifteen thousand. Of the fourteen different grape types planted on the estate, Rivenburgh and his team are most enthusiastic about Tannat, which is commonly found in Uruguay and in the Basque-influenced regions of France near the Pyrénées. Tannat is very tannic, and in the United States it has been most successfully utilized in Rhone blends at notable wineries such as Bonny Doon and Tablas Creek in Paso Robles,

California. The folks at Bending Branch are banking on Tannat becoming a sought-after varietal wine. And having tasted their 2011 vintage, I believe they're on to something.

Whether or not Tannat turns out to be a viable long-term bet boils to down to consumers' willingness to expand their palates and try new things. I've found that most wine drinkers, even seasoned ones, are devoted to a handful of varietals at most. But nearly fourteen thousand types of grapes are used to make wine around the world. How many of those have you tried? Hell, I do this for a living, and I doubt I've experienced more than fifty.

Most of the time you don't get to taste a bottle of wine before you buy it. Once you leave the store you're stuck with it. So despite the massive variegation of grapes out there, people tend to go with what they know. Rivenburgh points out that more and more wineries, tasting rooms, and shops are offering tastings and by-the-glass pours, giving more people the opportunity to explore at minimal risk. Case in point: I'd never tried a straight Tannat until I visited the tasting room at Bending Branch. Now I own several bottles from a variety of producers.

John Rivenburgh mentioned he used to be a Cowboys fan, but that after Jerry Jones took over, he gave up on America's Team. I'd like to thank Jerry Jones for doing his part to broaden the palates of football fans.

"You made the right choice," I said. "Eff the Cowboys."

He asked where I'm from.

"Philly?" He guffawed. "You'd have to be crazy to live there."

You don't know the half of it, buddy.

It took me eight days to get through Texas, and I could fill a whole book with material about the wine being made there. Shit, that might have even been this book if my brother, ex-girlfriend, mother, dad, stepfather, and dog had been able to keep their deceased/deranged/seared/amputated noses out of it.

I visited wineries from San Antone to Plains. I watched the Eagles whup the Cowboys in Dallas on Thanksgiving Day, ate at the Salt Lick in Driftwood, met a young winemaker in Elgin named Doug Lewis who I'm convinced is going to be a superstar, crashed a Victoria's Secret model's bachelorette party at William Chris Wines in Hye, visited Buddy Holly's grave in Lubbock, and fell head over boot spurs in love.

Not real love, mind you, in the traditional sense, where the other person, you know, like, is aware that you exist. But make no mistake, forever more my heart belongs to a lady named Amanda Cevallos. My buddy Wheels took me to a famous music joint called the Continental Club on South Congress Avenue where Amanda Cevallos and the High Hands were headlining. Amanda Cevallos has a voice like an angel and looks like a cross between a young Jennifer Lopez and Mazzy Star's Hope Sandoval. I'm positive that lusting after such a heavenly creature is a mortal sin, but dammit, if God rewound the tape and watched her sing "He Won't Stop Leaving Me Alone" up on that stage, I'm pretty sure he'd give me a pass.

I USED TO VOLUNTEER FOR 826LA, a nonprofit organization started in the mid-aughts by author Dave Eggers. 826LA is dedicated to helping underprivileged kids develop their writing skills. It's the sort of after-school program a lad like me might have benefited from. Instead, I learned about writing the old-fashioned way, from angry nuns who beat the fear of dangling modifiers and extraneous apostrophes into me with metal rulers and leather belts.

I can't mention the habit-wearing hags who helped raise me without giving a shout-out to the haggiest of them all, Sister Mary Gerald. Or shout-down, I should say. SMG is definitely six feet under by now. Back when I was a fifth grader known as Titman at the Resurrection of Our Lord elementary school, SMG was a barely-living legend. A cross between the Crypt Keeper and the Wicked Witch of the West, only meaner, SMG was an absolute terror in black and white, and she gave more Philly kids nightmares than Alfred Hitchcock.

There were certain things about Sister Mary Gerald the kids found endearing. You couldn't help but be impressed by her ability to remain upright for extended lengths of time despite a severe curvature of the spine brought on by being 193 years old. Her bony frame was a wonder to behold. An arthritic Kokopelli sans flute and fertility. She didn't walk so much as skitter across the room like a demented Monty Python animation.

I've never heard a voice like SMG's before or since. Imagine a busted muffler on a clown car driven by a banshee inside an echo chamber in hell. It was truly awesome in its sheer ability to disorient.

But the most entertaining thing about Sister Mary Gerald, as far as a group of eleven-year-old kids was concerned, was her senility. The old gal was in the winter of her life and wasn't wearing a jacket. She was always losing her bearings and forgetting names, or where she was, or who it was she had originally meant to smack across the face with one of those gnarled old hands of hers. Who better to instill knowledge in tomorrow's leaders?

Looking back, it's clear to me that she was in the grips of fairly severe dementia, which is sad. In my defense, it would have been easier to feel sorry for her if she had stopped hitting us for a minute. Apparently the Catholic Church did not consider her condition grounds for removal from her position of authority, though. They couldn't have given less of a shit about it had she been giving us all handjobs. Well, at least not until she made them. Give a shit, that is. Not give us handjobs. Father Doherty probably wouldn't have minded, though.

The way she made them finally give a shit was Rob Willard. The kid in the class with the big furry birthmark on his neck (there was always one kid in your class with a big furry birthmark on his neck). Technically it's called a congenital nevus, and Rob had finally, in fifth grade, after enduring six years of people making fun and pointing and petting it and naming it, gotten surgery to have it removed. I will never forget the morning he came into our classroom, just a day or two after his procedure, to deliver a note from the principal to Sister Mary Gerald. SMG snatched the slip and proceeded to spend what seemed the entirety of third period attempting to read it with her mole rat eyes and trifocal glasses. Finally, SMG looked up and waved Rob Willard away. It was unclear if she had divined the note's meaning or not. Knowing what was good for him, he quickly turned and darted for the door. Poor bastard almost made it too.

"Wait a minute, boyyyyyyyy!" she growled. This was followed immediately, I swear, by one of those eerie piano scales that portend doom in the movies. It's possible I was watching too much *Twilight Zone* back then.

The boy stopped in his tracks. The entire class sat up straight, tense with fear.

"Come over heeeeeeeeeerrrrrreeeee," she hissed, as the sky grew dark and thunder rumbled in the distance.

Rob Willard swallowed hard, turned around, and nervously edged toward her.

"You've got something therrrrrrreeee," she croaked, as he approached, squinting at him curiously and extending a twisted claw toward the young man's throat. He was frozen with fear. "Shameful. It's important that a young man maintain his appearanccccccce."

The entire class's stomach clenched as her gnarled digits found their way to his collar. Rob Willard opened his mouth as if to say something, but just then she withdrew her hand with surprising speed. I remember thinking that she must have decided it was nothing, after all. You got lucky this time, Rob Willard. But wait. No. His mouth was still open, gasping noiselessly while the face surrounding it turned suddenly, shockingly white. Time stopped for one lurid moment, then started again, as Rob Willard clutched at his throat, a look of sheer panic on his face, and blood streamed freely through his fingers.

Sister Mary Gerald was holding something aloft, studying it. Scowling at it. Completely oblivious to the suffering, bloodied boy in front of her. She turned to the class and a crooked smile cut across her face . . .

"A string on his collar!" she crowed. "Dispose of this," she said, handing Rob Willard his own neck stitches without looking at him, as though he were an abomination in the sight of the Lord. Rob ran from the room and SMG went on with the lesson as though nothing happened.

After I put this story in the book, I looked Rob Willard up on the Internet. It took all of five minutes. (Facebook be crazy.) He still lives in Pennsylvania, just outside of Philadelphia. And he's a surgeon now. Specializes in dermatology and surgical reconstruction, don't you know. You can't make this shit up.

"When I went back to the surgeon who excised the nevus he said 'that nun should be shot,'" Rob wrote, adding that he didn't think what happened in that classroom had any long-term psychological effect on him.

"But you became a skin surgeon!" I replied. "I mean, there has to be some sort of connection, right?"

"Nah," he said. "Just a coincidence."

As for Sister Mary Gerald, they didn't shoot her. Or fire her. Or take any disciplinary action as far as I know. Philly's motto should be "It's your fault you live here."

826LA DIDN'T SAVE ME FROM Sister Mary Gerald, but the idea that they would have liked to made me want to help the cause. In the fall of 2010, 826LA held a fund-raiser at the Writers Guild Theater in Beverly Hills. It was called "I Found This Funny: An Evening of Music and Comedy" and was hosted by Judd Apatow, the comedic thermonuclear device behind such films as *The 40-Year-Old Virgin* and *Knocked Up*. The event featured appearances by numerous luminaries including Eggers, Garry Shandling, comedian Aziz Ansari, and singers Randy Newman, Ryan Adams, and Fiona Apple. I, of course, was happy to lend my talents as well. And as a professional boozer, there is nothing I am better at than scamming free drinks. And as folks tend to be more generous at these things once they've got a little Chardonnay in them, I was asked to secure a wine donation. I sent e-mails to some contacts in the wine biz, and before you could say "some people are just awesome" we had our sponsor, Bear Flag Wines of Modesto, California.

On Saturday, about a week before the fund-raiser, some friends took me out for an extended brunch because apparently that's what friends do when you're a few weeks removed from tragically losing a younger brother. My friends wouldn't leave me alone, frankly. And there seemed to be a direct correlation between people's level of sympathy and the amount of food they felt compelled to try and shove down my throat. "Eat, eat! You need to eat!" It was a constant refrain. If they weren't taking me out for meals, it seemed like someone was always swinging by the apartment with homemade lasagna or chocolate chip cookies or noodle salad. And I'm eternally grateful for that. The Road to Healing is paved with companionship and calories. And Cabernet.

I got home a little before sunset. I had a solid buzz going, and felt like keeping it that way. Elizabeth was working at the restaurant and wouldn't be back for several hours. This was Me time, and I was determined to spend it with my most tolerable Me. Grief counselors and psychologists and oh, say, anyone who cares about you will tell you that alcohol is not a healthy way to deal with loss. Which is why I moved my home gym over next to my bar. Barbells cancel booze. That's just physics.

Judge me if you want, but in the weeks immediately following my brother's death, I found that Buzzed Me was easier to get along with than, say, Weepy Me or Angry Me or, worst of all, Woe Is Me. That dude was a real drag. A real American whine-o, if you will (HAW HAW HAW, kill me). So I went ahead and poured myself a generous slug of red wine, put on my headphones, and headed to the roof deck.

I'd been spending a lot of time up there, especially when I couldn't think straight enough to read, sleep, or even watch TV. I was keeping a good lid on the freak show most of the time, but my head was in a real weird place. I had nightmares. Flashbacks. Difficulty concentrating. Irritable as a Gwar fan at a Sting concert. But up on the roof I could see the sand and the ocean, the beachgoers and boats. The infinite horizon and all its possibilities. A lot of the time back then, I felt like I was being slowly smothered. But for some reason I could breathe on the roof. I'd call it my Happy Place if there was such a thing then. We'll call it my Least Crappy Place.

When people would come visit, I'd invite them up. Sometimes I could read worry on their faces. Other times confusion. Especially if I'd managed to crack a smile. *He's smiling? Up here, of all places?* My buddy Z was the only one to come straight out and ask me.

"How do you sit up here and look at the ocean that killed your brother and not fucking lose it?"

"Dianetics, Z. How would you like to take a free personality test?"

"How would you like a punch in the head?"

"I'll take it if it means I don't have to eat any more noodle salad. I mean seriously, why the fuck do people keep bringing that over here? I lost my brother, not my sense of taste."

"You got good friends is why, you ungrateful bastard."

"I know," I said and collapsed into a ten-foot-deep puddle of tears.

Thinking about my friends and how good they were to me? Guaranteed waterworks. But I never once blamed the ocean for what happened to my brother. I have even, on darker days, entertained the notion that it saved him. Which might sound strange, because Brian drowned, and I'm pretty sure drowning is no walk in the park (with the possible exception of someone who drowns in a water park). But I'm a firm believer that there are fates worse than death. Especially when there's heavy drinking involved. I have had a front-row seat for the demise of many drunks and addicts in my life. Some went slowly and painfully; others took people down with them. Some checked out fast and violent. But when the deck got passed to Brian, he drew Ocean. Like I say, it could have been much worse.

I've read numerous studies that assert drowning is one of the "easiest" ways to die, which is to say, least painful. That's the kind of cheery literature you get into when you're dealing with this kind of thing. But come on, the only people who know what drowning feels like aren't around to give us a blow by blow. And even if they were they couldn't compare it to being shot or stabbed or cuddled to death by puppies (which is, as we all know, the most adorable of deaths). Still, even though my logical mind knows it's probably bullshit, it's comforting to believe that Brian's death was peaceful.

At his funeral in Pennsylvania, someone lamented that Brian's death could have been avoided. Bull fucking shit. I'm no expert in thanatology, but I am certain the death rate for human beings is still holding steady at 100 percent. We are all of us corpses-in-waiting. The Walking Dead. Future worm buffets.

Brian was destined to shuffle off this mortal coil just like the rest of us. He just shuffled a little faster than most. Thirty-one years old and in good health (if you don't count the alcoholism) probably sounds young to you. But he wanted a cheap thrill at 2 A.M., dammit, so he jumped off the Venice Fucking Pier. No more than a hundred yards from shore. At least that's how far out on the pier we found his watch and wallet. Brian was six foot two and in good shape. Played sports competitively his whole life, and he was a good swimmer. Forty-nine times out of fifty that big motherfucker makes it back to dry land safely, no matter how loaded he might be. Not this time though. Not in the early morning hours of July 5, 2010, when he splash-landed right into the roiling guts of a powerful rip current that grabbed him and, with brute assuredness, took him right the hell out to sea.

My brother Sean once asked me if the authorities had

given any indication of how far out the current had taken Brian before it finally let him go.

"Far enough," I said. We left it at that.

When talking about my brother's death, people tend to attach labels like untimely, senseless, and tragic. And it's all those things. If you want, you could throw in shocking and unfathomable. But when I think about how he died, though, the two words that tend to come to mind are *fucking* and *stupid*.

Brian was in trouble. I'd known that for a long time. But I didn't do anything about it. He drank too much. And sometimes when he drank too much, he did really fucking stupid things. It was obvious to me and anyone close to him that Brian was headed to one of two places: Rehab or Big Trouble. And here's what's fucking stupid. I chose to wait for the latter to lead him to the former. That was my fucking stupid plan. Just sit around like a fucking stupid idiot and hope he got so trashed and did something so terrible he'd have no choice but to stop getting blotto.

I did this despite knowing that all those years ago, the thing that ultimately made my dad realize he had to call it quits wasn't *drunk driving a cement truck off a bridge and losing his arm*. It was my uncle—my dad's brother—who one day threw him up against a wall and pleaded with him to stop. To save himself and his family. It was the ultimate expression of brotherly love.

Me? I opted to wait for Brian to come to that realization on his own. It seemed easier than being proactive. Don't want to be a buzzkill, man! If I ignored the problem, I was spared the awkwardness of confronting him about it, not to mention confronting my own habits and behavior. Plus, Brian was a fun drunk. Drinking gave us a lot of good times I wouldn't take back. I knew the party couldn't last, but I was in no hurry to hasten last call. Brian was thirty-one. Lots of people are fuckups at thirty-one and still turn out all right. Eventually, he'd stop drinking.

And what do you know, he did. And I never even had to confront him about it.

So I'm up on the roof with my wine and the day was getting ready to call it a night, but not before it did some showing off. The sun burning a red hole through the horizon like a giant cigarette butt tossed on the Venice boardwalk.

Rumours is Fleetwood Mac's best album. "Dreams." "The Chain." "Go Your Own Way." From top to bottom, pure gold. But my favorite track from *Rumours* has always been "Never Going Back Again." Lindsey Buckingham wrote it after his messy and public breakup with Stevie Nicks. It's a simple song about complicated feelings, and it features one of the most enchanting guitar riffs ever laid down. Only a handful of songs can touch it. Jimi Hendrix's "Castles Made of Sand." Nirvana's "All Apologies." But none have ever gotten to me quite like "Never Going Back Again."

> *Been down one time*
> *Been down two times*
> *I'm never going back again*

The song came on in the waning moments before the sun disappeared into the sea. I closed my eyes as Buckingham picked his way through the intro.

When I opened them again, there he was. Brian. Sitting in front of me in the chair, rocking gently, and smiling. I'm not talking about an image of him, a memory. I mean, he was really there, in the flesh. Alive. Undrowned.

My Logical Brain said I'd had too much wine. Brian couldn't be there.

"But that's him!" I protested.

"You've suffered a devastating loss," my Logical Brain said. "You're experiencing some sort of PTSD-induced hallucination."

"Bullshit!" I shouted.

"Well, then, you're drunk."

"Shut up," I said.

"If that's really Brian, then prove it. Reach out and touch him," my Logical Brain said.

I wanted to, but I couldn't do it. I was afraid that if I touched him, he would disappear. Brian seemed to understand how scared I was. He smirked as if to say, "What a pussy." Then he gave me a reassuring nod. It said, "It's okay, man. Let's just enjoy this."

The song is only two minutes and fifteen seconds long. Some people can hold their breath longer than that. I bet Brian had. No doubt he'd held on as long as he could. He was a tough motherfucker. Lindsey Buckingham wasn't singing anymore. The guitar plucking was louder. The big finish. But wait, what's the next song on the album? Fuck! I know this. It goes "Second Hand News," "Dreams," "Never Going Back," and . . . "Don't Stop"! Brian loves that song. It'll soon be here. Better than before. Yesterday's gone. And here we are, up on the roof.

But he wasn't. I looked over and saw an empty chair.

My friend Jonathan is an actor, best known for portraying the Most Interesting Man in the World in a high-profile ad campaign for a Mexican beer. Jonathan and his wife, Barbara, were living on a sailboat in Marina Del Rey. After Brian was cremated, my brother Sean and his wife, Erin, came to visit and we all went out sailing. We took some of Brian's ashes with us on the boat so we could sprinkle them into the ocean. Some kind of peace offering. We sailed out about two miles from where Brian made his fateful leap. Jonathan wrote down the coordinates in his logbook. I joked that when I kicked the bucket, I wanted them to chuck me in there too. Same spot. Oh, and fuck the cremation, by the way. Put my corpse in a trash bag and tie a cinder block to it. If I'm going out, I'm going out in Irish luggage, motherfuckers.

It was windy and the sea was rough that day. Sean had put the ashes in a Ziploc. That, too, seemed appropriate. None of that fancy urn shit for us Dunns. Trash bags and Ziplocs is how we roll.

Sean busted out his stash of Brian and made the obligatory joke about cutting up some lines and snorting them like Keith Richards did with his father's ashes. Everyone laughed for a second and then got quiet. I looked around and saw us rocking in this vast expanse and the whole thing felt ridiculous. We had a bag of molecules and we got onto a bunch of other molecules and used it to float on top of some other molecules so we could put these molecules in those molecules because these molecules are supposed to be special. Then Sean dumped out the Baggie and the wind blew it back all over us. Same trick as at the river. It always looks so perfect and sad in the movies.

After we got back to shore, the most interesting molecules in the world and their wife came with me to the 826LA fund-raiser. Being around people was still a little dicey, but live music is powerful medicine and Randy Newman is a big shambling panda made of love and bourbon. At the end, Judd Apatow came out and thanked everyone in the packed theater for contributing to the cause. He encouraged us to stick around for the after-party in the lobby where they'd be serving Bear Flag wine. I felt like a contingently nonshitty human for almost an entire minute for having played a part in getting it there. Then just when I thought the lights were going to come up, Apatow said there was one more performance to go. From his neighbor. Guy by the name of Lindsey Buckingham, who walked out on stage with his guitar, waved to the crowd, and started picking out the intro to the third track off side one of *Rumours*. The one between "Dreams" and "Don't Stop." It's called "Never Going Back Again." Fuck you, molecules. You made me cry in front of Judd Apatow.

I LISTENED TO "NEVER GOING Back Again" several times on my trip, and each time I did I would take the mason jar with my brother's ashes from out of the center console and place it up on the dashboard, to give Brian a view.

As the trip went on we talked more and more. Once, during one of the loneliest stretches of the journey, on the interstate between central Nebraska and Des Moines, after we listened to Fleetwood Mac I reminded him about Goal Line Stand, the game we used to play in the living room when he was four years old and I was fourteen. I'd back up and toss him a Nerf football. He'd catch it, then square up and charge right at me, intent on knocking me down and scoring.

I was ten years older and three times his size, but I never took it easy on him. So Brian rarely got past me. But he never got pissy when he was thwarted. He seemed to relish the challenge. I'd "tackle" him, and we'd grunt and growl and make all sorts of noises just like the real football players on TV. But no matter how many times he came up short, Brian would get back up on his feet, hand me the ball, return to the starting position, and give it another go. Over and over again.

The point was not to burnish my reputation as a run stopper. I was never much of a football player. (Put me in a bowling alley, though, and I was a regular Earl Anthony.) Nah, I loved Goal Line Stand as much as the kid did. Every fourth or fifth try I'd grab hold of Brian and pretend to struggle to bring him down. He'd screw on his meanest football player face, little legs pumping, arms outstretched, trying to get that Nerf football across the piece of masking tape that served as the goal line. Even then, he had a truly impressive drive. Trying to get to the goal line was better than actually making it. And then, just when Brian had exhausted every bit of energy he had trying to break free, I'd let him go.

Touchdown.

PLAINS, TEXAS, SITS ABOUT FIFTEEN miles from the New Mexico border and it's where I spent my final night in the Lone Star State. It was December now and chilly as hell. But I spent the evening drinking wine in a barn with a bunch of farmers, and if that doesn't warm you up, nothing will. I highly recommend the experience to anyone with an interest in doubting his own manliness. I understand that "wine farmer" might not top your list of tough bastard professions, but it sure as shit should.

I was staying way out on Neal Newsom's ranch in the house he keeps there for guests. I was its only occupant that night, which suited me just fine. Apparently December in West Texas isn't the high season for wine tourism. Go figure. The guesthouse is lovely and well appointed, but it is in the middle of nowhere. Actually, pretty much all of West Texas is in the middle of nowhere. And Newsom's ranch is in the middle of that.

I parked Carl Vehicle and unloaded my stuff. On a whim, I brought Brian along. His jar was down to about a third, thanks to our visit to Buddy Holly's grave back in Lubbock, where I'll admit I'd been a little profligate with my spreading.

Out back of the guesthouse there was an old abandoned

homesteader shack. Besides that there were no visible signs of civilization. Grazing cows dotted the landscape at various intervals. *Here it is,* I thought. *I said I was moving to Nowhere. This is about as close as I'll ever get.* Then, being an accomplished photographer (read: I have Instagram on my phone), I went out to get some shots of the homesteader shack.

As I captured my moody, squared-off, film-grained black-and-whites, I thought about the lunatic who once lived there. What his daily routine was like, what he ate, where he crapped, the fact that this guy had lived in Nowhere back when it really was Nowhere. Maybe before it even had a name. And how he'd managed to make a living. Unless of course, he hadn't. It's possible this was the home of some poor sucker who'd been sold a bill of goods. Told that he'd be part of a thriving community and all it would cost would be his life savings. Then he ended up here, trying to make the best of it, before dying of an infection he got after cutting himself shaving. Shaving for no one.

Then, as I turned, I saw a giant, hairy beast, not ten feet from me. Startled, I took a step back into a depression in the dirt, stumbled, and fell on my ass. Heart pounding and flustered from the fall, I looked up to see a bunny. Okay, maybe not a bunny exactly, but a rabbit nonetheless. I came to understand that the area was populated with jackrabbits. Which, in my defense, are furry, are sort of strangely large (thanks to the oversize ears), and can technically be classified as beasts, if you're a soft-hands journalist who's lived in cities his entire life. For his part the rabbit just looked at me with a mixture of pity and disgust. *Man,* he seemed to say. *I'm not even close to afraid of you.*

Neal Newsom's family has been farming and ranching in West Texas for generations. What began in the 1980s with three acres of Cabernet Sauvignon has now grown into 150 acres of Merlot, Sangiovese, Tempranillo, Malbec, Pinot Grigio, and more. In addition to producing their own wines, Newsom and his wife, Janice, supply grapes for a number of Texas wineries, including two of the state's largest, Llano Estacado and Becker.

That night he invited me out to his barn—or "Barnery" as he calls it—to bend an elbow with some of his compatriots. Among the locals I met in the Barnery that night was Neal Newson's winemaking mentor, Bobby Cox, a walking encyclopedia of grape growing with a big bushy mustache to go along with his big everything else. Imagine if Wilfred Brimley got on the juice and cofounded CrossFit. Bobby's been growing grapes and making wine in West Texas since 1973 and is one of the state's leading viticulturalists and winery consultants.

Bobby's wife, Jennifer, who was also at the Barnery Summit, is what's known as a "supertaster." Supertasters, as the name suggests, have an extremely heightened sense of taste. And while this might sound like an awesome superpower, in practice it's not all that fun. For supers, everything is turned up to eleven. Sugar is sweeter, sodium is saltier, and bitterness is death on a stick. Supers are less likely to enjoy alcoholic drinks, coffee, and rich desserts. But, man, is Jennifer ever aces at identifying wines. With a sniff and she can tell you everything from the varietal to what the guy who picked the grapes had for breakfast.

We sat on folding chairs around a folding table in the shadow of two large tractors. Nearby was an antique weather radar, the kind most people had in those parts before satellites and computers. Neal said he still used his old rig to control the famed Marfa lights, the mysterious glowing orbs that appear in the desert outside the town of Marfa, a four-hour drive south of Plains.

Everyone brought wine (everyone but me, that is), all

locally produced. Jet and Gay Wilmeth of Tokio, Texas, brought along several bottles made at their Diamante Doble Vineyard, as well as at the custom crush facility they co-own, Texas Custom Wineworks. They're big fans of Italian varietals and believe West Texas, with a climate similar to central and northern Italy, is one of the best places in the world to grow Trebbiano and Sangiovese.

They are also passionate about the politics of farming. According to Cox, the long-standing government subsidies for cotton farmers in the state were the main thing stopping West Texas from becoming one of the country's preeminent wine-growing regions.

"California growers would say to me all the time, why are y'all still growing cotton? It's a Third World crop," Cox said. "Well, I'll tell you why—because the government was paying folks to stick with cotton. If they didn't, they'd grow grapes."

As Newsom pointed out, the return on investment in water costs alone is ten times greater for grapes than any other crop. He says agricultural mainstays such as cotton, peanuts, and corn are all "horribly water inefficient." Plus, who needs clothes and food when you have booze?

But change may be afoot. Government subsidies for cotton were halted in 2015, and the farmers I spoke with in Plains all feel strongly that West Texas has the potential to rival California, Washington, and Oregon in wine production as cotton fields give way to vineyards. "The conditions out here are just too right for it not to happen," said Newsom. "The elevation, the hot days and cool nights, the shallow, sandy red-clay soil over limestone. These are the conditions grapes thrive in."

Still, Newsom said it wasn't just a matter of wanting to. Transition like that can be tough. And times are already tough enough for the farmers out there.

"A lot of folks are interested in growing grapes now," he said. "They see it as a way to save the farm. But it won't. Vineyards are a long-term investment. It takes eight or nine years to see a return on your money, and that's without any bad weather years setting you back." This for a population that's already on the wrong end of the economic stick. "Some farmers in these parts just don't have that much time left," he said, shaking his head.

For those that can stick it out, though, the future could be bright. Cox noted that West Texas might not be as pretty as Napa, but it's got Northern Cal–like potential for producing epic wine. "It's a beautiful thing to see," he said. "And it's been a long time coming."

"Plus, we've got Louie Gohmert here," Newsom quipped, citing one of Texas's more colorful (i.e., batshit crazy) politicians. "Kidding!"

The impromptu Barnery Summit went until 11 P.M. or so, which I got the impression was pretty late round those parts. I got my fair share of crap for being a Yankee. But they didn't seem to mind being razzed for being some of the most virile specimens of American men I'd ever laid eyes on. I figured we were even.

WHEN NEWSOM DROVE ME BACK, I was struck by what a long, dark drive it was to get out to where I was staying. As the guesthouse swam into view in his headlights, it struck me this was precisely the kind of place where people get killed in horror movies. When I restrained myself from asking Neal to keep me company until morning, I felt my testosterone level rise by 30 percent.

As the last of his tire noise died away in the night, the stars felt so low I could touch them. I was struck by the profound emptiness that America still contains, as well as the incredible fortitude of the people who choose to spend their lives here. Then I heard rustling noise somewhere off to my left and scurried inside, my testosterone levels dropping to normal. Maybe a little below.

There's nothing to worry about, I told myself. There is literally no one out here. And that means there is literally no one to be afraid of. Just go to bed, and in the morning you'll get to see that spectacular wide open plain again and the jackrabbits will be jackrabbits again, not giant, hulking Sasquatch monsters coming to sate their savage libidos with my eyeholes.

Somehow I got to sleep, visions of Sasquatch eye-babies dancing in my head. At 2 A.M., I woke to the sound of a vehicle coming up the dirt road. Fuck. Here we go. Judgment night. In the depths of my fuzzed-out brain I envisioned a tribunal of the kind, but brutally honest folk of West Texas. It was time to pay for my sins. Not for the lust and the sloth and whatnot. That stuff don't amount to an ant fart. Naw, son, you got to answer for what you did to people. Or, rather, what you didn't do.

The sound of gravel under tires that had been rising suddenly stopped. I pulled the curtain, just enough to peek out the window. A pickup truck sat idling right next to Carl Vehicle, its headlights illuminating the house.

"Out here, we take care of our own. You had a baby brother to protect. Where's he at, anyway?"

"In this jar. See, I brought it into the house so he could—"

"Lemme get this straight. Your baby brother is a pile of ashes now. Because of drinking."

"Yes, sir."

"You're telling me you ran around like a damn fool,

scratching out your stories about how much fun you were having and all the places you were going and the parties you were hosting, and your brother . . . what was his name again?"

"Brian."

"And Brian is sat home watching you. Watching you conquer the world from a bar stool."

"I wouldn't say I conquered—"

"I ask you a question, son?"

"No."

"All right, then, I'll make a statement. You were bigger. You were the one who decided who won and who lost when you played Goal Line Stand. He mighta been four inches taller, but he never knew anyone bigger'n you."

The pickup outside was still idling. Sizing up my estrogen-mobile no doubt. Taking stock of the California plates. Doing some kind of terrible dismemberment calculus. I wanted to be anywhere else. Hydroplaning on the Jersey Turnpike. Hearing about how the aliens in Mom's attic poisoned her oatmeal again.

"But we're here to discuss your real sin, son."

"What's that?"

"The only sin worse than not being there when he needed you."

Fuck fuck fuck fuck fuck.

"Carrying him around after he don't."

I heard the truck shift into gear. The rear lights came on. It was backing up, now turning around. And off it went into the night. I waited by the window a good five minutes after it was gone, but the tribunal seemed to have ended.

The next morning I went back out to the old, blown-down homesteader cabin. This time I didn't take any pictures. It was a ruin. A relic of a time that had long ceased having a hold on the present. The person who lived there had dreams, ambitions. Their fortitude had made it possible for the generations that followed to prosper on the same land. Never in a million years would they have dreamed they'd see grapevines rising out of the clay. And they never would have credited those vines with the survival of the family farm.

Life is change. Standing still is death. At least it looks the same to everyone else. It was time. I took all I had left of Brian and poured him in a neat pile in the middle of the cabin's ruins. He'd be safe out there in Nowhere. And if I ever needed to visit, I knew where he'd be.

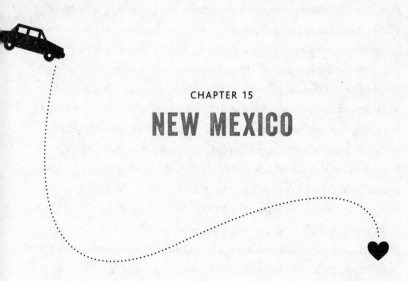

CHAPTER 15

NEW MEXICO

"I HAVE NOT BEEN COMPROMISED BY THE LIZARD PEOPLE."

My mom was always terrified by Bugs Bunny. I think she was worried he was going to convince her it was actually duck season and she'd end up blowing her own beak around to the back of her head. Yeah, that chaotic trickster vengeance thing really got to her. Because when someone messes with Bugs Bunny, his vengeance is sure, swift, and elaborate. And that fuzzy fucker has no concept of proportionality. Say you're practicing for your big opera performance. You've worked hard, spent a lifetime preparing to express yourself in song. But you better hope you don't sing too loud during rehearsal. Because if you wake Bugs up from a nap, that goddamn demon rabbit will drive you insane, embarrass you in front of thousands, then destroy the opera house, presumably killing you, the orchestra, and the audience. Bugs Bunny was NAP-PING. You knew the rules.

Mom loved Road Runner, though. The lines of good and evil are easier to parse. The hero is barely even there. Just the faintest whisper of personality, embodied by an idiot grin and superhuman speed. The Road Runner's primary charac-ter trait is his ability to remain unfazed by the fact that the same deranged, yet highly creative coyote has been stalking him across the desert for forty years with a bloodlust that would make Patrick Bateman blush. Why does Wile E. Coyote want this one bird so goddamn badly? Are roadrunners that delicious? Is this one particularly succulent? Is this the first roadrunner he's tried to kill? Or has he eliminated all other roadrunners in the world and is having trouble with the last one? Is he incompetent or merely experiencing an uncanny string of bad luck? Does he even remember why he's chasing this fool bird? It matters not.

What matters is the object lesson that is enacted again and again in every installment. The coyote is always foiled, but never by the Road Runner. He is only ever defeated by him-self and his wicked desires. Had the coyote not pursued the Road Runner, he would not have ordered a giant wrecking ball rig be delivered to the desert, thus making it impossi-ble for him to be flattened by said wrecking ball. Had he not tied a rocket to his back, that selfsame rocket would not have blown him up after crashing headlong into a mountain. Wile E. Coyote is the ultimate Catholic, summoning his own doom through his sinful urges. Jesus didn't die for Wile E. Coyote's sins. Wile E. Coyote did. Over and over and over and over. I think Mom found that comforting.

So while Bugs seemed to torture her, when she watched

Road Runner, Mom would just smile, shake her head, and tsk a little. Figures. Stupid Coyote. When you gonna learn?

I felt more coyote than roadrunner as I entered New Mexico on US 380. The gravity-defying rock formations and sandy colors of the landscape around there look an awful lot like the desert scenery from the cartoons. And while I didn't see any wrecking balls or rocket debris, around eighty miles in I did start to see signs promoting various attractions in the town of Roswell, home of the mysterious Area 51 air force base and site of the 1947 weather balloon crash that definitely 100 percent had nothing to do with our government covering up the fact that they shot down a UFO and recovered a crew member whom they experimented on, leading them to engineer a human/alien hybrid named Arnold Schwarzenegger who would eventually be sent back in time to kill John F. Kennedy to stop him from revealing the truth about the space program and the secret moon base manned by Buzz Aldrin clones and their army of robot sex slaves. Let me reiterate. ALL OF THAT IS 100 PERCENT FALSE AND I HAVE NOT BEEN COMPROMISED BY THE LIZARD PEOPLE. I'm just saying, Arnold was born in 1947. Coincidences are for people who can't handle the truth.

So you tell me. Is it coincidence that the International UFO Museum and Research Center just happens to be in Roswell? Wake up, people.

Frankly, all I wanted to do was push on through to Albuquerque, where I had resolved to make some left turns to honor the almighty Chaos Rabbit and jangle Mom's nerves. But as I rolled through Big Roz, I saw a sign for a wine store called Pecos Flavors. Like I'm going to be able to pass that up.

Pecos Flavors is a funky little place located right on Roswell's main drag. As you'd expect, they carry novelty items like Alien Amber Ale and Galactic Cabernet. Gotta keep those conspiracy tourists loaded. But Pecos's shelves are also stocked with wine from a number of excellent New Mexico producers such as D.H. Lescombes and Tularosa Vineyards. I picked up a bottle of Jemez Red from Ponderosa Valley Vineyards in northern New Mexico. It's a blend of Baco Noir (a hybrid of Pinot Noir and, I assume, bacon), Ruby Cabernet (a cross between Cabernet Sauvignon and Carignan), and Nebbiolo. It's no 2009 Léoville-Barton, but it's a solid flavorful little bottle with plenty of bold fruit flavor and more than a little backbone and it sells for just $20. It's one of my go-to wines when people doubt there's good juice in the nontraditional winemaking regions of the USA.

It's also one of my go-to wines when people say California is the "traditional" winemaking region of the United States. Because people have been cultivating grapevines in New Mexico for over four hundred years (or in European terms, ten minutes), making it the oldest wine-growing region in the United States. There are nearly thirty wineries across the state that produce four hundred thousand gallons of vino annually. Still, most of us have never tried New Mexico wine. There's only one explanation. Those goddamn aliens.

Aliens were also likely to blame for the fact that Dan Dunn, the world's foremost expert on becoming an expert on American wine, had only allotted enough time to swing by a single winery on his way through New Mexico, the country's oldest winemaking region. It definitely wasn't because the road had worn me down. Or because I was dog tired and ready to go home. Or because a representative from the Lizard People had gotten in touch, none too subtly either, and made it clear that the "dreams" where I'm fellating Arnold Schwarzenegger will continue until I stop sniffing around their home base.

Frankly, at this point in the journey, I wasn't sure of my own address. Oh wait, yes I was. Dan Dunn, 1 Carl Vehicle, USA, USA. (USA! USA! USA! USA!)

But I did know this: if you were to only visit one winery in New Mexico on your exhaustively complete inventory of the nation's vineyards, it ought to be Gruet. These guys are the leading purveyor of sparkling wine this side of Sonoma County.

I knew I'd have to break into the bubbly at some point on this trip. Sparkling wine is sometimes called the "happy accident" by winemakers, due to its serendipitous origins. And how's about this for a detail you'll think I made up, but I assure you is 100 percent true: "The Happy Accident" was my family's pet name for me when I was just a wee lad, due to my sparkling personality and serendipitous origins. Sparkling wine is my spirit animal. We're blunder brothers!

Primitive societies blamed the mysterious appearance of bubbles in their wine on phases of the moon and evil spirits. My mom's family blamed the mysterious appearance of me in their midst on the same two things (not to mention fizzy beverages).

The same way my teenage father never intended to stick a baby in crazy Charlene from down the block, it was never anyone's intention to foster fizz in fermented grape juice. But once they got a taste for how rewarding it was, they figured why not do it again, only this time intentionally and without treating it quite as terribly. Which explains both Dom Perignon and my giant network of siblings from all the other various couplings that followed Dan and Charlene's teenage backseat frolic. The fact that the first sparkling wine was probably a stomach-turning abomination is where this metaphor breaks down. (Shut up, it does.)

Carbonated happy juice became a growing concern around

350 years ago, when a lot of wine was being exported to England from the Champagne region of France. Thing is, it gets cold in Champagne in the fall after the harvest. So cold that often the wine's fermentation would stop prematurely, leaving residual sugars and dormant yeast in the barrels, which was then bottled up tight and shipped to warmer climes. However, when the bottles warmed up, the increase in temperature woke up the yeasties who started eating up all the leftover sugar and crapping out alcohol and carbon dioxide as per usual. A second fermentation. Only now, since it was in a glass bottle instead of a nonairtight cask, when the excess CO_2 couldn't escape, it went into solution in the wine, creating the classy gassy glass of headache we love so well today.

Now you may hear stories of a French Benedictine monk named Pierre "Dom" Perignon, and how he was the first to declare the sparkling tendency of wines from Champagne as a desirable trait by shouting, "Come quickly! I am tasting stars!" And while it is tempting to make fun of the homoerotic overtones of such a statement by a man of the cloth who spent most of his adult life cooped up with other men of the cloth and an unlimited supply of fizzy, fizzy wine, I assure you I would never sully the legacy of Dom Perignon. Instead I consider it a testament to his legacy that it wouldn't be out of place to hear someone exclaim his famous catchphrase in a West Hollywood cruising spot.

And in all fairness, credit for popularizing Champagne rightfully belongs to seventeenth-century London hipsters, the first to embrace the sweet wines that had gotten their fizz on during the long journey across the English Channel. Eventually, of course, secondary fermentation was induced intentionally and became known as the "Champagne method," or *méthode champenoise*.

FIVE FACTS ABOUT SPARKLING WINE

1. All Champagne is sparkling wine, but not all sparkling wine is Champagne.

2. A 750 ml bottle of sparkling wine contains roughly 49 million bubbles. The pressure from all those tiny gas balls causes corks to pop at an average velocity of 40 mph.

3. When in doubt, use any of these five simple go-to modifiers, to describe what you're drinking: complex; balanced; layered; intense; well-rounded. We've been over this before, but it bears repeating.

4. Marilyn Monroe once took a Champagne bath. It reportedly took 350 bottles to fill the tub, which subsequently took its own life. Its last words were, "I'll never top this."

5. The indentation found at the bottom of many wine bottles is called a punt. Modern glass technology has rendered the punt functionally useless, but it endures primarily because wine consumers, unlike football fans, equate punts with quality.

Today's most celebrated sparkling wines still come from the historic province in France where bubbly was born and are made primarily with Pinot Noir, Pinot Meunier, and Chardonnay. The juice from the Champagne houses of Krug, Cristal, Perrier-Jouët, and, of course, Dom Perignon are staples on exclusive wine lists the world over. But in recent years, as wine's consumer base has increased, so too has the demand for sparkling stuff produced for a couple bucks less, regardless of its pedigree.

As you may have noticed, I consulted "Sommelier to the Stars" Chris Sawyer (how them stars tasting, Chris?) regularly throughout the trip. I should remind you that Chris hails

from Sonoma County. When I asked about the state of bubbly in America, he pointed to the fact that many of the great
Champagne houses have purchased vineyards in Northern
California in recent years, which he says is a sign that New
World sparkling wines are becoming a force to be reckoned
with. "The coastal areas of California have the ultimate climate and soil conditions to produce great sparkling wine,"
he said. "There are things we can do here that they can't do
in France, such as ripen the grapes to perfection year in and
year out. And we can do it more cost effectively." Fair enough,
Chris Sawyer, but can you ride a bike in a striped shirt and
mustache while carrying a brace of onions and a baguette?
Have I found your Kryptonite? Or as the French pronounce
it, Le Cheez Whiz?

After Chris pointed out that my stereotypes of French
people were super racist and I pointed out that French isn't so
much a race as a disease and he pointed out that this was also
probably overly harsh and I pointed out that I was just having
a little fun because come on, look at those shirts and onions
and bicycles, and he pointed out that my entire conception
of France comes from Looney Tunes and I mentioned that
my mother hated the Chaos Rabbit and he shouted Aha!, I
knew we'd get to the bottom of this. He singled out acclaimed
California producers Schramsberg, Domaine Carneros, and
Roederer Estate among the finest this country has to offer.
You'll find they're staples at many of the country's higher-end
fine dining establishments. To my surprise, though, Chris was
also effusive in his praise for Gruet, which is made in Albuquerque. Chaos Rabbit country.

Too bad I'm a goddamn coyote. And just like old Wile E.
trying to chase the Road Runner into a landscape he'd painted
across the highway, I was hitting the wall. Carl Vehicle could

refuel whenever he got thirsty, get an oil change and a little radiator fluid, but my internal fuel light was on, as was my Check Engine flag. My battery was struggling to get things going every morning, my front end badly needed adjustment (a man gets lonely on the road), and my rear differential left a lot to be desired. Plus, I had begun to talk almost exclusively in car metaphors. Basically, I needed to get off the got damn road for a while. But at this point, the only way out was through. Through the Land of Fucking Enchantment. But I was only going to be able to handle one New Mexican winery at best. Carl Vehicle, I command you, take me to Albuquerque.

Gruet's Blanc de Noirs is absolutely dynamite. It's light, festive, and pops with crisp fruit flavor. Pop a bottle at brunch with some Kumamoto oysters and send me a thank-you note. Plus, it retails for under twenty bucks a bottle. If they slapped Napa or Champagne on the label, people would happily pay four times as much. It's definitely the best bubbly value in America, maybe even the world.

The Gruet family, *quelle surprise,* hails from France. My previous comments about their home country notwithstanding, they are a wonderful group of folks. Over dinner at the Hotel Andaluz in downtown Albuquerque, assistant winemaker Sofian Himeur plied me with much bubbly and tales of his grandfather, the company's founder, Gilbert Gruet.

Gilbert grew up in a small town called Bethon, where he dreamed of someday having a Champagne house of his own. Gruet et Fils started producing bubbly in Bethon in 1952. Thirty years later, while traveling through New Mexico, Gilbert met a group of European winemakers who had successfully planted vineyards near the town of Truth or Consequences, 170 miles south of Albuquerque.

"Back then New Mexico really, truly was the Wild West.

And you can imagine how intimidating it must have been for someone coming from a small village in France," said Sofian. "My grandfather was a risk taker, though, a real badass. He saw something in this vast, uncultivated land. Opportunity. He had a very clear vision of a future few others could have even imagined."

The land was inexpensive, the opportunity golden, and the town name too colorful to pass up. Gilbert decided to plant an experimental vineyard with Pinot Noir and Chardonnay. A year later, he and his wife and kids relocated to the great state of New Mexico and a fabulous success story began.

"To me, Gruet, and the success we've had so far, it's what America is all about in the eyes of so many people around the world," Sofian said. "My family came here because there was opportunity. Everyone worked their asses off to make it happen. And it happened—last year we sold a hundred twenty-five thousand cases. We're making amazing sparkling wine in New Mexico, man. Life is good!"

Indeed it is. And it only got better that night because, man, did we ever drink a lot of amazing sparkling wine in New Mexico.

To further convince myself of my coyote-like ability for self-inflicted harm, the only other thing I did of note during my twenty-four-hour stopover in Albuquerque was pay a stripper at Knockouts to massage me. No weird stuff and no happy ending. Just a firm kneading of my aching neck and shoulders, during which I may or may not have lost track of time. If you were curious about what this kind of thing will run you in New Mexico, twelve songs plus tip will still run you $150, even when all her clothes stay on.

But one thing was clear. I needed to get out of New Mexico before I ended up ordering anything else from Acme.

CHAPTER 16

ARIZONA AND
THE CALIFORNIA DESERT

"NEVER HEARD THE WORD
IMPOSSIBLE."

As I pulled back onto Interstate 40, my pal Jaybeau Jones over at SiriusXM's "70s on 7" dialed up a doozy: Cyndi Grecco's "Making Our Dreams Come True." You might know it as the theme song from *Laverne & Shirley*. It's one of my top secret shame songs. Those are tunes that come on the radio and make you think that for the sake of your dignity and the dignity of those around you, you should change the channel. And then instead of changing the channel, you roll your windows up and you crank that terrible embarrassing shit as high as it will go and sing along at the top of your lungs. Others on my personal list are Belinda Carlisle's "Heaven Is a Place on

Earth," "All Star" by Smashmouth, Lou Bega's "Mambo No. 5," Creed's "Higher," Hootie and the Blowfish's "I Only Want to Be with You," pretty much everything Britney Spears has ever recorded (but especially "Oops I Did It Again"), "The Sign" by Ace of Base, "Tubthumping" by Chumbawamba, "Blame It on the Rain" "by" Milli Vanilli, and the all-time champion, "Nookie" by Limp Bizkit.

Often when I ask people for their secret shame songs, they get confused and tell me their shameless songs. For instance, my buddy Scott told me his was "Don't Stop Me Now" by Queen. This is not a secret shame song. It is a shameless song. Secret shame songs are actively terrible (see list above), but you cannot help yourself. You hide yourself from the world like a junkie or a crackhead or a cake fart fetishist (look it up, it's a thing) and indulge in your sexy, sexy sin. Shameless songs, on the other hand, fill the world with so much awesome that you are compelled to act like an insane person. I have seen Scott sing "Don't Stop Me Now" at karaoke. It's pretty epic. And when you can sing the gayest song in the world (and please know I mean that as a compliment) at the top of your lungs while you dance like no one's watching even though everyone is totally watching, you, my friend, are dealing with a shameless song. "Nookie" has essentially the same message as "Don't Stop Me Now." That message is "I like to fuck. A lot." But where "Don't Stop Me Now" is an exuberant celebration of grabbing life with both hands, your mouth, and your dick, "Nookie" is a rapey frat boy playing Edward 40 Hands with George Zimmerman. Fun for a minute, but you know things are going to get ugly before midnight.

So yes, Laverne and Shirley. My favorite line from the theme song to the show is "Never heard the word impossible."

I love how optimistic it is, despite the fact that it is an irrefut-
able lie. Because besides the odds against Cyndi Grecco never
having run across that particular word before, the word is *in
the goddamn song* that Cyndi Grecco wrote. The only way it
could even have been true at the moment she wrote the thing
would be if she had just made up a random string of sounds
that happened to correspond to an English word. Me? I've
never heard the word *graptigulous*. But no one cares. I guess
Cyndi just got lucky. But you know what? While it's extremely
unlikely that Cyndi Grecco has never heard that word, you
know what it's not? Impossible.

I was in Arizona.

What kind of lunatic would try to grow wine in motherfucking Arizona?

LOCATED ON A STEEP EMBANKMENT in the Black Hills of Yavapai
County overlooking the Verde Valley, Jerome, Arizona, is as
picturesque a place as there is in this country. About a half
hour west of Sedona and an hour south of Flagstaff, Jerome
began as a mining community in the 1870s. By the early twen-
tieth century there were over ten thousand occupants all
looking to get at the copper in them thar hills. When the
boom busted during the Great Depression, Jerome very nearly
became a ghost town, but managed to keep it together. Today
it's a sleepy hamlet with less than a thousand residents, many
of them artisans and specialty shop owners. Its primary indus-
tries are tourism and wine. Both do brisk business, thanks in
no small part to Maynard James Keenan.

You may know Keenan as the front man and driving force
behind three high-profile bands (Tool, Puscifer, and A Perfect
Circle). What you may not know is that he also makes wine.
Really, really good wine. It turns out Northern Arizona is a

surprisingly propitious place to grow grapes. But we almost never found that out, because when people started planting grapes there, everyone said they were crazy.

Several years ago, IGN interviewed Keenan and asked him about what possessed him to start a winery in Arizona. He said it came down to business. "This is a prime spot for vineyards," he said. "An untapped resource. But the master plan is to have the Merkin Vineyards Bed and Breakfast set up for when California drops in the ocean. Beachfront property and the New Napa Valley."

Well, okay then. Good to have a plan.

I, for one, am happy to know MJK will be the one picking up the pieces once the Golden State slides into the sea. He's the kind of guy who doesn't wait around to be told what he is or isn't allowed to do. The guy joined the army to pay for art school. Went to West Point Prep, in fact, where he both wrestled and sang in the glee club (both of which they take pretty damn seriously at West Point Prep). Later, during the Tool years, he composed a song that uses the Fibonacci sequence as its underlying structure. I have no doubt the guy could be president if he wanted, and that the world would be a better place for it. Trouble is, he has a crippling allergy to bullshit. And elections in the United States are one long, uninterrupted bullshit bath (for both the candidates and the people). But damn, what I wouldn't give to see him deliver a State of the Union.

I first talked to Keenan when I did a piece on him for *Playboy* and he gave one of the most entertaining interviews of my career. Naturally when I got to planning out this trip, he was at the top of my list. Then, when I told him I'd be coming through Arizona, the first thing he did was ask if I wanted to crash at his place. Have I mentioned that winemakers tend to be preternaturally lovely people? Have I mentioned that Maynard James Keenan is extremely straightforward and doesn't make a big deal out of things? The tasting room for Caduceus Cellars and Merkin Vineyards (the twin pillars of Keenan's budding wine empire) is close to the top of the hill on Jerome's Main Street. As I drove up the winding road an early Tool hit was blasting from Carl Vehicle's speakers. "Why can't we not be sober? Why can't we drink forever?"

Why can't we not indeed?

Maynard was waiting with several bottles opened along with a spread of charcuterie and cheeses. If every drive had ended like this, I might have wanted to stay on the road.

A restless, relentless creator, Keenan is known for his prodigious work ethic and prolific output. But it's one thing to crank out a ton of songs, it's another to crank out a ton of songs people actually want to listen to. That same combination of creative intensity and high standards is also evident in his winemaking. During our marathon session, we tasted twenty Caduceus Cellars and Merkin Vineyards wines, all of which were very good, some of which were spectacular (the Nagual del Marzo and Oneste in particular), and Keenan told me he took the same approach to making wine as he did to making music. His aim is to create something thick, dense, rich, complex, engaging, emotional, and spiritual. Coming out of anyone else's mouth, I'd be ready to diagnose a severe case of BMS (bullshit modifier syndrome), but as far as I can tell, Maynard has no interest in trying to fool anyone. When he says something, he means it. And he is always ready to back up his opinions. When it comes to wine, his vision is very much borne out in the bottles he produces. It's the best Arizona juice I tasted. And that's actually saying a lot. While I was there, I also spent some time with my pal Craig Outhier, who works at *Phoenix Magazine* and has tasted just about everything produced in the state. Craig kindly offered to put together a brief guide to Arizona's winemaking regions, a favor I repaid by promising him a free copy of this book, which I'm sure I'll forget to send. Sorry in advance, Craig.

....

THE BEST WINE IN ARIZONA

By Craig Outhier, Editor in Chief, *Phoenix Magazine*

Hollywood director turned Arizona winemaker Sam Pillsbury tells a story about his early foray into desert winemaking. "In the year 2000 when I planted my first vineyard, there was a skit on *Saturday Night Live* about the ten surest ways to lose money," he says. "One of them was 'plant a vineyard in Arizona.'"

Luckily, Pillsbury and his colleagues have thick skins. And in less than two decades, they have managed to effectively reverse the conventional view of Arizona viticulture. I may be biased, but with over eighty bonded wineries sporting a wide variety of styles, it's not a stretch to call Arizona the fourth-most-important U.S. state for winemaking after California, Oregon, and Washington. On a gallon-for-gallon basis, AZ doesn't produce as much wine as New York, but I'll take the earthy Rhone-style reds from the Chiricahua foothills over the cloying, seder-ready stuff that makes up the bulk of the Empire State's output.

I had to beg Dan to even make a stopover here on his fancy wine voyage. And even then he only did it because he scored a personal tasting with the Tool guy. Dan's a starfucker, but I love him. And I love Arizona wine even more, so here's a quick and dirty AZ wine country primer.

VERDE VALLEY

Located about two hours north of Phoenix, this high desert river valley boasts the state's highest concentration of tasting rooms, distributed among the towns of Cottonwood, Cornville, and Jerome. Home to well-known Arizona labels like Page Springs Cellars, Arizona Stronghold, and Caduceus Cellars, Verde Valley offers the plushest wine tourism of Arizona's three growing regions, with a lively strip of boutique hotels and indie restaurants in Old Town Cottonwood, and a flourishing arts scene in Jerome. It's also where many of Arizona's rock-star winemakers reside, and I'm not just talking about the literal one that runs Caduceus Cellars. Eric Glomski of Page Springs and Michael Pierce of Saeculum Cellars can both rock out with their rootstock out. If you go, don't miss Four Eight Wineworks, which is a bit off the beaten path in Clarkdale. It's a wine incubator conceived by Maynard James Keenan that produces and markets wines for four up-and-coming labels. 907 Main St., 928-649-2007, four8wineworks.com

SONOITA/ELGIN

Located about forty-five minutes southeast of Tucson, Sonoita/Elgin is Arizona's first and only officially designated American Viticultural Area (AVA). Anointed one of America's top ten wine trails by *USA Today,* it offers more of an on-location, visit-the-vineyard experience than Verde Valley. This is where you'll find award-winning pioneer label Callaghan Vineyards. A winemaking Methuselah by Arizona standards, Kent Callaghan got under way in the 1990s and delivers the region's most consistently excellent juice. His *Wine Spectator* scores have cracked 90 on occasion. It's also home to rising stars Kief-Joshua Vineyards and spunky upstart AZ Hops & Vines, which is owned and operated by a pair of sisters who dubbed one of their muscato releases "Fluffer." The dry, straw-colored beauty of Sonoita hints at the dominant varietals—plenty of Syrahs, Grenaches, and tertiary Rhone styles, and some lesser-known Spanish grapes like Graciano.

WILLCOX
The most rustic (read: *Bonanza*-y) of the three wine regions, Willcox is the state's grape basket and shining hope for the future. Sitting on roughly four hundred square miles of loamy farmland about an hour east of Tucson, the region produces the majority of Arizona's wine grapes, shipping most of them to the Verde Valley and other regions. Rent a bike and explore the "Willcox Bench," a spacious run of farmland featuring four wineries including Pillsbury Wine Company, Sand Reckoner, and Bodega Pierce. If the day ends with you in a sleeping bag on Pillsbury's floor, sleeping off his Wild Child red and processing his stories about directing Nicolas Cage in the 1991 erotic thriller *Zandalee,* that's on you. Willcox is beginning to develop winemaking infrastructure of its own, along with the high-end restaurants, guesthouses, and entertainment options that promise to help Willcox blossom into a leading wine tourism region in the coming years.

While driving from one of Maynard's vineyards in Cottonwood back up the hill to Jerome, he told me about how Tool, the band that made him famous, came to be. Maynard had moved to L.A. and found work doing interior design for pet stores. At night he used to go to shows in L.A. As an opinionated guy, he had no compunction about letting people know if he thought a particular band sounded worse than a screaming baby on a plane. And at that time a lot of bands genuinely sucked. I mean, there's always a lot of shitty bands around, but this was right at the cusp between the glam metal hair bands that had owned MTV and the self-loathing grunge revolution. Guns N' Roses was still the biggest thing going, but change was in the air (for proof, check how Axl's hair morphed between *Appetite for Destruction* and *The Spaghetti Incident?*) and suddenly all the Poison and Ratt wannabes were scrambling to change their image to "alternative." Maynard felt this indicated a lack of artistic commitment. One night at a show somewhere on Sunset Boulevard, a guy overheard Maynard sounding off and called him on his aggressive attitude. "If it's so fucking easy, why don't you get up there and do it?"

And Maynard thought that was a fantastic idea.

He knew guitarist Adam Jones through a mutual friend. They met the other guys through other friends. Then they recorded the first Tool record. A few years later, in 1999, he became the first and only person to front two different bands on the main stage at Coachella—with A Perfect Circle on opening night, and with Tool to close the festival.

Basically, when Maynard says he's going to do something, he does it. And he does it real fucking hard. You think you can start a band? Actually, I think I can start a band that head-lines COACHELLA. You think you can make wine? Actually, I think I can make wine IN ARIZONA.

And just so we're clear, I'm not blowing sunshine up May-nard's ass in the hope of scoring VIP passes next time Tool goes on tour. I think he exemplifies everything that's wonder-ful about American winemaking. The original, upstart feeling of the early California pioneers. The tenacity of the people who decided to make the purple nectar in unconventional places. The total freaking obsession. Because besides family, it feels like everything else takes a backseat to his oenological pursuits. He has a winery connected to his house, he does not tour or record music during harvest, and his vacations are almost always centered around wine. He talked for hours about everything from blending to rootstocks to submerged cap fermentation. Sometimes it was all I could do to keep up with him. He told me that he recently spent five days hosting a group of journalists, taking them all over the state in an effort to promote Arizona winemaking. When I asked him why he'd bought vineyards that were so spread out, he told me they weren't all his. He took those journalists to competing vineyards. A bunch of them.

When I asked why, he looked at me like I was being thick. "It's important to me that this place gets its due," he said. "Arizona is producing world-class wine and I want people to know about it."

We spent several days hanging out and drinking lots of juice. I actually did most of the drinking, as Maynard was the designated driver. But I was able to recharge my batteries a bit. We visited his vineyards as well as the Bunker, his home winery. Over the time we spent together I also came to appreciate that Maynard shares my impatience for the more useless members of the human race. One day he wore a T-shirt he'd designed emblazoned with a list of 101 THINGS TO DO WITH YOUR HIPSTER DOUCHEBAG, most of which would be uncomfortable, if not fatal ways to treat another human. In other words, entirely justifiable. Let's just say I have strong feelings about the hirsute denizens of our cities "cool" neighborhoods.

"I wanted it to say hipster fucktards," Maynard said. "But I figured more people would hear the message this way."

"It's getting bad," I replied. "Feels like L.A.'s been infected by Brooklyn and Portland. They should all be rounded up and forced to shave their beards and mainline gluten."

I'll admit, I was carrying around some animus left over

from a few weeks before my trip began, when a friend had dragged me to a party at an art gallery in Silverlake. If you live in Los Angeles, this will happen to you eventually. Silverlake is an area that since the early aughts has played host to vast herds of wandering *Mustachicus doucherans* (or as they're commonly known, hipster fucktards). Correspondingly, over the same period in Los Feliz we'd seen a striking die-off of the ill-favored, less-evolved *Skinjeanalus lattefrothis*, an entire species that now appears to have been an evolutionary cul-de-sac. The sad fact is that Los Feliz's hipsters are yesterday's fucktards. Darwin don't play.

Still, it was a party, and parties offer opportunities. Like the opportunity to trap everyone inside and set the place ablaze. But while future generations might have hailed me as a visionary, I still clung to one or two vestiges of politesse, so I did my best to mingle with those creatures, drifting into a conversation with a diminutive Asian dude named Tae-Song and a woman who looked like an adult version of Marcie from *Peanuts* (if she dyed her hair purple and developed an eating disorder).

Tae-Song said he worked in banking. Or maybe it was Bangkok. It was loud in there. What I do recall is his Jens Lekman T-shirt. Marcie didn't divulge what she did for a living, but I'd bet a case of mustache wax and a fixed-gear bike she was in psychology. She started analyzing me the second I told her that for a decent chunk of my adult life I'd made my living by drinking.

"Do you think maybe you've got anger issues? Do you use alcohol to quell that anger?" she posited, after I'd finished enumerating the many elaborate and unnecessary surgeries I believe should be performed on IRS auditors.

Now between you and me, the notion that I have anger issues is ridiculous. Yet somehow, despite my linguistic training,

I couldn't conjure up the word *ridiculous* at the time. Instead I went with something more along the lines of "Go fuck yourself, four-eyes, and eat a ham sandwich while you're at it." Luckily I said it without irony or sarcasm, so Marcie, being a full-blooded *Mustachicus doucherans*, couldn't hear me.

What she also couldn't seem to grasp, no matter how much I shouted, snarled, and shook my fists, is that I don't use alcohol to quell my anger. On the contrary, alcohol stokes the precious inferno of fury that rages inside me. That fire goes out, and I'm out of a job. That's beside its side benefit as a defense when I'm out and about. It's the emotional equivalent of a skunk's anal scent glands, only with colorful profanity instead of stank spray. Both can clear a room if it becomes necessary.

And out there among the spayed and neutered urbanites that are attracted to the shining shores of Los Angeles, believe me it comes in handy. People in L.A. fear anger more than they fear earthquakes, car crashes, or terrorist attacks. For my money, it's the single worst thing about the place. The more anger that comes out as nature intended (through your lungs and fists), the less comes out the side door (through the passive-aggressive nuspeak that passes for business lingo these days). Fuck those simpering ball-less fucks and their tiny dogs. Hard. With a broken beer bottle. See? How much better is that than stuffing it all down into your gullet and turning it into cancer? As my dear old uncle Murph used to say before the enlarged blood vessels in his esophagus burst, "An angry drunk is a happy drunk."

I told Maynard he'd done the right thing by not putting "hipster fucktard" on his shirt. The term is dreadfully insensitive. I mean, what about the ordinary, everyday fucktards who have probably never sported ironic facial hair or gone to see bands they hate on purpose? It's unfair to tar them with the hipster brush. We decided that henceforth we would simply use "hipster" to describe these obnoxious poseurs. The "fuck-tard" is implied.

"By the way," I said. "You got any secret shame songs?"

"What's that?"

"Songs that you hate yourself for liking."

Maynard thought about it a moment.

" 'Boyz' by M.I.A.," he said. "You know it?"

"She's the 'Paper Planes' chick, right?"

"Yep. 'Boyz' is on the same album. I never lost so many friends so quickly as when I admitted I like that song."

I made a note to check it out on Spotify.

"What's your cheesy song?"

I told him.

"*Laverne & Shirley* was a good show," he said.

"Schlemiel! Schlimazel! Hasenpfeffer Incorporated."

"More wine?"

"I've never heard the word *impossible*."

"Bullshit, you haven't."

I was sad to leave Jerome and Maynard, but there's only so much you can impose on a genius winemaker rock star. It's about a five-hour drive from his place in Arizona to Joshua Tree National Park. And somehow, even after fifteen years in California, I'd never been. Finally I was going to make good on a promise I made to myself twenty-six years ago.

WHEN *RATTLE AND HUM,* THE U2 concert movie, came out in the fall of 1988, I was so excited I went to the very first show-ing they had at the GCC Northeast Cinema. You know the one, out by where Sam Goody's used to be at Welsh Road and the Roosevelt Boulevard. Philly's Irish runs deep, so the place was packed, and there were more than a few telltale *psshhh-*

hhhhhhht!!s as the mostly underage crowd popped the beers they'd stolen from their parents and took surreptitious swigs from pint bottles of Jameson. Two fights broke out before the trailers even started. The second was between the original fighters and the people who'd been trying to break them up. The manager came in to talk to us.

He got as far as shouting "Fighting will not be tolerated! Alcoholic beverages will not be tolerated!" before realizing he was way out of his depth. As the crowd booed him into oblivion, he beat a hasty retreat as several empty beer cans flew at his head.

Rattle and Hum was directed by Phil Joanou and is a collage of live footage, studio outtakes, and band interviews that U2 guitarist the Edge described as a "scrapbook." I found this a bit puzzling as the scrapbooks I made as a kid tended to contain more bottle caps and fewer giant stadiums filled with screaming fans. They also usually didn't cost several million dollars to produce. Usually. Reviews were mixed. Some saw it as U2's shining moment, when they seized the mantle as the world's biggest rock band. Others thought that the gospel choir was a little much and that Mister Down-and-Out in Dublin might be developing some kind of messiah complex. It was a turning point for a lot of fans. Those who wanted U2 to remain small and scrappy were disappointed with the changes. Others just couldn't resist the music these kids were making. Bono can be, without a doubt, a pompous, egotistical, self-aggrandizing parody of himself. But motherfucker can *sang*. Adopting all those African AIDS babies didn't hurt either. That was him, right?

In the years since, the band's been through a lot. But I think you have to give it to them for just not stopping. Those same four guys have been playing together for nearly four decades. And sure, their last few albums have been tepid piles of recycled pap, but they're still not doing badly on the Mick-o-meter. As I write this, the Rolling Stones have sucked for twice as long as they were amazing. And I'm being generous and leaving *Undercover* in the good bucket. U2 put out unbelievable records for twenty years, mediocre ones for fifteen, and they're still fantastic live. As far as I'm concerned, they're in the black.

Rattle and Hum is not the best thing U2 has ever done. That would be the rendition of "Bad" that closed their 1985 set at Live Aid. Bono wears a mullet and a pirate shirt. The Edge has hair. (If you haven't seen it, YouTube that shit right this second.) But I'm not here to defend the film's artistic merits. I'm here to talk about what they did in that movie theater that day. First of all, they shut the room up right quick. The crowd had chanted "Start the show" until the trailers started. When those came on they started with a steady, sonorous two-note chant, almost like a foghorn: "Fuuuuuck ooooooooooof, fuuuuuck ooooooooooof." When the movie's opening shot came on, however, there was a brief bout of cheering and excitement, followed by complete, obedient silence. Except for the guy who shouted "Diiiiiiiick" at the top of his lungs when Bono came on-screen. I'm pretty sure he got lynched.

The first half of the movie, everything's in black and white. There's some good stuff in there—the band in Harlem recording "I Still Haven't Found What I'm Looking For" with a gospel choir; a visit to the legendary Sun Studios in Memphis; and an emotionally charged performance of the epic song "Sunday Bloody Sunday" at Madison Square Garden, to name a few—but a lot of it shows a shift away from the nervy energy of *Boy* and *The Unforgettable Fire*. It's hot, but it doesn't quite burst into flames.

Then, about an hour or so into it, the film fades to black, and for a few seconds there's silence. I recall wondering if the movie had ended. I could feel my disappointment curdling into rage when I heard the opening strains of that familiar chorale-like sustained synthesizer—the ethereal intro to "Where the Streets Have No Name," off *The Joshua Tree* album. Words in white appear over black:

SUN DEVIL STADIUM
Tempe, Arizona

A drum kit on a riser silhouetted against a red light. One by one, shadows of each band member flash across the backdrop as they take the stage, Adam Clayton, Larry Mullen Jr., the Edge. The sound of the synthesizer steadily rising. Larry Mullen hits the hi-hat and smacks his drumsticks together, setting the beat . . . TISSS, one, two, three, four, five, TISSS, one, two, three, four, five, TISSS, one, two, three, four, five . . .

The Edge picks a few teaser notes, like chimes, before unleashing a repeating six-note arpeggio driving with the drum beat. White lights begin to strobe onstage. The camera lingers on the Edge, and Bono enters the frame behind him. The crowd at Sun Devil Stadium roars, as does everyone in the movie theater. My heart is beating faster. Something is going to happen. Something big. The Edge starts strumming his guitar faster. Larry Mullen thwacks the hi-hat several times in rapid succession. Bono yells as Mullen hits the kick drum. Adam Clayton thumps the bass and with a burst of sound and color the propulsive pre-verse arrives.

A wide shot. All the house lights go up. My chest was pounding. Up on the screen, a hundred thousand people bouncing in unison to the rhythm of this delirious anthem that sounded, to my ears, like a joyride to heaven.

I want to run
I want to hide
I want to tear down the walls that hold me inside

And I did. I wanted that.

It was a shamanic moment. These four people had channeled all the energy of the universe down through my skull in a white hot lightning bolt of knowledge that lit me up from the inside, projecting out through my skin and bathing the walls in the savage truth of me. A giant, complex, quiescent set of information, ideas, consequences, and actions immediately perceived in toto, showing me precisely what was happening to me from a single, perfect observing point outside time and space. I wanted to run. I wanted to hide. I wanted to tear down the walls that hold me inside. I wanted to get the fuck out of Philadelphia.

"It's all I can do," Bono sang directly to me. And I knew it would not happen today, or tomorrow, or next week, or next month. It didn't have to. But I would, beyond any doubt, be getting the hell out of this place. It was all I could do. I had no idea where I was headed. *Tempe looks friendly,* I thought. And like it might be pretty close to some nameless streets. But where wasn't important. What mattered was that I wasn't stuck. I didn't have to stay here. The bus driver would let me off wherever I wanted. All I had to do was reach up and pull the cord. It had been over my head the entire time.

I will forever be grateful to U2 for "Where the Streets Have No Name." Even thirty years later it reminds me that wherever I am, whatever I'm stuck in, whatever my current crisis, it doesn't have to be forever. I am the one driving this car. I am the one naming these streets. Or ripping down the signs others have put up. It's not abuse, it's mental illness. It's not tragic, it's unsurprising. It's not love, it's a hole you're trying to fill. It's not heartbreak, it's the pain that was always there. It's not alcoholism, it's a career. (I'm still workshopping that last one.) Sometimes I wonder how my life would have turned out had I not gone to see *Rattle and Hum* that day.

Then I remember, I wasn't saved by seeing *Rattle and Hum* that day. I was saved by not going to see *Punchline*. Sometimes you don't know you're dodging a bullet.

I PULLED OFF THE ROAD at the Cholla Cactus Garden in the middle of Joshua Tree National Park. The first thing I saw when I got out was a sign that said, THIS CACTUS IS HAZARD-OUS. DO NOT TOUCH FOR YOUR SAFETY AND THE PROTECTION OF THE RESOURCE. The gorgeous cholla is commonly called "jumping cactus" because it is covered in thousands of light, hollow spines that detach in clumps and seem to try to jump onto your skin, hair, clothes, and anything else they get near. If there is moisture on your skin (like if you're, say, alive), the tiny spikes will actually curl up once they pierce the skin, making them very difficult to remove. It's one of those beauti-ful things in life you don't dare get close to. I was tempted to take a picture of the sign and text it to Elizabeth along with "don't you wish I'd been wearing one of these when we met?" I decided against it. She didn't need the aggravation. And neither of us would have heeded the warning.

So here I finally was. Joshua Tree. I'd sworn to myself I'd get here one day. It was a tribute to the music that helped me see the state I was in and that I had to change it. And somehow I'd managed to live in L.A. for a decade and a half without ever getting out here. There's that old Dan Dunn commitment for you.

But this place didn't look like an Anton Corbijn photo. It was a desert. And if there was one thing I didn't need another of, it was a desert. I've just had one, thanks. I'm full. I mean, you do realize why no one lives out here, right? Slowly at first, then in a searing rush, all the light that had flooded out of me all those years ago in the GCC Northeast movie theater in

Philadelphia sucked, sickeningly, back into my head. And the world had dirtied it up something terrible.

I had pictured this as a shining moment of triumph. Late in my long journey I would consummate a promise I made to my younger self. It would be profound. It would be moving. Morgan Freeman would probably do the narration and it would make me tear up, but in that manly way where you're sensitive, but also tough, so your eyes get wet, but no tears fall and then you suck those tears back inside and use them as fuel for your next CrossFit class. It turned out that the stark, lonely, black-and-white Joshua Tree of my dreams, birthed from the images on the album cover, was just another brown landscape, only when you were actually there, there was a chance some asshole cactus would decide to hitch a ride in your pee-hole. Oh, and the streets totally had names. This one for instance was called Pinto Basin Road. Inspiring.

I felt none of the things those images had made me think I'd feel. They weren't real. They had been manicured and manipulated for my consumption, and I had eaten it up happily, used it as fuel for my escape. But now that I was here, it was clear that this was someone else's place, not mine. Instead of being full of contentment and freedom, this moment was full of dust and clouds and tourists. And here I was trying to force my own meaning on it. It was like trying to masturbate to a fetish I wasn't into. If you've tried it, you'll know: even if you start with the worst of intentions, you just can't get it up for the German scat stuff.

How did I get this far with this weird piece of "Joshua Tree is special to you" dogma stuck in my head? I hadn't been freeing myself of Catholicism and provincialism and panspermatism (I'm still not convinced humanity didn't begin with an alien sneeze), I'd just been trading it for another piece of "truth" that didn't come from inside me. I started feeling a little sick. I'd been too occupied with my own struggles, my pain, and my self-satisfaction to see it. No one can tell you what your life is supposed to be or what it's supposed to mean. Not a parent, not a preacher, not a girlfriend, not a band.

All the dirty light in my head was making me dizzy. I went back to Carl Vehicle and sat in the AC for a while, just to get my bearings. I'd romanticized Joshua Tree the same way I'd romanticized my relationship with Elizabeth. Seeing things that weren't there because I wanted them to be true. It's the same reason I told my buddy Justin not to come meet me at Maynard's winery. I like Tool just fine, but Justin is an absolute maniac. To him, Maynard is Jesus, George Washington, and John Lennon all wrapped up in some sort of perfect existential burrito. But Maynard ain't no burrito. He's just a dude. A supertalented and driven dude, sure. But at the end of the day just a guy doing what he loves and raising a family. And when people treat you like a symbol, not a person, I would imagine it's pretty fucking annoying.

Wonderful, then. I'd based the back half of my life on a lie. When people told me I was going to come undone on the road, I didn't think they meant I'd actually realize genuinely painful things about myself.

I'd planned to take a long hike around Joshua Tree and stay in the area that night, but I suddenly had the urge to see Buna. If I got a move on, I could be walking her on the beach three hours from now. If she remembered who I was. "Home, Carl," I commanded, as I put him in gear one last time. No stops. Straight shot. It was time to go home.

Well, okay, maybe I'd make one stop. Might need to get gas. And pee. Pick up some snacks. See if I could find another bronze ram's head to match Michael Stipe. There's no such thing as a straight shot. You just tell yourself that there is. For the same reason you should never meet your heroes or visit the locations on the covers of your favorite albums. It ruins the illusion.

And as I rumbled off down Pinto Basin Road, heading out of the park, another thought occurred to me. Respect the illusion. The fun of seeing a magician is not in knowing how it's done, it's in being willfully fooled. You pay money and ask the man to fool you and when he does it, you're happy. Whether or not Joshua Tree was objectively meaningful to me was beside the point. The idea of it had been powerful enough to propel me out of the life my parents had accidentally planned for me and into something new. And it had done that, despite the fact that it wasn't "real." The life I made for myself outside Philly might not always be great, but it was different. And it was almost certainly an improvement, no matter how much it might suck sometimes.

If I were smart, I never would have come to Joshua Tree. I would have let it stay, bright and shiny and eternally new in my mind. Instead I had been the punk kid in the front row asking how the trick was done. Asking over and over until he gets to see the fake deck of cards and the magician's pocket full of aces. Happy now?

Actually, yes I was. I'd learned an important lesson. And I resolved to use it. It was time to create a new illusion. The place up north of Joshua Tree I neglected to visit. I decided I'd call it Joshua True. And except for the name, it's exactly like the place I'd imagined, the one that's been calling me since that day in Northeast Philly. And it can keep calling for all I care. I'm never going near the goddamn place. It means too much to me.

"IT'S ONLY GOING TO GET
BETTER WITH AGE."

CHAPTER 17

THE END OF THE ROAD

I considered many ways to end this book, but I'm going to go with the truth. Which is not to say I don't regret not using my surprise twist zombie apocalypse ending. That's the one where Brian, John, Piglet, and the kitten I ran over in South Carolina (I don't want to talk about it) all reanimate along with Dad's arm and Dennis's leg. Only instead of returning as mindless corpses with an insatiable appetite for human flesh, they'd just have an insatiable appetite for tacos and video games. They'd come over to my place every Sunday afternoon to hang out and eat Pacos and play FIFA Soccer. I know, you're thinking, where's the twist, but check it out. All we'd drink would be beer, because this is where I'd reveal that *I don't even like wine.* I know! Crazy, right? Turns out the real reason I spent three months crisscrossing America was to try to score chicks on Tinder.

Don't worry; I survive the zombie apocalypse and so do

you. Because the undead limit their assault on civilization to grade A assholes who deserve to be gorged upon. Think Wall Street executives and Ted Nugent and that dickcheese who cut you off on the highway last week. And to answer your question, no, Elizabeth is not zombie fodder. Neither is Jack.

Except, *last minute super twist*! They get Jack after all. It's really sad, except for the part where he totally deserves it.

Back in reality, though, last I heard Elizabeth and Jack were still together and she'd gotten promoted to executive producer on a network reality TV show. Jack was still bartending, taking acting classes, and waiting for his big break. I hope he gets it too. Preferably a femur, or an ankle. But I'll take a few ribs if that's all you have.

It's tempting to say I'm happy for Elizabeth, but I'm not sure I am. What I am is not *unhappy* she's happy. Which is progress. This is a genuinely incredible woman who brought far more light into my life than darkness, and at a time when I needed it most. I can't imagine how things would have turned out had she not wound up next to me on the flight home from Brian's funeral. And I'm glad I didn't have to find out. Dealing with his reanimated corpse at LAX would have been far, far more difficult than it already was.

THREE MONTHS, ONE WEEK, AND two days after I pulled out of Southern California on the road to Nowhere, I passed the historic VENICE sign strung across Windward Avenue at Pacific. I was back. The Eighth Annual Pebble Beach Food & Wine festival was just around the corner, so naturally I began sinking all my time into fretting about screwing up in Pebble Beach. To keep up a head of steam with this I made sure to not actually put any work into figuring out what I was going to say or do during my presentation. If you're prepared, it's nearly impossible to fret, and without fretting I'd have entirely too much free time on my hands, and I'd end up a drug addict or a fitness freak or a Scientologist.

As the time got shorter, the situation became ridiculous. Looking back on it, I think I didn't want to admit that the journey was done. I'd grown attached to being just a little bit outside society. Not having a set daily routine. Waking up to new scenery most days. Pebble Beach had always symbolized the end of it, the point at which I would have to make choices about what was next. Where I would live. Which shitty day job I would have to take to keep myself in Sokol Blosser Pinot (a man has needs). Of course, Pebble Beach wasn't just a symbol, it was also a practical reality. In a month . . . wait, now it's a week . . . wait, now it's a few days . . . I would be getting up in front of what was probably the most wine-educated audience in America. And I was basically just some mook who rode around in Carl Vehicle for a while. I didn't have a sommelier's license. Unless you count the one I stole from Daniel Johnnes while he was in the bathroom. (Like he can't get another one.)

As I mentioned before, virtually everyone I told about my wine expert ambitions had the same basic reaction—what I was doing was awesome. I never got tired of hearing these misinformed plaudits. You know what they say, when life gives you undeserved compliments, let them go to your head and warp your sense of self-worth. Looking back, after they stopped saying nice things about me, those same people usually went on to say something along the lines of "blah blah, filtration blah racking blah blah brett," and other winemaker-ish blather. I learned to cherish the time I spent with my eyes glazed over. It was good to get a little me time after all those hours spent alone in my car.

Okay, so I'm exaggerating slightly, but I did start to get a bit paranoid about the fact that out on the road, where no one talked to me for too overly long, many of the people I spoke with had products to promote, and the majority of them displayed the natural politeness found so abundantly outside our major cities, so faking it was a pretty easy proposition. Basically people took me at face value, and no one was probing me for gaps in my wine knowledge. Except during my close encounter while driving past Area 51 in New Mexico (who knew aliens were so into Meritage?). At tastings across the United States, I'd honed a raft of bullshit modifiers like a set of ninja throwing stars, and they sure made it look like I knew what I was talking about: *complex, flabby, tight, food friendly, earthy, unctuous, opulent,* and *suppulescent.*

I made that last one up, by the way, and I encourage you to use it. I tried to throw it in at as many tastings as I could. And you know what? Over my entire trip, only Chris Brundrett of William Chris Winery called me on it and then only because he grew up on a cattle farm in Texas and knows bullshit when he smells it. All of which is to say that it really doesn't matter what you say when you taste wine. *Unctuous* is not made up, but it might as well be. On Robert Parker's website, he says the word is appropriate to describe "rich, lush, intense wines with layers of concentrated, soft, velvety fruit." Sounds pretty tasty, but that definition only shares a single word with the original meaning, which is rich or fatty, and has since become a negative way to describe an ingratiating, overflattering person (i.e., that the person themselves is greasy or oily). So when you say a wine is "unctuous," you could mean it's rich and has a viscous mouthfeel, or you could mean that it's too eager to please (like those big jammy Zinfandels that go down real easy, but lack true complexity). I heard it used so many times on the road that it essentially lost all meaning.

It became oddly comforting to me, though. One of the few constants in my peripatetic existence. It became something of a mantra for me. When I was having a tough time on a drive, I'd just start saying it on loop and make my own EDM track.

In any case, even though it started out as a joke, I don't see any reason suppulescent couldn't be the next unctuous if we all get out there and start using it. Hell, it actually means more to me than unctuous at this point. (Unctuous unctuous. You feeling that molly, yet?)

If you haven't already guessed, I spent almost the entirety of the time between the end of my trip and the start of my seminar at Pebble Beach musing on things like unctuous and suppulescent while doing what I do best: talking about knowing how to talk about the fine art of talking about talking about wine.

My anxiety mounted in inverse proportion to the amount of time I had left to prepare. I was paralyzed by what felt like an inevitable mortifying failure. At Pebble Beach it would be difficult, if not impossible, to camouflage my deficiencies as a wine authority with verbal legerdemain (see also: this entire book) or by using the strategy that had served me so well throughout my travels whenever someone was on to me: jumping in Carl Vehicle and driving away. I was going to be the one that everyone in the room was looking to for enlightenment. They were coming to hear things. Smart things I was supposed to say and know about wine. Whereas people expected me to be full of knowledge, the only thing I am absolutely certain I'm full of is shit. Why else would I become a writer? As the great Aristotle himself observed in *Poetics*,

writing is the art of sticking your head up your own ass, sucking up all the shit that's in there, chewing on it for a while,
then going to the bar. It's possible I don't have that quote
precisely correct.

The seminar I was scheduled to deliver had been dubbed
"Dan Dunn's American Wino." The title was not my idea. I
think it sounds like I'm going to be showing off some hapless
soul I picked up down on Skid Row and paid twenty bucks
to do unspeakable things to me onstage. But the festival
organizers pushed hard for it, and by the time I'd finished
arguing with them, the programs had been printed. Feel
free to call it whatever you want, they said. Everyone at the
festival will know its real title. I'm not sure what their problem was with the original title I offered: "Titman's Winetastic
Revenge." You wanna talk gratuitous? Changing the name of
someone's seminar. *That's* gratuitous. In the end, I adopted
a Shakespearean outlook—what's in a name? That which we
call a Rosé by any other name will still taste great in a spritzer
on a hot day in July. So Dan Dunn's American Wino it was. I
didn't even ask them to put an "an" in the middle.

A couple days before leaving L.A. for Pebble Beach, I
started pecking at a draft of what I wanted to say. I arrived
at the festival's headquarters, the Inn at Spanish Bay, two
days before my event and spent much of the time holed up
in my hotel room anxiously tweaking it. And masturbating.
I tend to do that a lot when I'm nervous or stressed out or
fatigued or awake.

When I wasn't beating myself up/off in my room, I walked
around the resort. The festival had taken over the place, and
therefore I viewed everyone I encountered as a potential
future inflictor of ridicule.

"Hey, how's it going?" someone asked.

"You mean, besides the fact that I have no idea what kind of cheese to pair with Sancerre?" I snapped.

"Well, you could try a . . ."

"GET OFF MY FUCKING BACK, MAN!!!"

I'm sure Robert Parker has forgiven me by now. He knows how stressed out I get.

The day before the presentation, I decided it might help if I went to check out some of the other presentations. This turned out to be the worst idea I've had in years. And I used to be into competitive sauna. "The Nose Knows" not only featured a dizzying dissection of the olfactory system and its importance in tasting wine that I didn't fully understand, I couldn't even keep up with the questions from the audience. The leader had apparently run afoul of some controversial issue regarding how long you should rest your nasal cavities before tasting wine after a nasal endoscopy. I wasn't quite sure why they were angry, but it was clear that whatever he had said had chummed the water, activating the crowd's bloodlust. Which, it bears pointing out, was mainly expressed through polite disagreements and lots of troubled "hmmmm . . ."s. Still, their fury was palpable. And as he wrapped up, the speaker was doing the verbal equivalent of the hunched run someone makes to the last helicopter out of a war zone. I consoled myself with thoughts that these guys were heavy hitters. I'm a lightweight. People probably wouldn't be interested in my session.

Leaving the seminar I ran into Dave Bernahl, the founder of Pebble Beach Food & Wine. He asked if I was excited about tomorrow. When I said I was, he said I should be because my event had sold out. "No pressure!" he joked. To which I said nothing, but internally, I did something very important. I resisted vomiting all over one of the most important people in the wine industry.

The morning of my presentation I woke up at 5 A.M. and couldn't go back to bed. The placid churning of the surf coming from ocean was the background radiation of the universe turned up to 11 and boring its way into my skull. Is 5 A.M. too early to crack a bottle of wine? What if I pretended I was still up from the night before?

After a few more hours of self-recrimination (Why didn't I take that sommelier class before I left?) and prayer (Dear Elvis, I know I skipped Graceland when I came through Tennessee, but hear me out . . .), it was time to head to the Inn at Spanish Bay. My OK Corral. My Waterloo. My Rumble in the Jungle (except for the fact that I had no claim to a title, was surrounded almost entirely by white folk, and was facing no opponent other than my own laziness and low self-esteem). Luckily, there was still time to jump in Carl Vehicle and drive away. And then suddenly there wasn't time to jump in Carl Vehicle and drive away. It. Was. Starting.

And it went really well.

Seriously, weirdly well. It felt like it was over in a not-unpleasant flash. The crowd was lively. I got laughs where I was supposed to, which is to say whenever I needed to distract from the fact that I am not a walking font of wine wisdom. Which is to say, most of my talk. I even managed to incorporate some actual interesting information. And suddenly, America's leading expert on talking about talking about becoming a wine expert had done just that (though I'm still not entirely clear on what that is). And the audience, I'm relieved to say, drank it up (along with several cases of happy juice from select producers around the country). Afterward, Dave Bernahl approached me and said he couldn't be happier with how everything had gone. He even invited me to reprise the Wino seminar at a companion festival he was producing a few months later in Los Angeles.

"Sure," I said. "Why not?"

"Great!" he said. "Let's make it happen!"

It didn't. But for no apparent reason other than neither Dave nor I ever bothered to follow up.

It turned out that doing it once was enough for me. For well over a year, my entire being had revolved around getting to Pebble Beach and delivering the greatest wine-soaked soliloquy in human history. So much had gone into it—mapping out the route, arranging three months' worth of lodging and winery visits and interviews, getting rid of my apartment, packing up my stuff, securing dog care, driving across the whole goddamn country and back again, all the note-taking and soul-searching and ass-aching. All the book writing.

And after all that, the thing I had been working toward lasted from 3:45 to 4:45 P.M. on a Saturday afternoon in April 2014. Do you remember where you were at 3:45 on April 11? Of course you don't. Nobody does, including the people who were there (I had to look up the date and time when writing this).

Don't get me wrong. I'm thrilled the seminar went off without a hitch. I put a lot of work into it, and people paid good money to attend. Several winemakers I'd met on the road came a long way on their own dimes just to be there, and I would have hated for them to be disappointed. And the audience genuinely seemed to dig it. It was a lot of fun talking through what had turned out to be one of my life's great adventures.

Plus, who wouldn't relish the opportunity to stand up in front of a room full of his fellow citizens and sing the praises of the greatest country on earth? (Put your hand down, Noam Chomsky.) My heart swelled with actual pride as I traced the connection between the early pioneers who headed west in covered wagons in search of a better life, and modern-day farmers in West Texas ripping up their cotton fields and planting Sangiovese and Aglianico in the hopes of someday competing with the best stuff from Italy. And sure, there's no real reason to believe we're ever going to make better wine than the Italians. But that can't stop us from *saying* we make the best wine in the world. Just ask the guys running our flawless, world-leading health-care and education systems. If America has a superpower, it is radical self-delusion. And without it we would never have achieved any of the monumental feats this country has accomplished over the years. Winning World War II. Pioneering the atom bomb and nuclear power. The wit and wisdom of Larry the Cable Guy.

We might be crass, we might be crude. We might rank in the low 30s on many important metrics of civilization. But dammit, we've got pluck. On the can-do spirit scale, we're still Number One. And we like to get tanked. Put those two things together and you've got yourself a recipe for success. Or at least great wine. Sure, Vermont doesn't have the cachet of California, but there's good stuff happening up there. And just like vineyards take ten years or so to really establish themselves and start producing top-quality grapes (actually precisely like that; actually precisely *because* of that), in ten years, I predict that the domestic wine landscape in this country will look radically different from what you see today.

There are cynics who'll say this country is in decline (and not just because Fox News is paying them to say that), but tell that to Greg Kempel who started Maple River Winery in Casselton, North Dakota. He's making wine with whatever fruit he can get his freezing cold hands on, from chokecherries to gooseberries. You think Greg Kempel gives a crap about what's happening over in Bordeaux? Hell, he'll probably kick your ass for even suggesting he knows where Bordeaux is.

When it comes to wine in this country, a lot of people put a lot of stock in what Robert Parker has to say. But I prefer to listen to the other great Parker this country produced. One Mr. Trey Parker. I think he spoke for everyone, especially all the American winemakers across the land, when he wrote the following words in the modern classic *Team America, World Police:* "America. Fuck yeah!"

....

THE WINO COUNTDOWN

The time has come to conclude the informative and actionable wine-centric sidebars you've come to know and either love, resent, or ignore. I hope they've been halfway informative. When they weren't, I hope they were funny. And when they weren't either, I hope they were short. Here are, in my entirely subjective opinion, some of the coolest wineries I visited on my trek across the USA.

MCRITCHIE WINERY & CIDERWORKS (THURMOND, NC)

Sean McRitchie cut his teeth in the vineyards of Oregon's lush Willamette Valley, but claims he didn't truly come into his own as a winemaker until he relocated to the rugged foothills of the Blue Ridge Mountains. "I thought I was this tough guy having worked in Oregon," he said, "but the weather here is humbling. It's tough to farm in North Carolina." Tough indeed, which is all the more reason to be impressed by the delicious wine and hard cider produced at this family owned and operated winery in the Yadkin Valley.

ST. JULIAN WINERY (PAW PAW, MI)

One of Michigan's oldest and best wineries was started back in 1921 by an Italian immigrant named Mariano Meconi. Today St. Julian produces everything from raspberry wine to apple cider, but their most felicitous offerings are part of the Braganini Reserve Collection. I was particularly impressed with the Meritage, Riesling, and Porpetto, an iced Traminette with an aromatic bouquet of peaches, mangos, and lemon zest that has a long fruity finish, not unlike the end of "Wake Me Up Before You Go Go."

CHIMNEY ROCK (STAGS LEAP DISTRICT, NAPA VALLEY)

Winemaker Elizabeth Vianna told me "there is no better place to be on earth than a winery at harvest." Wise words, Ms. Vianna. Elizabeth Vianna also showed me the difference between a block of Sauvignon Gris grapes fermented with X5 yeast (funky grapefruit) versus CY3079 yeast (thicker mouthfeel, sweeter), which was a turning point in my understanding just how complex the business of making excellent wine is.

GLENORA WINE CELLARS (DUNDEE, NY)

New York's Finger Lakes region poses a host of challenges to winemaking, from moist humid days in summer to the occasional deep freeze in the springtime. And while diseases such as powdery mildew and petritis are "happy" there, according to Glenora's winemaker Steve DiFrancesco, there's no place else he'd rather ply his craft. "There's viticultural diversity here you won't find anywhere else," he said, before ticking off a list of vinifera, hybrids, and native grapes that thrive in the vineyards around Seneca Lake. DiFrancesco's Pinot Blanc is a triple threat, composed of juice fermented in three types of vessels: a concrete egg, delicately flavored oak barrels, and a stainless steel tank.

DUCHMAN FAMILY WINERY (DRIFTWOOD, TX)

Just one of many fantastic wineries I was amazed to find scattered across Texas. Duchman winemaker Dave Reilly is convinced that the sky's the limit for Italian varietals in the Lone Star State, and after tasting his award-winning

Montepulciano and Aglianico, I'm inclined to believe him. As an added bonus, Duchman is located just minutes away from one of the world's great BBQ meccas, The Salt Lick. I think I know where I'm going to retire.

....

I DID HAVE ONE UNEXPECTED moment in the middle of my talk, when we'd gotten around to Texas. I told the story of going to visit Buddy Holly's grave at the municipal cemetery in Lubbock. How I'd arrived there in the middle of a sunny Sunday afternoon and been struck by the fact that there wasn't another living soul around. I get that Holly had been dead for fifty-five years, and Lubbock isn't Grand Central Station, but still, not one other person?

I hadn't planned to get into it, but somehow it just came out. I told the audience that my brother had died unexpectedly and that I'd taken a mason jar filled with his ashes along with me on the trip. I also told them about how I laid the jar with Brian's ashes right next to Buddy Holly's gravestone—which is engraved with the rocker's actual surname, "Holley"—and that while snapping pictures I found myself humming "Oh Boy!" And that I sprinkled more of his ashes on that spot than I had anywhere else along the way. I realized too late that I had ventured into shaky territory here. I could feel the emotion rising in me, the walls closing in just the tiniest bit, the yawning maw of the universe opening under my feet. So I moved on to Shelburne Vineyard, which makes an incredible Marquette Reserve, and, hey, let's uncork some of this stuff, huh?

What I didn't tell them about was the conversation Brian and I had there. You're used to this kind of thing by now. I was worried it was going to be a little much for the uninitiated.

Brian told me that he hadn't seen Buddy Holly in the after-life. In fact, in all the time he'd been dead he hadn't met a single celebrity. I guess things there are pretty similar to the way they are here. Somehow the famous people are always hanging out someplace just slightly cooler than you are.

"What about limbs?" I asked.

"Limbs?"

"Yeah, you know . . . Dad's arm, Dennis's leg, whatever body part the drummer from Def Leppard is missing. Have you encountered any expired limbs?"

"You're fucking weird, dude," Brian said.

"You mean weird like 'standing over Buddy Holly's grave talking to a jar of dirt' weird?"

"I'm a whole person, asshole!"

"You *were* a whole person," I corrected him.

"Whatever. I don't know where the limbs go. Someplace else. I'm not in fuckin' charge."

I started humming "Peggy Sue." Or maybe Brian did.

"If you could have done one thing before you died, what would it have been?"

"Not jumped off that pier," he replied immediately. "Idiot."

"No, I mean, if you were going to die no matter what, but you got to do one last thing. What would it be?"

"Oh, right," Brian said. "Bucket list do-over. Hmmmm . . ." While he gave it some thought I hummed a few bars of "La Bamba" by Holly's ill-fated traveling companion Richie Valens.

"Well," he said, "if I could have done one last thing I guess I would have told you guys—you know, our family—how much I love you. Called or texted or something. Does that count? It's technically more than one thing."

"Yeah, man," I said. "It counts."

"Oh, and I would have had a karaoke showdown with Bill Murray."

"That's two things."

"Why you gotta be so stingy with the do-overs?"

"You have to limit it somehow, right? That's how life works."

"Is it?" he replied. And I didn't have a good answer.

That was the last time we spoke on the trip. Or since.

FIFTEEN MINUTES AFTER THE TRIUMPHANT conclusion of "Dan Dunn's American Wino" (Pro tip: When in doubt, always close with free booze), I was outside on the patio at Spanish Bay enjoying a stunning view, a glass of fine bubbly, and the company of a delightful woman I met that weekend. She remained on my mind for quite some time afterward, but I hardly gave the seminar another thought until it came time to draft this chapter. And though I may have had a Texas-sized panic attack beforehand, the truth is, whatever happened there, even if it had gone horribly, mortifyingly off the rails, nothing could diminish the transformative experience I had getting there. Ralph Waldo Emerson said life is a journey, not a destination but, man, destinations can sure come in handy when you're out of your mind with loss and don't know where to put your feelings. When it comes to these matters, I prefer a quote by a young fellow named Dan Dunn: "Don't Stop Believing" is a Journey not a Bon Jovi. Which is to say, nothing sticks to you when you're flying down the highway at eighty miles an hour listening to rock and roll.

Can I honestly say there isn't a single soul on earth who knows more about American wine than I do? Hell no. But in all honesty, I don't want to be that guy (no offense, guy). This trip taught me that I am most definitely not the sharpest somm in the snootytorium. My nose routinely fails to detect the overtones of cat piss and lilac that seem obvious to others. And my bottle memory is terrible. I had an awful time keeping names, vintages, grapes, and such straight.

On the other hand if I need to know that name of the cashier I talked to in Pawley's Island, South Carolina, it's right there. (Imogene, if you must know.) I'm shit at remembering wines, but I'm great at remembering people. And I'm okay with that. In fact, understanding it led to me identifying the one signature skill I did develop over the course of my journey. And I think I might just be best in the world at this one: personality-based wine assessment. Or wine-based personality assessment. I swear, this is not a case of JAATOOHAAW (Just Another Asshole Talking Out Of His Ass About Wine). I'm looking into starting a life-coach business, using this as my primary psychological modality. I believe that, by finding the kind of wine a person *should* be drinking then comparing it to the wine they *are* drinking, you can find a way to charge people hundreds of dollars an hour to get drunk with them. It's important work.

And it helped me figure out where the hell I'm supposed to live now. A couple seconds of thought will tell you that the only town where this concept has a chance in hell of succeeding in is L.A., where you can set up shop at the corner of Crazy, Wealthy, and Shit-Hot California Wine. Livingston, Montana, remains one of the favorite places I visited on my trip, but its combination of self-reliant, nonneurotic folk, and terrible local wine would be poison for my new business. So I won't be moving there. Same goes for Oregon. Sure, they've got the wine for it, but trying to tell a hipster what kind of wine they should be drinking is a losing proposition.

I'm still working out the nitty-gritty of my theory, but essentially I classify wines like I classify people. Every bottle is a mixed bag, just like every person. I started practicing my technique way back in Santa Barbara with Kurt Russell (who is a 2002 Kistler Pinot Noir all the way). It took me a day and a half to figure him out. Now, minutes after meeting someone, I have them pegged for a producer and a bottle.

Me? I'm a Blenheim Vineyards Rosé. Tart, refreshing, and a damn good value. As I mentioned earlier, Blenheim is in Charlottesville, Virginia, and is owned by Dave Matthews of all people. I didn't get to meet Dave, but that fits my profile as well. I get to all the right places, but my timing is usually a little off.

My mother is the Brianna at Miletta Vista Winery in St. Paul, Nebraska. Those grapes had a hell of a time developing in extremely harsh conditions. But somehow, against the odds, they made it. The white wine they yielded is the ultimate underdog. It doesn't have the pedigree or breeding of a Pinot Grigio from California or even a Viognier from Virginia. I regularly talk to wine industry people who have never even heard of the varietal. But that didn't stop that Little Wine That Shouldn't Have Been Able To from being named "Best of Show" at the 2012 U.S. National Competition, held in the epicenter of American wine, Sonoma, California. The Brianna beat the odds and somehow got Miletta Vista out of St. Paul and to a place it could thrive. Not unlike what Mom did for me.

When I was up in the Oakville District of Napa Valley, my winemaker pal Chris Carpenter gave me a bottle of 2011 Cardinale Cabernet Sauvignon. "It's a little tight," he told me. "Hold on to it a while. It's only going to get better with age." That wine, to me, is Elizabeth. Or, rather, my memory of her. When I hit the road, I was pretty tight about that memory. But it's gotten better with time. Hell, give it another twenty years and I'm sure I could write a book about how she went on to build an incredible life for herself, filled with purpose, love, and satisfaction. It's clear to me now that these qualities are probably best pursued somewhere away from me.

Jack, on the other hand, is like the Merlot from Newport Vineyards in Rhode Island. First, it occasionally gets swallowed in Elizabeth's hometown (I think they go back there for the holidays), it's wimpy and thin, and no matter how much time goes by I doubt I'm ever going to like it. No offense, motherfucker.

My dad was always beer, not wine. And now he's in AA, so he's neither. He is, however, the strongest cup of coffee I ever had.

Clothilde reminds me of the Domaine Pinot Noir from King Estate in Eugene, Oregon, in that I swore I was gonna go back there and get some, but I never did.

To me there's not a wine made in America that compares to Daniel Johnnes. And even if there were, I wouldn't dare mention it. He might bludgeon me with a bottle of 1999 Le Tertre Roteboeuf. And that would be a terrible way to treat a bottle of that magnitude.

My cousin Dennis doesn't remind me of a specific wine so much as he does wine tastings. Years ago when you'd go to a wine event, you'd often encounter formally attired men and women who'd swirl their wine and examine the "tears" that flow down the inside of the glass. Back then, the myth of those droplets indicating a wine's quality still persisted. Today, though, you rarely hear anyone say "nice legs" about a wine. Or about Dennis. "Nice leg" just doesn't have the same ring to it. And if we're being honest, his has never been all that great.

Brian is the 2010 Screaming Eagle that someone gave me as a gift a few years ago. More than any other wine in my modest collection, that's the bottle I've been holding on to for a special occasion. There have been a few significant causes for celebration over the past few years that almost rose to its level, yet I held on to it. The 2010 vintage was supremely popular, and they didn't make much of it. An American cult wine if ever there was one. I was determined that when the time came to pop that cork, it had to be to commemorate one of the most important things that ever happened to me. I've found, however, that identifying those is more than a little tricky.

And one day, a few weeks after Pebble Beach ended, I stopped seeing the point in waiting. *I'm opening this bastard today,* I thought to myself. *Because fuck it. Every day's important.*

I stuck it in my bag and headed to the beach in Venice. Which is where I'm living again, by the way. Couldn't very well remain a citizen of Nowhere forever. Makes laundry a total pain in the ass.

I've talked about two songs that remind me of Brian, "Nightswimming" and "Never Going Back Again." The third is "Learning to Fly" by Tom Petty & the Heartbreakers. Specifically the version off *The Live Anthology.* I had it on my headphones as I walked across the sand to my usual spot. It was a warm spring day that already felt like summertime. I sat, cracked open the Screaming Eagle, and poured myself a slug. Took a sip. Well shit, this really is an incredible wine. To describe it in a word, *flawless.* In three words, *best wine ever.* Seriously, I cannot recall ever having tasted anything quite as satisfying as that wine. And the fact that I could confidently identify the elements that made it so powerful and distinctive—the hint of crushed rocks, the highly concentrated black fruit flavor, the unobtrusive yet integral trace of oak—well, that made it just that much more special.

Along with the Screaming Eagle, I'd brought a book with me, Haruki Murakami's *The Wind-Up Bird Chronicle.* Scott recommended it. I can't imagine why he thought I'd relate to it. It's about a hapless hero who, after losing his cat, goes on a strange, hallucinatory adventure, which deals with a wide spectrum of heavy subjects along the way. It's the kind of book that makes you believe that everything is possible. Not anything. Everything.

So when I looked up and saw Brian about a half mile away, standing on top of the Venice Pier, giant grin on his face and fixing to jump, I was only a little surprised. This time it wasn't 2 A.M. and the sea wasn't angry and I wasn't at home in bed asleep. And Brian knew exactly what he was doing. He looked over to make sure I was watching, and then he waved and shouted "Later!" before turning to face the sea and executing a perfect swan dive. Only instead of plummeting into the ocean, after a small drop, he swooped out over the water, fingertips skimming the foam, the breeze blowing back his hair, cackling like a madman. Learning to fly.

A showoff might have taken a lap over the beach, peacocked for the hardbodies, and blown the hippies' minds. Not Brian's thing. He headed straight out to sea, swooping and gliding on the shimmering air, until he was just a dot. Then a speck. Then he was gone.

"Cheers," I said, raising my red solo cup.

What kind of asshole brings glass to the beach?

ACKNOWLEDGMENTS
RAISING A GLASS

Scott Alexander. It's difficult to find the right words to convey just how grateful I am for all you've done to help transform this latest flight of fancy into a reality. So I've left space in the margins for you to add those words yourself. I have no doubt you'll nail it. You always do.

Curtis Robinson. You're still the finest *Aspen Daily News* editor who ever lived. And if there's a better "venue research" guy in the business, well, I hope he sees this and reaches out to me.

Scott Gould. Who says agents are a bunch of sleazy suck-fish? I do. I say it a lot actually. But never about you, buddy. You're one of the good ones. Thanks for sticking with me all these years.

Josie Freedman. Here's to the film adaptation I hope somebody's making. Put some of the money toward that dream home in Healdsburg.

Brittany Hamblin. You convinced the brass at Harper-Collins to shell out actual currency for this tome. So this is your fault. But not all your fault . . .

Ain't that right, Sean Newcott? Thank you, thank you, thank you. And thank you again. You did a hell of a job editing the book and keeping me in check. It couldn't have been easy.

Marcos Efron and Michael Waghalter. For that thing you did that ultimately led to this thing.

Same goes to you, Rob McElhenney and Glenn Howerton and the rest of the "Sunny" crew.

Tom Caltabiano. You owned Pebble Beach Food & Wine.

Dave Bernahl. Without you, there wouldn't have been a Pebble Beach Food & Wine.

Kurt Russell. For that time we did two radio shows in a row. That was cool.

Maynard James Keenan. Whenever I'm feeling low, I watch the "Safety Dance" video, and suddenly everything is okay again.

Justin Silver. Three words: World Dog Awards.

Alana Bly. We'll always have Virginia.

Natalie Oliveros (a.k.a. Savanna Samson). That kiss!

Adam Carolla, for warning me of the very real threat of psychos posing as vintners.

To all the people—some old friends, some new—who opened their hearts and homes and bottles of wines along the way. I cannot thank you enough for all you did to help make this possible . . . Lisa Mattson, John Jordan, Christopher Sawyer, Drew Bigda, Jenny Peters, Mary Wagstaff, Kanchan Kinkade, Deborah Clifford, Peter Work, Karin Warnelius-Miller, Elizabeth Vianna, Ashley Teplin, Jeremy Baker, Claudia Wade, Dan Brennan, Tom DeVaul, Ken and Gail Albert, Shona Lothrop and Pat LaClair, Jeff Knapp, Eileen Wong,

Patrick Reuter, Alex Sokol Blosser, Alison Sokol Blosser, Emily Saveraid, Chris Carpenter, Trey Busch, Jerry Solomon, Charles Smith, Michaela Baltasar, Hannah MacDonald, Linda Trotta, David O'Reilly, Joe Benyak, David Oldham, Jenna Hudson, Josh McFadden, Sofian and Crystal Himeur, Daniel Johnnes, Denise Clarke, Katie Roller, Laury Poland, Christina Roberts, Steve DiFrancesco, John Wagner, Anthony Lerner, Ian Blackburn, Sam and Robin Sebastiani, Michael Coats, Scott Wagner and Beckie Tilden, Ashley Trego, Alfred Eames, Danielle Emerson, Amy E. Ciarametaro, John and Jamie Parsons, Michelle Prevost, Geralyn Hashway, Patrick Zimmerer, Kim Whistler, and Louise O'Brien.

Oh, there's more . . . Mike Miller, Mick and Loretta McDowell, Jada Williams, Becca Hensley, Cassandra Earle, Casey Hough, Marcheta Keefer, Jamie Claudio, Jen Sigal, Rachel Martin, Jenni McCloud, Vanessa Casas, Rutger de Vink, Jim Law, Jonathan Wheeler, Allison Conway, Dave Kostelnik, Steve Monson, Luca Paschina, Brigitte Bélanger-Warner, Dave Matthews, Gabriele Rausse, Ann R. Tuennerman, Megan Uram, Monica Seide, Heidi Witherspoon, Emily DeFoor, Martha Ezzard, Georgia O'Farrell, Lisa Ezzard, James Seib, Catherine Markel, Lincoln Case, Beverly Stotz, John Rivenburgh, Nichole Bendele, Chris Brundrett, Doug Lewis, everyone at Rose Hill Manor, Xandria Lorenzo, Greg Bruni, Neal Newsom, Krystin and Jared Herrera, Amanda Cevallos, and Chris Turner.

If I've forgotten someone, insert name here: _____.

Thanks for your couches and spare bedrooms (and, of course, good company) Greg Lewis, Dave Zierler, Brian Hightower, Sammy Hewins, Stinky, Jenny Hirsch, Mike Surcouf, and Rich and Mia Andreoli.

For being there when I needed to see a familiar face . . . Fred

Pichel, Emily Blue, Jasmin Hakes, Larry Olmsted, Charles Joly, Jeffrey Morgenthaler, Craig Owens, Pat Cunningham, Barbara Joan Nardi, Grace Graham, Bob LaBrum, Marc Dent, Bill Nickels, Sean McGovern, Rosalina Pong, Gita and Falcon, JC, Chrissy Stock, Dennis McGlinn, Mike Dunn, Marty Swanson, Michelle Evans, Bridget Evans, Lucinda Sterling, Tim McAteer, Autumn Marie Dean, and Alex Dalton.

Yvonne Rankin. For the music.

Helen Fielding. For all the wonderful e-mail.

Tom Fitzpatrick. For keeping me afloat.

Everyone at Food & Wine and Food Republic.

My family. I'm convinced most of you are clinically insane. Don't ever change.

Jessica. For the good times, mostly. Though the bad stuff did inspire good material.

And finally, Thomas Jefferson. You were right. America is a hell of a fine place to make wine.

ABOUT THE AUTHOR

Dan Dunn is the author of the books *Living Loaded: Tales of Sex, Salvation, and the Pursuit of the Never-Ending Happy Hour* and *Nobody Likes a Quitter (and Other Reasons to Avoid Rehab): The Loaded Life of an Outlaw Booze Writer.* His work has appeared in *Playboy, GQ,* the *Los Angeles Times, USA Today, Maxim, LA Weekly,* and *Newsday.* He lives in Venice, California, with his fears, insecurities, and dog.